Early Childhood in Postcolonial Australia

CRITICAL CULTURAL STUDIES OF CHILDHOOD

Series Editors:
Marianne N. Bloch, Gaile Sloan Cannella, and Beth Blue Swadener

This series focuses on reframings of theory, research, policy, and pedagogies in childhood. A critical cultural study of childhood is one that offers a "prism" of possibilities for writing about power and its relationship to the cultural constructions of childhood, family, and education in broad societal, local, and global contexts. Books in the series open up new spaces for dialogue and reconceptualization based on critical theoretical and methodological framings, including critical pedagogy; advocacy and social justice perspectives; cultural, historical, and comparative studies of childhood; and post-structural, postcolonial, and/or feminist studies of childhood, family, and education. The intent of the series is to examine the relations between power, language, and what is taken as normal/abnormal, good, and natural, to understand the construction of the "other," difference and inclusions/exclusions that are embedded in current notions of childhood, family, educational reforms, policies, and the practices of schooling. *Critical Cultural Studies of Childhood* will open up dialogue about new possibilities for action and research.

Single-authored as well as edited volumes focusing on critical studies of childhood from a variety of disciplinary and theoretical perspectives are included in the series. A particular focus is in a reimagining and critical reflection on policy and practice in early childhood, primary, and elementary education. The series intends to open up new spaces for reconceptualizing theories and traditions of research, policies, cultural reasonings, and practices at all of these levels, in the United States, as well as comparatively.

The Child in the World/The World in the Child: Education and the Configuration of a Universal, Modern, and Globalized Childhood
Edited by Marianne N. Bloch, Devorah Kennedy, Theodora Lightfoot, and Dar Weyenberg; Foreword by Thomas S. Popkewitz

Beyond Pedagogies of Exclusion in Diverse Childhood Contexts: Transnational Challenges
Edited by Soula Mitakidou, Evangelia Tressou, Beth Blue Swadener, and Carl A. Grant

"Race" and Early Childhood Education: An International Approach to Identity, Politics, and Pedagogy
Edited by Glenda Mac Naughton and Karina Davis

Governing Childhood into the 21st Century: Biopolitical Technologies of Childhood Management and Education
By Majia Holmer Nadesan

Developmentalism in Early Childhood and Middle Grades Education: Critical Conversations on Readiness and Responsiveness
Edited by Kyunghwa Lee and Mark D. Vagle

New Approaches to Early Child Development: Rules, Rituals, and Realities
Edited by Hillel Goelman, Jayne Pivik, and Martin Guhn

Comparative Early Childhood Education Services: International Perspectives
Edited by Judith Duncan and Sarah Te One

Early Childhood in Postcolonial Australia: Children's Contested Identities
By Prasanna Srinivasan

Early Childhood in Postcolonial Australia

Children's Contested Identities

Prasanna Srinivasan

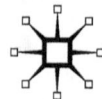

EARLY CHILDHOOD IN POSTCOLONIAL AUSTRALIA
Copyright © Prasanna Srinivasan, 2014.

All rights reserved.

First published in 2014 by
PALGRAVE MACMILLAN®
in the United States—a division of St. Martin's Press LLC,
175 Fifth Avenue, New York, NY 10010.

Where this book is distributed in the UK, Europe and the rest of the world, this is by Palgrave Macmillan, a division of Macmillan Publishers Limited, registered in England, company number 785998, of Houndmills, Basingstoke, Hampshire RG21 6XS.

Palgrave Macmillan is the global academic imprint of the above companies and has companies and representatives throughout the world.

Palgrave® and Macmillan® are registered trademarks in the United States, the United Kingdom, Europe and other countries.

ISBN: 978–1–137–39217–6

Library of Congress Cataloging-in-Publication Data

Srinivasan, Prasanna.
   Early childhood in postcolonial Australia : children's contested identities / by Prasanna Srinivasan.
     pages cm
   Includes bibliographical references and index.
   ISBN 978–1–137–39217–6 (hardcover : alkaline paper)
    1. Children of minorities—Australia—Social conditions. 2. Children of minorities—Australia—Language. 3. Srinivasan, Prasanna—Childhood and youth. 4. East Indians—Australia—Social conditions. 5. Ethnicity—Australia—Psychological aspects. 6. Human skin color—Social aspects—Australia. 7. English language—Social aspects—Australia. 8. Early childhood education—Social aspects—Australia. 9. Postcolonialism—Australia. 10. Australia—Race relations. I. Title.

DU120.S64 2014
305.800994—dc23
                                                                    2013047570

A catalogue record of the book is available from the British Library.

Design by Newgen Knowledge Works (P) Ltd., Chennai, India.

First edition: June 2014

10 9 8 7 6 5 4 3 2 1

*I dedicate my Ganga to
Glenda, a "white transformer," who extends her hands
for many boundary crossers.*

Contents

Series Editors' Preface — ix
Acknowledgments — xi

Introduction: Who Am I? Who Is My Ganga? — 1

1 Ganga: Our Beginnings, Our Context, Our Stories — 9

2 Boundaries Speak: othering, Othering, øthering Australian / Not Australian — 23

3 Complex(ion) Speak: I Am White, I Am Australian. Pookey Is Black, She Is Not Australian — 55

4 Forbidden Fs Speak: You Know What Australians Think If You Say You Are a Muslim — 75

5 Tongue Ties Speak: I Am Australian, I Speak Australian — 101

6 Terra Strikes Speak: We Can't Let Everyone in, This Is Our Country, Shouldn't We Have a Choice — 117

7 The "Whiteness Truth": We Have to Do Something — 141

Epilogue: But Remember She Is Saying, "I Don't Like Brown Skin, I Am White" — 155

Appendix: Ganga's Key "Boundary Speakers" — 167
References — 171
Index — 181

Series Editors' Preface

We are delighted to welcome this volume to the Critical Cultural Studies of Childhood Studies series, as it embodies our intentions for the series and its emphasis on cultural studies of childhood and sensitivity to power and postcolonial dynamics in early childhood research contexts. *Early Childhood in Postcolonial Australia* draws from a highly creative study, employing critical personal narrative, cultural studies of childhood and early education, and participatory action research methods. Prasanna Srinivasan frames the volume within postcolonial contexts of migrant and indigenous others' experience in Australia, using the metaphor of "Ganga" in powerful ways to unpack both her interpretation of a wide range of data and her troubling of multiple constructions of the "other," through a multilayered analysis of boundary identities and postcolonial subjectivities.

Srinivasan combines qualitative data collected in the participatory action research tradition, including an array of rich and relevant quotes from children and their teachers, with her poignant voice, theorizing, and personal narrative. Her powerfully nuanced self-disclosure and interrogation, side by side with an excellent command of relevant theories, makes a strong contribution to critical cultural studies of childhood—and of adults who share children's life spaces, particularly in child care and preschool settings. We appreciated her struggle with "whiteness," privilege, and other subjectivities, and her use of what might be termed "Third space" to unpack both her experiences as "other" joining dominant culture institutions and those of children and teachers with whom she conducted participatory research.

While highly applicable to the Australian early education context, this volume also has implications for similar debates and tensions around what should be emphasized in the care and education of young children—particularly minoritized or othered children in postcolonial contexts. Drawing upon the power of ideological "othering" (Althusser, 2008) in shaping cultural identities and practices, Prasanna Srinivasan unveils ways in which her "postcolonial partialities" become reinvigorated in ways that uncover power dynamics and multiple identities. Combining postcolonial, poststructural feminist and critical race theories to discursively analyse and interpret subjective identity practices with "Ganga," her inner voice, Srinivasan transforms "boundary speakers" into postcolonial subjects, 'Other Australian' (OA) and 'øthered Australian' (øA) to represent the "crisscross of our discourses, strategies and material effects of our contest by engaging with the 'Postcolonial estuary of contesting 'Australian.'" (8) In doing so, *Early Childhood in Postcolonial Australia* contributes to the ongoing reconceptualization of early childhood in ways that have relevance for many disciplines and postcolonial contexts.

BETH BLUE SWADENER
and
MARIANNE N. BLOCH

Acknowledgments

I would like to sincerely thank everyone and everything that has made Ganga realizable in the form she is now. I stop from naming anything or anyone with a fear of omitting someone or something that has been equally critical in getting this together.

I leave this page with my heart filled with gratitude for every experience, every being, and everything that has become Ganga,

prasanna.

Introduction: Who Am I? Who Is My Ganga?

> *The Ganga, especially, is the river of India, beloved of her people, round which are intertwined her memories, her hopes and fears, her songs of triumph, her victories and her defeats. She has been a symbol of India's age long culture and civilization, ever changing, ever flowing, and yet ever the same Ganga.*
>
> —Jawaharlal Nehru, First Prime Minister of India

This book is not just a compilation of what was exchanged, and theoretically interpreted and understood through my doctoral study about cultural identity discourses in Australian early childhood settings; it is the story of my Ganga and me, and I situate my voice within and without what is shared by us as culture narrators.

Who Am I: My Subjective Experiences

I first introduce my "self," also my "other," before I introduce my study. I am a Hindu Brahmin, who grew up in postcolonial India, a society that was crisscrossed by caste system, religions, invasions, and colonialism. I grew up in a Brahmin household. However, I was told by my grandfather from a young age about the evils that Brahminism created to hierarchically segment and dominate a society through its caste system. The particular knowledge that Brahminism epitomized was meticulously woven into every individual around not just the subjects of Hinduism and its varied denominations, but also those outside. Thus, whether we were in or out of this system, we were responding to the structures of Brahminism. I was groomed to be an insider who could speak with those outside, and contest *varnashrama*, the color, character, attribute, labor-based caste system that still dominates the minds of Indian peoples (Ilaiah, 2004). When the Brahminic scriptures taught me to believe that everything is an illusion, my grandfather took me aside and read poems by Subramanya Bharathi (1882–1921) that contended that the very concept is arguably an illusion too, and gave me permission to contest the immediate realities around us. Outside my household was the society that was still coming to terms with the aftermath of colonialism, the postcolonial independent India that had successfully overthrown British India in 1947. Thus, color and colonialism had occupied my mind and my emotions for a very long time, and it followed me to Australia when I migrated with my husband and my young son in the late 1980s.

In Australia, as a family we experienced skin color–based exclusion from time to time. My children were excluded from play as being "dirty," by their peers at kindergarten and school, due to their skin color. When I complained, the kindergarten teachers reassured me that it was a matter of children's innocent curiosity and nothing else. I walked away silently. After about ten years in Australia, I became an early childhood practitioner and color and colonialism followed me there too. I was asked to keep my "black" footprints off the "clean" floor by the cleaner at the kindergarten (early childhood settings, providing sessional educational care for children between the ages of three and five), where I worked as a teacher. I made a complaint, and the kindergarten committee explained that the cleaner must have thought that I was a parent and would not have made that comment had he known that I was a teacher there. For me, this implied that the comment itself was pardonable, but what was wrong was that it was said to a teacher. I was hurt, as a parent, as a teacher, and most of all as a "black" subject. Mine and my children's "brownness," our permanent reality, was thus repeatedly subjectified as "unclean" interruptions that had to be excluded from "clean" imaginations. I knew how I felt, but I didn't have the concepts to outline why that committee member felt differently about the same comment. I saw color, the color of the committee, which I hadn't noticed till then—they were all "white," with clean white footprints. Around the year 2006, I was introduced to postcolonial and critical race theories, by my "white" teachers, and I found my voice to "speak" colors. My introduction to these theories gave me the language to express my experiences of color and colonialism and those of my family in Australia. I now know that in those experiences, my children's "white" peers and the "white" cleaner were "othering" our "blackness" as something that would tarnish their otherwise "clean" surroundings. "Whiteness" has historically seen non-whites as primitive, fearful, or exotic (Taylor, 2004), and after all, the colonizers dominated and controlled the colonized by regarding them as uncivilized and barbaric or mysterious and quaint (Said, 1978). And as "non-whites," we were being colonized by "whiteness" in Australia. Most of all, I also understood at this time that the "white" teachers at kindergarten and schools were simultaneously "normalizing" this behavior with romantic visions of childhood innocence and curiosity. Thus, the teachers perpetuated the children's exclusion of our "blackness" with their silence and inaction. I embraced these postcolonial and critical race theories due to everything that I was and everything that Australia was at that time. Thus, through all of the above experiences and my theories that were external to me, my "other" became my "self," my ideology, my philosophical paradigm that I strongly drew upon to make meaning of what we experienced in Australia and beyond.

My family began to use my postcolonial language to discuss our lives in Australia. My son one day exclaimed with frustration, "*Hybridity is a reality for us amma, but it is an imagination for white people.*" I began to reflect on what he meant by this, and what was his hybrid reality, which was an imagination for "white" people, and many more questions followed within my "postcolonial self." Will hybridity ever become a reality for all of us, and what inhibits hybridity from becoming everyone's reality? In these reflections my doctoral study began in 2008. I developed my study in order to engage with the complexities of enacting with cultures in early childhood settings, for me, my son, and all the children in them. I had always distinguished my family's cultural layers, our multilingual practices, our values toward elders, books, arts, and music against what was practiced here, in Australia, as I definitely identified differences between the two cultures. However, with my knowledge of "othering" growing as I became more and more familiar with postcolonial literature, several questions flowed persistently in and around me: Isn't this the distinguishing procedure that colonizers used, to dominate their "other"? Did that mean I was guilty of "othering" too? Although on one hand I believed that "othering" was a colonial discourse, I could not reconcile with leaving it there, as I knew I was as guilty of the same segregating discourse as my distinguishing colonizer. I wanted to challenge and change the practices that I thought of as being inadequate to engage with different cultures. But who was I to decide? Wasn't I inevitably trying to control what I saw as "different"? The distortions in my postcolonial vision continued right till the end of my doctoral thesis, and they still occupy my mind as I write this book.

Who Is My Ganga: My Ganga and I

I had completed the data collection for my doctoral study and I met with my supervisors to discuss a way in which I could start writing about this dynamic process. That morning Glenda and Margaret, my supervisors, suggested that I should look into using a metaphor to engage with the complexities of what my study was and had become. After all, a metaphor enables the user to link meaningfully various unfathomable, yet related domains, as it allows one to understand complex concepts by providing a mental map of the linkable elements (Liu and Owyong, 2011). I chose Ganga as my metaphor.

Ganga is the largest river of the land now called as India, and the people of India not only realize her physical power, but they also relate to this power spiritually. Ganga's power has been etched into the minds of her people by myths and histories told and retold for thousands of years, and they still remain in circulation in India's contemporary society. Despite river Ganga's heavy pollution, which is an environmental and biological threat, India's Ganga is still revered for her sanctity, and worshippers still immerse themselves into this river to cleanse their sins. Even when the scientific realities claim her waters as being a mortal threat to human, animal, and plant lives, her subjects cling to the mythical imaginations to seek immortality in her waters. I grew up with the river Ganga, her myths, her stories, and her sanctity, and I hold Ganga very close to me—Ganga is my story, my reality, and my imagination. Thus, Ganga to me represents our paradoxical truths, realities, and the imaginations that we embrace and claim as "truths" due to our subjective affiliations. Ganga as a metaphor symbolized my research experience and linked all those complexities for me, and as I began working with my data as my Ganga, I became her and she became me. After all, everything that was generated, surfaced, and consumed as my doctoral study was due to my presence, and therefore I generated my Ganga, and my Ganga interacted with me. What I analyzed and interpreted, in turn analyzed and interpreted me, as it surfaced the many that I was, and the many that I wasn't. With Ganga inside, I was able to discuss our complex discursive interactions, especially to make meaning of our subjective voices and our silences. Every time I engaged with my Ganga, I realized that she represented every aspect of my study—as

Jawaharlal Nehru said, *"ever changing, ever flowing, and yet ever the same Ganga."*

India's Ganga is fluid, changing what she encounters and changing with what she encounters; she is multiple, having varied origins, flowing through different nations and called by different names; she is sublime, having the power to divide and unite boundaries; yet, she is stoic, always present, and always occupying the thoughts of her subjects, and always flowing toward the ocean. Thus for me, my Ganga represented me, my study's origins, my theoretical frameworks, my action research, my data, my ideologies, my analyses, my discussions, and my final union with all postcolonial subjects. Ganga allowed me to be receptive to change, and change to reach my destiny. One who experiences India's Ganga brings her waters in a small pot to remind themselves of their compelling tryst in her rippling swirls. And I offer this small pot of my Ganga to the readers through this book, our stories.

My Ganga: This Book, Our Stories

This book is the story of my cultural identity quest in early childhood settings, which remained complex till the very end. To tell my complex story, I use Ganga, the largest river in India as a metaphor to denote everything, from my study's data to my mentor. Ganga became my inner voice to "speak" with and about the complexities that were inherent in the topic, the action research methodology, and in our subjective understandings and experiences with skin color and with cultures in Australia. By centralizing "othering" as a key process in enacting, shaping, resisting, and contesting cultural identities, I make meaning of my Ganga. I use different theoretical interests namely, psychoanalysis and social psychology (Lacan, 2002; Crisp and Turner, 2007; Elliott, 2007, 2010), Althusserian ideological influence (Althusser, 2008; Fairclough, 1992), and finally post-structural feminist theory (Foucault, 1972, 2010; Weedon, 1987) in combination with postcolonial (Said, 1978; Hall, 2003; Young, 2001, 2003; Loomba, 2005) and critical race theoretical paths (Frankenberg, 1993). I co-narrate how we, including children, spoke of people as "Australian" or "not Australian" to attribute different cultural identity layers to these categories. In doing so, I finally bring forth the different identity "truths" that surface and lead to the recognition of the ultimate "white truth," the "power" of "whiteness" in Australia.

In this book, I discuss how I channeled my Ganga through each theoretical interest, to surface different meanings, that enact, shape, resist, and contest "Australian / not Australian" identities. Chapter 1 outlines briefly the theoretical, sociopolitical, and methodological beginnings of my study, and its complexities, and the study's context (the study's duration, setting, and participants). I have also included some of the key terms that I have specifically used to define certain concepts. Chapter 2 explains briefly how I used the different theoretical tools to engage with the varied forms of "othering," how this influenced my understandings of "Australian / not Australian" categorizations, and our subjective realities and imaginations attached to these categories. Chapter 2 particularly presents the specific terms used in discussions and the imagery, "postcolonial estuary of contesting Australian," the final analytical tool that surfaced from and with Ganga. The varied theoretical concepts used in this stage of analysis are also discussed here. Chapters 3, 4, 5, and 6 discuss the key layers (skin color; food, faith, and festival; language; national boundaries) with which our cultural identities were distinguished and established, and I use sets of narratives that were significant in layering the attributes of "Australian" and "not Australian." Each of these chapters begins by discussing how that particular layer was used by narrators to reflect our categorical realities and imaginations. These chapters further lead to connecting the narratives with their ideological beginnings to finally surface the evidence of "power" with my dialogues with Ganga.

In these chapters, I initially "speak" with Ganga to interpret the role of "*othering*" in enacting "Australian" and "not Australian" identities by individuals and groups. I evidence the role of "othering" in establishing the layers of "Australian" and therefore the "not Australian" and vice versa within the theoretical space of social psychology and psychoanalysis. These theories justify "othering" as a normal, inevitable act of self-discovery and identity development. I illustrate how individuals (speakers) within cultural groups interact when they came together with their "Australian" imaginations and "not Australian" realities. The speakers' narratives set these categories apart, and yet remain as one to be dictated and dedicated to establishing the identity of "Australian." Most of all, I bring to note how our narratives are particularly controlled by those who spoke as "Australian," as they repeatedly reinforce the "Australian" imagi(nation), as and when this identity is disrupted even ever so slightly by speakers. I then reengage with the imagi(nation) narratives of "Australian speakers" to uncover the influence of political ideology using Critical Discourse Analysis (CDA, Fairclough, 1992). I unearth the power of ideological "*Othering*" (Althusser, 2008) in shaping cultural identities in Australia. I particularly focus on just the "Australian speakers" and how they respond to the ideological constructions of the identity "Australian" (national subject) and the "not Australian" (migrant outsider). This inquiry only rekindles and reinvigorates my postcolonial partialities, as I become determined to surface "power" that controls all our voices and silences.

I end each of these chapters with my inextinguishable postcolonial subjectivity, and I split and speak as and with Ganga. The "†" is my voice with fragmented †, to represent the many that † have become. † grapple with my own shortcomings that not only influence how † make meaning of events, but also how † therefore respond to events. In recognition of my commitment, † finally privilege my postcolonial subjectivity, and yet struggle to embrace this in its absolute form. † combine poststructural feminist, postcolonial, and critical race theory to discursively analyze and interpret our subjective identity practices with Ganga, my inner voice. † transform all boundary speakers into postcolonial subjects, "Other Australian" (OA) and "øthered Australian" (øA). † specifically use only "øthered Australian" narratives and the voices of "Other Australian" are embedded indirectly within my dialogues with Ganga. Through these dialogues with Ganga we surface the postcolonial elements with which we, the "øthered Australian," contest the "Other Australian" and the ideological "Australian." Ganga and † bring to light the "power" of "whiteness" and "Australianness" in "*øthering*" and contesting our identity layers. † present and represent the crisscross of our discourses, strategies, and material effects of our contest by engaging with the "postcolonial estuary of contesting Australian."

† try and make meaning of my experience with Ganga in the concluding chapter. † discuss the phenomenon "Australian," which was central to our cultural identity enactments, dividing and uniting who we were. We were many, yet we responded to this one image, "Australian," an illusion that was created and nurtured for ideological gratification and power. As Holmes, Hughes, and Julian (2007) stress, the conceptions of both "Australian" and "migrant" identities need to be changed to overcome racism and injustice. Here, † contemplate with varied forms of "othering truths" that interact and act with this complex phenomenon presented by multiculturalism and nationalism, especially in early childhood settings. † finally imagine

hybridity as a reality for all individuals and groups, and not reserved for some. I end my Ganga with how she began, *"ever changing, ever flowing, and yet ever the same."*

In the epilogue, our journey rebounds and I carry some of my Ganga back to the early childhood setting where she originated two years ago. I share Ganga with the staff (early childhood educators currently at that centre), and we briefly (re)contest our cultural identities. With my tensions that arise from my quest to decolonize, my inability to sever my colonized roots, and my postcolonial reality, I tell our cultural identity stories in this book. Our voyage in Ganga begins.

CHAPTER 1

Ganga: Our Beginnings, Our Context, Our Stories

> *The flowering of a truly national spirit in Australia is not an optional extra, but a major objective to be sought in the next few decades.*
> *My personal ambition is that all Australians of all backgrounds will always be proud.... to say... "I am an Australian."*
>
> —Grassby, 1973, pp. 8–9

In the following chapter, I set the context in which our contest for inquiring into our cultural identity stories began. I narrate how and with what I constructed my imagination, my pursuit to transform early childhood cultural identity practices with children and families, through my doctoral study. My study is a collection of stories that were exchanged in early childhood settings with young children, their families and the staff (early childhood educators), who educationally cared for the children. These stories reflect the everyday cultural realities and imaginations influenced by our real and yet imagined categorizations of collective identities for "self" and "other."

Cultural Identity Stories: Our Realities and Our Imaginations

I have always found it difficult to define what my cultural and national identity represented, especially due to my engagement with the histories of India. The land that had been fragmented and the united nation that it is now and yet remains fragmented in many ways. India as a modern nation was built by the colonizers, the "British Raj," to rule the population that had historically been diverse in its ethnic, linguistic, and religious makeup; a nation that still stands divided after it became free of colonial rule in 1947 (Keay, 2000; Sen, 2005). India, since then, is united as a country, yet divided by its national identity, "Indian," a reality, and yet an imagination when its multiple roots are traced. Therefore, it is very difficult for me to encapsulate and present the essence of "Indian" culture or what is being "Indian," in a definite manner. After all, culture is a difficult term to define, because it is abstract and evolutionary, yet it has become central to most conversations in today's society (Pang, 2001; Bennett, 2003; Rosaldo, 2006; Grant and Sleeter, 2007). The narratives in my study too were prolific with our cultural/ethnic/national identity conversations. This centrality of cultural narratives in today's society became the focus of my study and hence this book, as current societies are situated within constructs of the modern nation-state. According to Appadurai (2006), the modern nation-state, despite being constructed on the premise of multiculturalism and inclusion, is imbued with divisional ideas of nation and nationality. After all, constructs such as nation and national identity are built on notions of national sovereignty based on ethnicity (Appadurai, 2006). In many ways, fervent nationalism is juxtaposed to multiculturalism, as sovereign nation and national identity constructs do prescribe and ascribe such solidarity to individuals' collective identity. This then renders the development of fragmented multiple identities within one unified collective identity a difficult state to attain and accept, as specific ways of being and acting a specific collective or national identity is meticulously laid out. Anything outside what has been laid out always remains outside what has been conceptualized within those identity boundaries, unless these identity boundaries are repeatedly disrupted and reconfigured to result in boundless boundaries.

Although the creation of nation-states and national subjects has become today's reality, it is laden with complexities, especially due to global mobility. Colonization and globalization are phenomena that have resulted in much inside/outside movements across modern nation-states. This has caused individuals and groups from varied cultural and religious groups with congruous or discordant interests to come together within a shared space, the nation. In fact, Hall (1996) declares that colonization and decolonization have resulted in postcolonial societies with a population that is made up of colonizers and colonized and many others who are linked sometimes by such histories. Therefore, there are constant arbitrations, negotiations and contestations between individuals and groups loyal to their collective identities, on claiming ownership of that illusive construct, the national subject, as this identity is being constantly disrupted and challenged with dynamic movements. With his phenomenon becoming more and more inescapable, the sociopolitical institutions of sovereign nations dedicate much of their political discourses to owning and claiming unified, definite boundaries for their state and the national subjects within these states. These political repertoires in most cases invariably result in defining these national subjects as the insiders, and therefore define the outsiders with certain unspoken, but loosely specified physical characteristics, such as skin color, facial features, and accent, in other words, "race" ideologies. Thus, in relation to modern nation-states, as problematic as it may seem, the sociopolitical systems intentionally and/or inadvertently perpetuate "race" ideologies to construct and establish one's national, ethnic, or cultural identity. Hence, "race," a mere social construct, a dominating imagination, has become a reality in many modern societies, as it is often linked with color, ethnicity, religion, and language (Merenstein, 2008). Therefore, biological markers such as skin color, hair, and other physical attributes used in "race" discourse are used in discourse of ethnicity indirectly, and thus, one way or the other, culture and ethnicity gets fixed and bound by one's "race" (Gunaratnam, 2003). Taylor (2004) too contends that "race talk" has become a symbol of Western societies, leading to notions of citizenship, and it further centralizes the interactions of those who live within such societies around identity constructs such as ethnicity, nationality, culture, gender, class, and caste. In fact, conversational starters that aim to establish or mark one's ethnic origin with physical features have become accepted "curiosities" in many so-called multicultural societies. Thus, in many ways, "race talk" or identity imaginations based on skin color, ethnicity, and culture have become today's realities.

My study, our cultural identity contest began, and these identity imaginations based on "race" ideologies became very evident in the everyday narratives that were exchanged between children and adults in early childhood settings in Australia. Such identity exchanges became so central to our daily conversations in early childhood settings, that what began as a study of cultural identity enactments became a critical inquiry of our postcolonial realities and imaginations, the "race" categorizations of "Australian" and "not Australian." Our realities and imaginations were colonized by national ideologies, deeply and undeniably connected to the color and culture of "whiteness."

Australia's Australian: A Postcolonial Reality and Imagination

Australia is a land with an overt colonized past and covert colonizing present, a postcolonial reality for some and an imagination for others. Many groups that are linguistically, culturally, and religiously different come together within the national boundaries of Australia, and this diversity is constantly widening with newer groups and individuals coming to live in Australia temporarily and permanently. The Australian population is diverse in its ethno-cultural makeup with indigenous peoples, colonizers, or settlers and later immigration. More than 29.2 percent of Australian population was born overseas (Australian Bureau of Statistics, 2011). But, diversity and multiplicity is not a recent phenomenon in this land. Before colonial occupation, there were around 600 tribes living in this land, whose social organization was highly complex and linguistically diverse (Holmes et al., 2007), however with no national or political unity amongst the groups. Added to this complexity, there were also other ethnicities such as Chinese and Germans in the early 1800s living in this land along with many heterogeneous Aboriginal groups. After colonization, with "white Australians" (Catholics and Protestants of British and Irish origin) becoming absolutely dominant, ethnic minorities, such as Aboriginal Australians, Chinese, and Germans declined in numbers (Jupp, 1997). Thus, colonization and colonial occupation became a defining factor in the diminishing of social diversity with the centralization of "white Anglo-Saxon" as the dominant group. This group had absolute political power and control over not just this land now called Australia, but also its peoples. The establishment of Australian federation united the colonies to become one nation, Australia. But the "white" colonizers continued to rule and shape Australia and Australians' identity.

The Australian Natives' Association, one of the organizations that was instrumental in establishing the Australian federation in 1901, was made up of "white" men born in Australia (National Council for the Centenary of Federation, 2001) with no member from the Aboriginal population. However, the "native" status and the ownership hence claimed by this group of "white" men resulted in the establishment of this imagi(nation) on Aboriginal land, on Australia, and on the national subject, "Australian." The establishment of Australian federation presented an imagined understanding for the "white men" of British and Irish origin who then governed Australia that Australia was now free of its colonial past. However, the "white men" still controlled its colonized borders with white supremacy, which was in reality still attached to its colonial past. Thus, with an image of having established a unique Australian identity that set them apart from their British origin, the identity of Australia was controlled by the "white fellas" born in Australia, and not by the "black fellas," the original owners of this occupied land.

The Australian identity continued to be shaped by its current occupiers with overt racially discriminatory policies. The *White Australia policy* (1901) was drawn to overtly maintain the identity of Australia with "white Anglo Saxon," English-speaking image. With heavy-handed discriminatory political measures, the political rulers protected the colonial roots of this nation from being colored by those within this land and from outside. Later, as Makkai and McAllister (1993) point out, the gatekeepers of "white Australia" liberalized their borders to other European migrants, to make Australia economically viable. Tavan (2004) adds that it was only around the 1960s when Australia faced severe criticism from non-European nations of the world, did it reluctantly reconcile to opening its doors to Asian refugees. After the abolition of the *White Australia policy* in the early 1970s, the Australian politics moved from colonial, discriminatory discourses that established white supremacy, to moderate, tolerant discourses of multiculturalism.

The then Whitlam Labor government openly declared the demise of the *White Australia policy* and the beginning of a new era of multiculturalism and acceptance of cultural diversity. Since then, most sociopolitical institutions in Australia have adopted policies that speak of acknowledging, respecting, valuing, and celebrating indigenous cultures and the cultures of fresh migrants. Within the Australian context and the context of many countries like Canada, United States of America, and New Zealand that share histories of colonial settlement on indigenous lands, the development of Aboriginal or migrant identity can be very complex. This sociopolitical context requires the construction of "self" in relation to one's ethno-cultural identity within the discourse of nationalism. The resulting multicultural discourse encourages one to own the identity of his/her ethnic origin and become a national subject, thus demanding dual or multiple identities, a "migrant self" and a "national self," in oneself. This creates and proposes a complex development of sometimes juxtaposed value systems, especially for Aboriginal and migrant Australians, as it automatically positions Aboriginal Australians and migrant Australians as having cultures outside what is considered as uniquely Australian. Examining and responding to such strategic negotiation of one's identity in relation to arbitrating such juxtaposed value systems hasn't received much attention in multicultural education (Grant and Agosto, 2006). Yet, all these identity arbitrations, such as national, migrant, and Aboriginal identity built around the national imagi(nation) of modern statehood is vociferously expressed by the sociopolitical institutions in the name of upholding national interest and security. Moreover, they also occupy the minds of today's sociopolitical narrators. This national imagi(nation) stretches and penetrates all sociopolitical institutions, including the field of early childhood educational care and development, as modern nation-states commit themselves to developing such identities in young national subjects through pedagogical and curriculum guidelines.

Cultural Identity and Early Childhood Education in Australia

Early childhood is a stage during which identity ideas are exchanged and established with the use of social interaction using language. The conception of one's identity or an understanding of what one is, the development of "self" is seen by many theorists as something that is innate, unique, and desirable to humans (Crisp and Turner, 2007), a distinguishing capacity that sets humans and animals apart. Early childhood, in particular, is seen as a critical period for the development of one's identity, which is gaining a knowledge of who one is and affiliating oneself with social groups, defined by factors such as ethnicity, race, culture, gender, and class (Miell, 1995; Schaffer, 1996; Epstein, 2009). It is also a period during which social interactions with those around enables young children to construct understandings about the status of the group to which they belong in comparison with those to which they don't. Therefore, although one's identity development is regarded as innate and very human, it is also dependent on the identity messages that are available outside.

Education and educational setting is one such socially interactive medium that influences identity and more specifically cultural identity development. In Australia, since the advent of multiculturalism, educational settings including early childhood educational care settings have been recommended to embed national identity development along with curricular practices that promoted and supported Aboriginal and migrant cultures. Since 1980s, most educational settings in Australia had developed goals to adopt multicultural policies and practices as their priorities to enable all individuals to maintain their cultures and to educate everyone about Australian values. Their key aim was not just the socioeconomic progression of young Australians through education, but also education to eradicate racism and prejudice (see Australian Victorian Essential Learning Standards [AusVELS], Australian Curriculum Assessment and Reporting Authority [ACARA], 2009; Melbourne Declaration on Educational Goals for Young Australians, Ministerial Council on Education, Early Childhood Development and Youth Affairs [MCEECDYA], 2008). These documents recommend the promotion of a strong sense of cultural identity in children and families who have migrated to Australia, promote indigenous or Aboriginal perspectives, and overall epitomize the development of unified national identity as Australians. These overarching educational documents based on the realms of multiculturalism also influence the field of early childhood education in Australia. Drawing upon the early childhood theories of identity development and the above pedagogical recommendations, the Australian early childhood curricular guidelines (see The Early Years Learning Framework [EYLF], Commonwealth of Australia, 2009) encourage early childhood educators to engage in multicultural practices that are conducive to developing cross-cultural understandings whilst developing a sense of Australian citizenship. However, such multicultural educational discourse has been critiqued as being about maintaining the cultures of those that are seen as different from the centrally positioned "white" English speaking Anglo-Australian identity (Aveling, 2002; Leeman and Reid, 2006).

Studies conducted in Australian early childhood settings with very young children found that children from a very young age conceptualize and practice "race" categories and nationalistic discourses through their daily play behavior and interactions (see MacNaughton, 2001; MacNaughton and Davis, 2001; Skattebol, 2003). These studies also reveal that children as young as three to five years of age had hypothesized the physical attributes of the national subject "Australian," using which they included and excluded children in their educational care settings. Moreover, "whiteness" or "race" discourse played a central role in defining this national subject "Australian," and therefore, excluding the "non-white" as a "migrant other" was evident in children's expressions. Yet, the studies also confirmed that most adults who educationally cared for young children found it difficult to respond to children's discriminatory "race" discourses. Thus, children's narratives of national imagi(nation) remained uninterrupted in early childhood settings, as they were heard and discarded as insignificant or left unheard by adults in those settings.

The above became the core around which my doctoral study, which later morphed as Ganga, began. With my son's voice about our migrant reality and the "white" imagination in my heart, I set out to conduct my participatory action research with young children, families, and educators in early childhood settings. Still standing upon my postcolonial pedestal, a reality hidden underneath the mask of developmental and social psychology, I set out to inquire the role of benign "othering" in enacting cultural identities in early childhood settings.

Cultural Identity Sites: Where, How and with Whom We Contested National Imagi(nation)

The literature highlighted the gaps in pedagogical practices and the evidence of "race"-based exclusion in educational settings. They also spoke of the relevance of challenging the national imagi(nation) around which cultural identities were enacted in multicultural Australia. Therefore, my aim was to bring about collaborative action and transformation in daily early childhood pedagogical practices that supported cultural expressions equitably. Guajardo (2008), among many authors, believes that action research has a transformational effect naturally. I conducted qualitative, participatory action research (see Freebody, 2003; Martin, lisahunter, and McLaren, 2006; MacNaughton and Hughes, 2009) and worked closely and collaboratively with children, early childhood practitioners, and families in those participating sites. I was aware that such a study was less generalizable: as Denscombe (2010) aptly comments, the action researcher can never be impartial and separate self from what is happening by taking an unobtrusive stance. I recognized that all my research actions were going to be influenced by my theoretical underpinnings and my postcolonial experiences of color and colonization in postcolonial Australia.

I collected narratives, which distinguished and spoke of cultural identity attributes in early childhood settings. Narratives can be politically powerful, as they can mobilize groups into action (Reissman, 2008), and therefore this methodology, in combination with participatory action research model, best suited the key aims of my study. As soon as I began my data collection, I realized that narrative inquiry was central to my study, as narratives became descriptions of the dynamics involved in my action research cycles. Most of all, with narrative inquiry I was able to situate my voice within what was exchanged and analyze my own subjective responses and understandings of events, as they were observed and recorded. Using multiple methods, I collected cultural identity stories, which included extensive, informal conversations with and between children, educators, and families. Simultaneously, I used participatory observational techniques with which I triggered purposeful conversations with children, educators, and families to elicit their reactions and responses to particular cultural exchanges and expressions. I also conducted face to face individual interviews with educators to gather their attitudes and understandings of early childhood practices that supported children's cultural identity development. Field notes and journals in which I recorded not only the events as they unfolded but also my own immediate reactions to those events and observations became an insightful source that researched my own "self" and my subjective reactions, interactions, and interpretations.

Denzin and Giardina (2007) especially outline that including multiple voices, especially the researcher's subjectivity, makes the act of researching less colonizing. Being a postcolonial subject, who had always consciously and unconsciously opposed colonial domination, participatory action research seemed less colonizing to me, as it researched "self" and exposed "self" with "other." However, I reminded myself that this form of research can also be equally colonizing, as I planned to initiate change, having already established the existence of deficits in pedagogical practices that supported cultures and cultural identities in educational care settings in Australia. Authors offer varied strategies to overcome the colonizing nature of research experiences that "other" the experiences and voices of the researched. Reinharz (2011) particularly urges the researcher to become conscious of her layers, the "research self, personal self and situational self," and question how one is contextually labeled and is labeling the researched. For me, it was beyond these labels, as I had the power to record and analyze the emotions and feelings felt by all involved, with the use of my theoretical and experiential learning. Mills and Gale (2004) encourage one to explore the space between the researcher and the researched, especially while writing, as this is when the researcher has the power to eliminate "self," to engage in the colonizing act of "othering." I wrote in such a manner that I analyzed and theorized my own emotions and how I responded and made meaning of events as they happened. Yet, I still felt that every research act was a colonizing act, as the data from the "researched other" was collected by the "researching self" with a quest to uncover particular truths. The "researching self" dissected what was said, and unsaid, in the name of analysis and wrote for and about the "researched other" to be divulged with the outer world. I wanted to expose my "othered self" and my "othering self" and observe how these fragments within myself influenced the generation, interaction, and interpretation of and with data. Hence, I wrote about my "self," by situating my "self" among and with the "researched other." I began to introspectively have such conversations during every point of engaging with data. Conversations with my own "self" became integral to my study to bring forth the constant clashes and twists within myself. Such endless, silenced, internal conversations erupted as cultural narratives were exchanged between speakers and later during documentation and contemplation of daily events and even now as I embark on externalizing these by writing this book. Exposing my non-severable "postcolonial self" still continues to occupy my mind, and I do not want to justify or validate any of my research experience as something that is devoid of my subjective emotions.

Ganga emanated from the two long day care centers (early childhood settings that provide educational care for children between the ages of zero and five) in Melbourne metropolitan area that consented to participate in my study. I specifically chose to conduct this study in centers with two or more children (focus was on children aged between three and five years old) whose families had migrated from India to Australia. In total, there were four focus children from one centre (one boy and three girls, all in one room) and three focus children from the other centre (one girl in *kinder* room and two girls in pre–*kinder* room). Although all the children in the group including focus children, their families, and participating staffs were informed of my study, I included the narratives only of those who gave consent to participate. Those children who assented to participate chose their own pseudonyms. I spoke predominantly in Tamil and Hindi, and sometimes in English with my focus children and families. The data collection phase began in May 2010 and ended in December 2010. I initially spent two whole days a week in each center and worked only in the rooms with focus children, their families, and educators at the settings. After about six weeks from the date of commencing my research, one centre withdrew from this study. The reason for this was that they felt that the ideas I exchanged with children challenged Santa believers (see chapter 4 on Forbidden Fs for details). They agreed that I spoke the truth, but speaking my truth was a mistake and a problem. I then spent four days a week in the center that continued to participate in the study until the end of that year.

I embraced my participatory action research methodology and my narrative inquiry very close to me with intentions of collaborative action and liberation from national imagi(nation). I imagined that it was possible to bring about changes in current early childhood pedagogical practices, as now I not only had my lived experiences, which I could theorize, but also my live data gathered collaboratively, which I could validate and theorize with children, practitioners, and parents. Yet, as I practiced my research, I saw "difference," in our histories, in our theories, in our experiences, in our subjectivities, and in our colors, through and with all my "other," and this made the procedure highly complex and volatile. Before I continue with the stories that flowed from our realities and imaginations of cultural identities, I present the terms that I frequently use to tell our stories with Ganga.

Cultural Identity Signifiers and Terms

I describe some of the significant terms that I use in this book, and why and how I have used them. These terms are used in chapter headings and frequently throughout this book to represent specific conceptual ideas and meanings that I recognized as being central to my discussions.

Boundary: As central as the term "culture" is to my study and the functioning of today's society, I found it very difficult to use this as a term to represent the way in which we expressed our collective identities. Moreover, I felt that those constructs were highly problematic, as they oversimplified the realities of those who embodied these concepts in their daily lives. Therefore, I used the term "*boundary identity*" to represent "culture" constituted by our geographic, linguistic, ethnic, and religious origins. The participants, including me, became "*boundary speakers*," and the narratives that I gathered became "*boundary speaks*." Stemming from this chief concept are the following terms, which are significant in representing the layers of our boundary identities.

Boundary streams: These are the predominant themes embedded in boundary speaks, around which boundary speakers frequently enact boundary identities of self and others. Boundary streams are central to the discussion of Ganga, as these are the many layers that we, as boundary speakers, used to depict the boundaries and persona to each other, and the discussed boundary streams are *Complex(ion)*, *Forbidden Fs (Food, Faiths, and Festivals)*, *Tongue ties*, and *Terra strikes*.

Complex(ion): The strongest stream, *complex(ion)*, skin color was used by boundary speakers and children, including focus children and adults, in their boundary identity, especially national identity definitions. Complexion literally means one's skin color or the natural tone of one's skin; however, here I name this as complex(ion), for it played in complex ways and was, many times, closely affiliated to one's innermost emotions and feelings.

Forbidden Fs (Food, Faiths, and Festivals): The three aspects namely food, faiths, and festivals were frequently included and interpreted by boundary speakers as key features of one's cultural attributes, closely related to the daily enactment of one's boundary identities. I discuss the three Fs: Food, Faiths, and Festivals as one stream, because on many occasions they were inextricably woven directly and indirectly by us, as boundary speakers. If the stream complex(ion) opened up the conceptualization of "Australian" and "not Australian" at a glance, this stream entrapped us within the boundaries of these identities. Yet, it seemed to be considered by many boundary speakers that it needed to be silenced or excluded within the realms of public, everyday discourses. I sensed that legitimizing any open discussion or practices of food, faiths, and festivals was closely linked to whose boundaries these represented and how. And therefore, I group and name these as the Forbidden Fs. Our understandings of these identity layers were intense, deep, and sometimes unresolved.

Tongue ties: Tongue ties was one of the smaller streams that contributed to Ganga's boundary course through its boundary flows. This stream was most significant in establishing the language of "Australian." I named this stream as "Tongue ties" because the "boundary speakers" "tied" or restricted the public expressions of one's linguistic background with notions of speaking and hearing "Australian."

Terra strikes: This "boundary stream" was abounding with the boundary speakers' commitment to their borders—"terra," the national territory and identity. Thus, this stream exposed the interplay of fear and desire for multiplicities within what was considered to be the space of "Australian." The boundary "speaks" depicted our desires, fears, and challenges and our sense of ease in challenging or being challenged.

The "boundary speaks," which I use in the following chapters, are narratives, which I collected through field notes, participant observations (informal and purposeful interactions and silences with focus children, children in the group, families, and staff), and open-ended interviews with staffs. The sample size is very small. Therefore I have chosen not to link the narrators with their corresponding centers to maintain their anonymity. The background information of the key "boundary speakers" that Ganga encountered is included at the end of this book.

In what follows, I elaborate on the theoretical tools using which I inquired with the narrators and narratives of national imagi(nation), masking and unmasking my postcolonial subjectivity. I particularly discuss how I used the different forms of "othering," and their theoretical links, in making particular meanings of the narratives that spoke of the realities and imaginations of "Australian" and "not Australian."

CHAPTER 2

Boundaries Speak: othering, Othering, øthering Australian / Not Australian

> *In language, there are important connections among saying (informing), doing (action), and being (identity). If I say anything to you, you cannot understand it fully if you do not know what I am trying to do and who I am trying to be by saying it. To understand it fully you need to know who is saying it and what the person saying it is trying to do.*
>
> —Gee, 2010, p. 11

I began with my postcolonial lens, because of which I was already exposed to terms such as "othering," "Self," and "other" in particular ways. These terms relate to the relationship between the colonizer, "Self," and the colonized "other," and how the process of "othering" established and perpetuated colonial dominance and hegemony discursively. I began to wonder whether I was engaging in the same binary discourse that I critiqued using my postcolonial interests. I therefore adopted theories of social psychology and psychoanalysis, with intentions of decolonizing my biased vision and justifying my ways of distinguishing what was around me from who I was and we were as cultural enactors. I began to engage with Ganga by accepting that "othering" was an innate unavoidable process in the development of one's personal and social or collective identity (for me this represented ethnolinguistic/cultural/national identity). However, as my inquiry with Ganga became deeper and deeper, I realized that I could not accept such simple interpretive conclusions about how we categorized and attributed "boundary identity" for each other. I searched for other processes submerged in Ganga that were influencing our "boundary speaks" in specific ways. From Ganga surfaced three different forms, "othering, Othering, and øthering." The following provides not just an explanation for my use of multiple theoretical tools to unravel complexities attached to our cultural interactions, but also reflects my inability to cleanse my postcolonial "self," which followed me till the very end.

OTHERING "SELF" AND "OTHER": CHILDHOOD INEVITABILITY

Children's awareness of who they are begins at a very young age. As soon as they begin to understand and use representational language, they understand their individual and social attributes such as gender, ethnicity, "race," and abilities. In social psychology, the development of one's identity is reasoned as a process of differentiating or discriminating or *"othering"* to establish what one is (self) and what one is not (other). According to Crisp and Turner (2007), "self" consists of "personal identity" (one's personality and temperament) and "social identity" (the social groups such as cultural, religious, ethnic, occupational, sports, etc. that individuals consider themselves to be a part of). These theories and those of psychoanalysis also suggest that young children's development of who they are is dependent on learning from "other" to ascertain and distinguish the attributes of "self" and "other" with language based categories or "othering" (Lacan, 2002; McKinlay and McVittie, 2008; Elliott, 2010). The role of "other" is played by significant adults such as family members and teachers, and peers, as they provide such categorizing language in the development of one's identity. In fact, pre-schoolers' awareness about negative judgments about their own group make them want to affiliate themselves with a group of higher status, and children gather this information from the media and those around them (Kowalski, 2007). Thus, young children and adults through the process of "othering," construct identity categories of individual *personal self and other*, and the *collective social self and other*. Epstein (2009) too claims the inevitability of not just children's construction of such identities, but also how they attribute particular understandings to specific identities. These identity behavior attitudes and understandings stem from their social and cognitive experiences with those around. Epstein outlines the complexity of children's identity development as follows,

> Research has examined young children's awareness of such relatively stable attributes as race, social class, culture, gender and disability. How children come to understand these characteristics in themselves

and others is based on many perceptual, cognitive, and experiential, or social factors.

(Epstein, 2009, p. 26)

Identity categories also dictate our behavior. Our cultural stories or "boundary speaks" convey the identity characteristics of "self" as much as those of "other." "Boundary identity," that is, our cultural or ethnic group subscription, greatly affects our behavior, as we modulate our behavior to fit the characteristics of our own group, and eliminate or exclude the attributes of those whom we categorize as outsiders (Hogg and Abrams, 2007; Wright and Taylor, 2007). These theories further argue that due to this innate need to classify and establish the common characteristics of the social groups of "self" and "other," the process of categorizing individuals into groups with predetermined attributes, stereotyping is inevitable when diverse groups come together. Prejudices and tensions that emanate due to such stereotyping are unavoidable, as each group tries to assert its position in the society with group loyalty; however such tensions can be reduced by bringing groups together through "re-categorization" (Crisp and Turner, 2007). Thus, social psychology theorizes the presence of "other" and the relevance of "othering" in modulating one's behavior and it further clarifies the evidence of group partialities and distinctions, and provides strategies to reduce biases and tensions between groups. The process of "re-categorization" brings members from both groups to become loyal to a new category, and now the members from diverse groups become bound by the identity behavior expectations of this new group. I argue that multiculturalism is one such phenomenon that brings diverse groups together within a nation and nationhood. As a nation, Australia's multiculturalism, therefore, presents and grapples with this inevitable "othering" that stems from varied cultural groups coming together. Most of all, Australia's socio-political system believes that itneeds to find strategies to "re-categorize" these groups to reduce the unavoidable prejudices arising from this phenomenon.

OTHERING "AUSTRALIAN" AND "NOT AUSTRALIAN": NATIONHOOD COMPLEXITY

The political establishment of multiculturalism in Australia in the 1970s resulted in many cultural or ethnolinguistic groups living together, yet also engaging in quite distinct cultural practices. From then on, the sociopolitical institutions in Australia had always recognized the differences in cultural practices and values between such groups. Australia's sociopolitical structures since then have strived to promote multiculturalism to manage varied cultural groups within its national boundaries. However, having acknowledged the differences in cultural groups and the tensions that may emanate from bringing varied groups together, the simultaneous construction of unified national identity also became a major political agenda (Stokes, 1997). Thus, the creation and the maintenance of one national identity—"Australian"—for all, through the "re-categorization" of diverse groups, became a political imperative to reduce apprehended clashes between cultural groups in Australia. However, identity development is an "othering" act, as it is about distinguishing and maintaining what "self" and "other" is and isn't (Hall, 2003). Therefore, every time a specific group is created, named, and attributed with certain characteristics, it also creates other groups that aren't the one that is created. Hence, this unification of "differences" with one single "Australian" identity still resulted in creating a dichotomous relationship between the group "Australian" and the rest of the cultural groups in Australia. The very creation and the maintenance of one specific group, "self," which is the "Australian" with the process of nationalistic "re-categorization," thus resulted in the creation and the maintenance of "other," the "not Australian" simultaneously.

"OTHERING" IDENTITIES: "BOUNDARY SPEAKERS" IN GANGA

The theories of social psychology and psychoanalysis enable one to identify the presence of *"othering."* We as "boundary speakers," consciously and unconsciously "spoke" of the dichotomous relationships between "self," the "Australian," and "other," the "not Australian," and vice versa. Through "othering" we defined our boundaries within the major themes, Complex(ion), Forbidden Fs, Tongue ties and Terra strikes. Thus, we spoke or were spoken to as "Australian" or "not Australian" with the identity of "Australian" as our reference point time and time again. Every time Ganga and I tried to name or unpack the identity "Australian" with those who "spoke" as "Australian," they "spoke" as, about, and for the maintenance of "Australian," always distinguishing the characteristics of "self" and "other." An effective "re-categorization" process should have resulted in the acceptance of varied attributes of all cultural groups as "Australian"; on the contrary, the "boundary speakers" constantly fixed the identity of "Australian." Due to this, the individuals who recognized "self" as "not Australian" either strived to become "Australian," or chose to exclude and remain "not Australian." On the other hand, those who "spoke" as "Australian" not only strived to maintain "self," they also engaged in the maintenance of their "other" with repeated exclusion or silencing of what was deemed by them as "not Australian." Any acceptance of the "not Australian" was only in comparison to "self," the "Australian," and how close the "not Australian" was to "self." Thus, the voices of the "Australian" had the power to decide who, under what circumstances, could be accepted as "Australian." The recognition of "othering" as the process that established the categories of "Australian / not Australian" did not unravel why the "Australian" always had the power to modulate the cultural enactments of all "boundary speakers." Hall (2003) proposes that the theories of psychoanalysis and social psychology do not recognize the hierarchical power relationships that result from the establishment of binaries. Having identified the presence of definite binaries of "Australian / not Australian" in Ganga, I became interested in recognizing the power relationship that dominated the minds of all "boundary speakers." Hence, it became necessary for me to "speak" about the *Australian speakers*," the "boundary speakers" who spoke to dominate the identity of "Australian" and consequently those of "not Australian." My postcolonial "self," which I had tried to suppress, resurfaced to seek the origin of this control.

"OTHERING" IDEOLOGY: SUBJECTIFIED BY LANGUAGE

Australia is a multicultural nation and this is a reality that is attached to precolonial, colonial, and postcolonial past and present. And yet, the cultural enactments of all "boundary speakers" were controlled by the imagi(nation) of "Australia's Australian." It is this "Other," the political origin, which conceptualized the identity of this nation and the national subjects. Our "boundary speaks" were littered with language that endowed the "Australian speakers" with enough power to not just shape the identity of "self" the "Australian," but, in doing so, they also dominated all "boundary identity" behaviors in multicultural Australia. I traced the political ideas that simultaneously established multiculturalism and superimposed this with nationalism, this unifying process of "re-categorization." *Ideology* is defined by Althusser as *"Systems of ideas that dominate the mind of a person or social group"* (1971 cited in Alister, 1990, p. 123). If ideology is considered as a compilation of ideas that rules an individual or a group, our "boundary speaks" were dominated by the ideas about the characterization of "Australian," and by "Australian speakers." Thus, rather than individuals or groups engaging in "othering," the ideology that is "Australian" engaged in "Othering" "self," the "Australian," and the "other," the "not Australian." The ideology or the set of ideas about "Australian" also endowed this identity with more power with repeated reiterations. Ideologies are perpetuated by those in power into the society by "Ideological State Apparatuses" (ISA), which in turn converts individuals into subjects through the process of "interpellation" (Althusser, 2008). It is "interpellation," the repeated bombardment of symbolic messages with language statements that are showered by ISA that creates loyal subjects out of individuals. Ideology is abstract and cannot exert power in the absence of individuals (Althusser, 2008). Yet, ideology is able to maintain its hegemonic power and control over individuals' behaviors through the conversion of individuals into subjects with "interpellation." Then the subjects internalize these and mobilize these ideas with their everyday texts and practices. Here, rather than locating "self" with mere social groups based on culture/ethnicity/"race," as proposed by the theories of social psychology, the "self" pledges their loyalty to a specific identity to become subjectified. The daily behavior of the subjects are now dominated with intentions of showcasing their loyalty toward this identity, and they become incapable of thinking otherwise, as they believe such unquestioning commitment is for the betterment of all. Being unconsciously dominated by a set of ideas or identity behaviors that restricts subjects from thinking outside these prescribed behaviors is termed as hegemony. And Loomba (2005) annotates the link between hegemony and ideology as follows,

> Ideology is crucial in creating consent, it is the medium through which certain ideas are transmitted and, more important, held to be true. Hegemony is achieved not only by direct manipulation or indoctrination, but by playing upon common sense of people.
> (Loomba, 2005, p. 30)

Hegemony or domination of subjects' thoughts and actions with ideological ideas not requiring aggression or physical power penetrates and permeates into the daily practices of the categorical subjects. Hegemony drives the subjects to believe that categorical presence and adherence is essential for everyone's well-being and they willingly succumb to these ideas (Loomba, 2005). To control the subjects' behaviors in a hegemonic manner at the everyday level, language that propagates these ideas becomes critical in mobilizing ideological subscription.

The construction of this nation and its national identity was a political conception, a set of ideas attached to Australia's colonial roots. Therefore, the political language statements that continued to establish this ideology, the imagi(nation) of "Australian" became significant in tracing behaviors of Ganga's "Australian speakers" who repeatedly spoke to maintain this nation's identity and that of outsiders, the "not Australian."

"Australia's Australian": National Subjection

The nation Australia was created through colonization of this land and its peoples, and the resulting colonial settlement took political control of this space. Once the nation Australia was politically created and unified, it was seen as necessary by the colonizers to control the identity of this nation state and its social makeup. Historically, the policies of Australia (Immigration Restriction Act, 1901 or the *White Australia policy*) established the Australian identity as English speaking, white subjects, by overtly and covertly prohibiting individuals and groups from its borders on the basis of their color and language (Tavan, 2004; Holmes et al., 2007). During the days of the *White Australia Policy* (1901), the political "interpellation" was dominated by "whiteness." In 1973, under Whitlam's Labor government, Australia actively took steps to overthrow the *White Australia Policy*. Al Grassby, the minister for immigration in 1973 declared Australia as a multicultural nation in his famous speech to outline its political stance toward cultural diversity.

Grassby (1973) spoke as the "Australian" subject, for and about "Australian" identity, by taking ownership of the nation and its identity, by asking the question "*Who are we in Australia?*" and his speech reached out to the nation and its people through the representation of this nation with the everyday term, "*family of nation.*"

> The concept I prefer, the "family of the nation," is one that ought to convey an immediate and concrete image to all. In a family the overall attachment to the common good need not impose a sameness on the outlook or activity of each member, nor need these members deny their individuality and distinctiveness in order to seek a superficial and unnatural conformity. The important thing is that all are committed to the good of all.
>
> (Grassby, 1973, p. 3)

Thus, with much aplomb Grassby touched the hearts of people with everyday language, "family," and recommended nonconformity to uphold diversity. Yet, he recommends that individuals overlook their differences in order to commit to the common goodness by declaring the criticality of all subjects to become committed to this "family of nation." It is this subjectification that is critiqued by Althusser (2008) as a strategy used by sociopolitical institutions to dominate subjects' behaviors, as the subjects are made to believe that the prescribed set of categorical behaviors is for the betterment of all in the society. Thus, this categorical language mobilized the ideology of nation to its national subjects while introducing the acceptance of multicultural diversity. The categorical distinction of the then migrants, the "not Australians," followed,

> They perceive different goals and pursue them in their own traditional ways. In short, they lead a way of life which, while in living touch with its ancient forms and impulses, is imperceptibly coming to terms with—or at least learning to co-exist....in our society.
> (Grassby, 1973, p. 6)

The new arrivals, the "not yet Australians" and their attributes were established as *"traditional, ancient impulses,"* the "difference" that set them apart from what he claimed existed in this society. Grassby ensured that the existing subjects of Australia, the "Australians" were reassured that the very "different other" will not be a threat to "self," as they will learn to adapt and coexist. The speech ended with Grassby's proclamation of future ambition for all "Australian" subjects.

> The flowering of a truly national spirit in Australia is not an optional extra, but a major objective to be sought in the next few decades.
> My personal ambition is that all Australians of all backgrounds will always be proud...to say... "I am an Australian."
> (Grassby, 1973, pp. 8–9)

Thus, as the doors of Australia opened politically to invite "difference" on one hand, it negated "difference" on the other through nationalistic ideology. We, including the "not Australian," thus aspired to be "Australian" subjects.

"Australian": Interpellation Subjectification

The ideologically driven aims of these statements continue to acknowledge and outline the current diversity in the social makeup of

Australia. Grassby's legacy, the "interpellation" of "Australian" subjects, still continues in subsequent immigration policies of Australia: "*A New Agenda for Multicultural Australia*" (Commonwealth of Australia, 1999), "*Multicultural Australia: United in Diversity*" (Commonwealth of Australia, 2003) and the recent document, "*The People of Australia: Australia's Multicultural Policy*" (Commonwealth of Australia, 2011). With a strong emphasis on unification and nation-building, the statements maintain and propagate the identity "Australian" that Grassby "Othered." They particularly acknowledge the contributions of "*all Australians*," and simultaneously bring to note that Australia's political tone should continue to be dictated by "*the heritage of Great Britain and Ireland*" (Commonwealth of Australia, 1999, p. 20). The statements then set out to nationalize and unify the languages in Australia with, "*English is Australia's national language. Because it is a significant unifying influence*" (Commonwealth of Australia, 1999, pg. 27). The more recent publication "*Multicultural Australia: United in Diversity*," reinstates Australia's diversity with the acceptance and celebration of "difference," and yet, it extracts the unquestioning unification and loyalty to what is uniquely "Australian," for the betterment of all.

> Australian multiculturalism recognises, accepts, respects and celebrates cultural diversity; "All Australians are expected to have an overriding loyalty to Australia and its people" and "Our commitment to and defence of Australian values of equality, democracy and freedom unite us in our diverse origins, and enhance the ability of us all to participate fully in spheres of Australian society."
> (Commonwealth of Australia, 2003, p.2)

Thus, those who speak for and as "Australians" are made to believe that such abiding commitment is altruistic, as it is for the goodness of all.

The more recent "*The People of Australia: Australia's Multicultural Policy*" slightly softens the image of the migrant outsiders, "not Australian," as future citizens of Australia. However, they are again urged to pledge their loyalty to this unique set of "our" universalizing common "Australian" values and rights.

> These key rights and responsibilities are enshrined in our citizenship pledge which requires future citizens to pledge their loyalty to Australia and its people, uphold our laws and democracy and respect our rights and liberties.
> (Commonwealth of Australia, 2011, p.6)

The focus here is more on extracting one's loyalty to *"Australia and its people, our laws, our rights"* to alienate the diverse values that are automatically present with many cultures coming together. Moreover, this citizenship idea also leads the subjects who already believe they are "Australian" to claim ownership and vehemently safeguard "our laws and rights." The outsiders who are yet to become "Australian" are left to believe that this subjective identity, which is highly sacred and desirable, needs their unwavering assurance in protecting it from those who may be seen as threats. Thus, the outsiders who are now subjectified as "Australians" become insiders who guard this nation and national identity from those perceived as intruders.

The current immigration document (see Australian Citizenship: Our Common Bond, Commonwealth of Australia, 2013) is released by the Department of Immigration and Border Protection. This change in the name of the political body that oversees immigration affairs reflects the nation's fear of outsiders. Hence, the softened "interpellation" rekindles the desire to become subjectified as "Australian" through the promotion of Australian citizenship to migrants. The opening lines very purposefully script the image of a unique Australian membership as follows,

> Australian citizenship is a privilege that offers enormous rewards. By becoming an Australian citizen, you are joining a unique national community.
> (Commonwealth of Australia, 2013, p. 2)

This "uniqueness" of "Australian" identity is stressed to awaken the subjects' desire to eagerly seek and conform to the subjective behaviors circulated, in the interest of their national membership. What follows exposes the origin of this desire by repeating the very same words, "*I am Australian*," with which Grassby expressed his personal ambition.

> Australian citizenship is an important step in your migration story. Becoming an Australian citizen means that you are making an ongoing commitment to Australia and all that this country stands for. It is also the beginning of your formal membership of the Australian community. It is the step that will enable you to say "I am Australian."
> (Commonwealth of Australia, 2013, p. 3)

With the citizenship aspirations alighted brightly in the hearts of migrants, the statements demand the continued assurance by the now converted subjects to dutifully protect the nation as it is. Thus, these citizenship ambitions universalize the diversity that migration presents in a hegemonic manner, as Loomba (2005) comments, without force or direct prescriptions. The colonial ambiguity that reflects the desire for multiplicity and the fear of the same is still present in current statements that acknowledge Australia's multicultural identity.

> While we celebrate the diversity of Australia's people, we also aim to build a cohesive and unified nation.
> Australia's national language is English. It is part of our national identity. Everyone in Australia is encouraged to learn and use English to help them participate in Australian society.
> (Commonwealth of Australia, 2013, p. 9)

The idea that as "Australian" one has to accept English speaking as a part of their identity is prescribed right under the statement that acknowledges diversity and later stipulates the need to unify those differences in the name of national solidarity. Thus the fear of losing national sovereignty is achieved by universalizing Australia's linguistic identity. Many countries in the world still remain sovereign modern nation-states despite being multilingual. However, by strategically positioning the demand for monolingual English speaking identity as the image of the nation, the "Australian" subjects are made to feel that such a mandate is justifiable. Moreover, this also compels the subjects to not only adhere to speaking English, but also to believe doing otherwise can become a disrupting factor within the nation.

This identity persona of "Australia's Australian," being an ideological aspiration, an imagi(nation), is abstract. Ideological "interpellation" alone is not enough for the circulation of these abstract ideas, as committed vehicles are necessary for the dispersal and the maintenance of these constructs, especially to recruit more willing subjects. They actively tried to either convert the "not Australian" into subjects of Australia, or resorted to maintain the exclusivity of the "Australian" identity. The "Australian speakers" in Ganga served as these vehicles, and by shaping and propagating these floating identity ideologies, they kept Grassby's imagi(nation) alive. The political ideologies, thus "Othered" or colonized the identity behaviors of this nation and all national subjects.

"Othering" Subjects: "Australian Speakers" in Ganga

Ideology represents mere floating ideas that are inanimate until they are activated and mobilized by subjects through their daily practice.

The ideological messages that are in circulation are always in interaction with the individual; therefore, a "culture free" environment is impossible (Spears, 1997). Analyzing how ideological messages on nationalism and national identity influence adults and children in settings requires the textual analysis of what was uttered by speakers and connecting these with ideological language statements. Critical Discourse Analysis (CDA) theorizes the role of language (including all forms of symbols), its connections with the wider social processes (Fairclough, 1992), and, most critically, how ideologies are embedded in individuals' language (McKinlay and McVittie, 2008). By positioning language as the central medium using which people in power gain and maintain control, CDA identifies how ideology maintains power in societies through everyday spoken language. CDA thus serves as a theoretical tool that links ideological with individual language to identify power and control embedded in language that categorizes and shapes or "Others" identity attributes in particular ways. And CDA uncovered such language use that "Othered" the identity of "Australian" in Ganga.

The "Australian speakers" responded to shape the identity of "Australian," especially when they recognized that this identity was being disrupted and challenged by speakers. They immediately distinguished what "Australian," their collective identity, stood for, to reinforce the attributes of this identity. These "Othering" identity ideas were embodied and propagated by "Australian speakers" with its colonial beginnings, its "whiteness," as it was when this nation and the national identity were conceptualized. Backed by political hegemony that repeatedly idealized national unity, they controlled the identity behaviors of both "self," the "Australian," and "other," the "not Australian." And as subjects who succumbed to the power of "interpellation," these speakers strived to protect this ideology, the "Australian" from being challenged or changed.

Yet, not all "Australian speakers" could be subjectified to keep the sovereignty of this nation and national identity intact. Spears (1997) argues that as much as individuals are influenced by social structures, individuals create social structures and therefore have the propensity to become social agents, who can resist or reinforce those structures. There were those who resisted and spoke as "Australian," and their "Othering" spoke of reshaping the identity for and with the "not Australian," the outsiders. Althusser's ideological explanation on subjects' unquestioning adherence to categorical behaviors was inadequate to explain such challenging behavior. These resisting subjects, who spoke as "Australian" confronted commonly accepted and consumed nationalistic ideas, and worked to transform these with children, staff, and families in early childhood settings. These "Australian speakers" were Ganga's *"white transformers,"* as they spoke with their "whiteness" to oppose being dictated by the "white Australian." Just like how the "Australian speakers" spoke to keep Grassby's national "self" alive, the "white transformers" kept my postcolonial "self" alive. My postcolonial "self" could not be extinguished, and I succumbed to this subjectivity of mine to speak with the resistors, the "white transformers," and my own voice of resistance. I stopped masking my postcolonial subjectivity and I began to acknowledge and freely express my inner "self," which is also an outer "other" borne out of the ruins of colonialism and colonization.

"Othering" and "Othering": Inadequate Inference

I listened to the voices of resistance, the *"white transformers"* within the same subjective category of "Australian speakers." This brought to surface my subjectivity, my ideological commitment, whose presence I had tried to suppress in the name of decolonization. Hence, despite recognizing the ideological power that colonized "Australian speakers," my postcolonial "self" refused to discard the resisting voices in "Australian speakers." Engaging with processes of "othering" and "Othering" alone overlooked our postcolonial contradictions and I needed to unite with the resistors not to be subjectified but to challenge unifying hegemony. I resisted being dominated by the ideology "Australian" and by subjects who claimed the ownership of this boundary identity and the boundary identities of "not Australian" in the name of national unity. I exposed my postcolonial partialities and allowed my "self" to be consumed and to consume my subjective interests, and yet I resisted postcolonialism in its absolute form. I instead resurged to unite my postcolonial Ganga in her absolute form with other theories of resistance to contest the ideological "Australian" that dominated our boundary identities.

Contesting "Australian" with Postcolonialism

As pertinent as it was to make meaning of Ganga's "boundary speaks" with postcolonialism, especially due to Australia's colonized history that subjectified and controlled the identity of its national subjects with political and cultural superiority, it can also be inadequate.

Postcolonialism distinguishes and discusses the relationship between the dominant "Self" and the dominating "other" In its original form, postcolonialism too discusses the process of "othering" using which hegemonic, colonial interference and domination of lands and its peoples was made possible. The case for postcolonial challenge to colonialism was strongly put forth by *Orientalism*, in which Said (1978) identified and deconstructed the colonial discourse of "othering." Postcolonial theories provide the language and theories to discuss the inequitable relationship between the colonizing "Self" and the colonized "other" with the establishment of "difference" in the colonized by the colonizer. The colonial violation of lands and its peoples are justified as "Self" is proclaimed as a superior, scientific, independent, mature, normal, liberal, capable, logical individual thinker, while the "other" is positioned as inferior, mysterious and exotic, suitable for display, for its linguistic, cultural, and religious traditions. This deficient "other" is excluded for its lesser attributes, and yet maintaining that "other" becomes imperative for the very existence of the colonizing "Self," as the development of one's identity hinges on constructing "difference." Most of all, dominating and controlling the "other" is made possible as it is deemed as being deficient. The dominant "Self" with institutional force has the power to control, impose, and maintain these ideas in varied forms from politics, to education, to everyday realities of "Self" and the orient "other."

In globalized, complex, neoliberal societies, which are affected by different forms of inequitable practices, what is postcolonialism and its current theoretical applicability is much debated. Prasad (2003) too acknowledges that *Orientalism* has been criticized by some for its use of stringent dichotomies, (Occident/Orient; West/East; colonizer/colonized) and its nonrecognition of the change in views of the West about the Orient with time. Loomba (2005) extends this thought further to argue that colonialism is a form of dominance and therefore, postcolonialism as a tool can be used to resist any form of domination (caste, class, gender, "race," and culture). However, the inequities in current societies, although existent, are indiscernible as the process of colonization operates in covert ways through the attribution of responsibilities of failure and success on individuals. Such covert forms of domination cannot be challenged with the use of original, dichotomous categories of colonizer and colonized alone. Yet, according to Young (2001, 2003) and Rizvi (2007), postcolonialism unmasks covert forms of colonial domination still present in current societies that may seem far removed from its origins of imperialism and colonialism. Viruru (2006) adeptly uses postcolonial underpinnings to problematize the establishment of "difference," as this leads to the justification of controlling the "different other" with institutionalized discourses. And Ahmed (2007), too, deconstructs the language of diversity and multiculturalism that establishes "difference" between cultures to uncover their role in perpetuating inequities. In fact colonialism creates and maintains cultural identities for all who are colonized but not the colonizer (Camara, 2008). Here, the constructed imagined "difference" in cultural attributes between the existing national subjects (colonizers) and the newcomers (colonized) offers a justifiable foundation to carefully design institutionally supported policies to exclude and act upon the deficient "different other" with force. This takes into account how the identification of colonizers from colonized and vice versa shifts with sociopolitical contexts, as conditions that legitimize colonization now hinge on what attributes are differentiated to either epitomize and dominate, or trivialize and subordinate by a set of ideas or ideology perpetuated by the sociopolitical institutions at that time. It hence becomes critical to identify and unmask ideologies of "difference" that permit colonization at that moment in time when identities are contested by subjective speakers in their everydayness.

When ideology or a set of abstract ideas colonizes and dominates the minds of the people to seek out "difference" between each other, then the colonizer/colonized relationship is between the ideological force and all its subjects. It is not just between the colonizing and colonized groups and individuals. Postcolonialism, thus offers a very strong foundation to identify how ideas based on cultural identity "difference" dictate the daily interactions between ideology and its subjects and between subjectivities in complex ways. Yet, I still struggled with my postcolonial ambivalence. To engage with this complexity I had to encounter my tensions within, my aspirations to cleanse my postcolonialism on one hand, and my inability to think outside this paradigm. It was futile to believe that decolonization was possible for me—as Loomba (2005) aptly comments, postcolonialism does not arise out of vacuum, but is a presence that stems from colonialism, and a subject who challenges any form of dominance is a postcolonial subject. I accepted my Ganga, in all her forms and voices, as I realized that being postcolonial was being colonized yet decolonized, and being colonial yet anticolonial, it was about embracing "hybridity" (Bhabha, 1994, 1996) to purposefully work against any form of dominance. With and as Ganga in my multiple postcolonial forms, I united with many who had done the same, to shoot from and shoot at ideological dominance with our postcolonial messiness.

My search to seek and unite critical theories with Ganga continued. And now with my firm decision to support my "white transformers," I sought theories that spoke of "white" complacence and resistance.

Contesting "Australian" with Critical Race Theories

Critical race theory challenges "whiteness," the dominant culture, the culture that is seen as "normal" and "right," particularly in colonized states. Frankenberg (1993) argues that the American society was built with "race" as a marker of difference, and this still influences the discourses of today in varied ways. Frankenberg not only recognizes how "whiteness" is normalized, but she also unmasks how the normalization of "Americanness" is recognizable by those who are not American or not "white." Unlike *Orientalism*, critical race theory enables one to speak out of the binaries, as Frankenberg proceeds to uncover the discursive strategies used by "white" speakers to perpetuate, negate, or actively work against "white" dominance. Like the American society, the Australian society too had been historically controlled by "whiteness" and its colonial past. Yet, it is very difficult to define "whiteness" or "white culture" within the context of Australia. I recognized its presence and influence as an outsider, a "brown other," but it was woven intricately with everyone's lifestyles and worldviews, including mine. Thus, "whiteness" is slippery and one has to be highly exclusionary and biased to identify and name its affective attributes on us, "brown / not Australian speakers." Yet, succumbing to its omnipresence due to its anonymous presence hurts us. As Rose-Cohen (2004) states, denying "white culture" hurts people whose cultures are silenced by "whiteness." Taylor (2004) too argues that escaping or avoiding "race talk" does not eradicate racism, as any antiracist work has to stem from the racial categories that it seeks to abolish. There were too many "brown" subjects in Ganga who were silenced by "whiteness," and avoiding "race talk" would be like fuelling "white" dominance. Like Frankenberg, I wanted to speak against the normalization and nationalization of "Australianness" by "whiteness," with the propagators, negators, and the resistors of "white" power in Ganga. I now allowed my Ganga to embrace critical race theory along with postcolonialism.

My "postcolonial self" united with critical race theory, and Ganga changed and became more purposeful to "speak" with the voices of subscribers and resistors of "whiteness" in Australia. For many like me who want to challenge systems of dominance and control, these theories offer a relevant space to discuss the hegemonic colonization of identities by "whiteness" in postcolonial Australia. However, using postcolonialism alone can limit one's discussions within the binary constructions of "Australian / not Australian"; "white/brown" binaries. Speaking with binary constructs is a colonial discourse, and I did not want to emulate my colonizer by doing so. Yet, I wanted to speak with experiences that are unique to certain groups in the society of Australia. Moreover, I also wanted to "speak" with the silences and voices of resistance evident in both the colonized (not Australian other) and the colonizer (Australian Self). If ideology is a set of ideas that dominates one's mind, then isn't my postcolonialism that keeps pushing me to work against dominance an ideology that controls my mind? Should I succumb to its power? I refused to submit to my postcolonial ideologies, and yet I wanted to do so to speak against "white" power. My ambivalence and my reluctance to speak against the colonizing, dominant "Australian speakers" and the dominated "not Australian speakers" in Ganga continued. I now critically analyzed my postcolonial subjectivity and challenged my own theoretical ambivalence to reconcile and embrace my stance.

- I am a postcolonial subject, for me decolonization is impossible because of my commitment to acknowledge and challenge colonial dominance. The effects of colonialism are still within and without, and therefore, I have the propensity to colonize, as much as to challenge colonialism. Denying this hurts me, hurts those who are colonized and the "colonial resistors."
- If I rationalize my interactions with my postcolonial vision, I engage with subjects with my postcolonial subjectivity. I regard them as colonizers and the colonized. This hurts, but at the same time it also liberates me and those I engage with. Who gets hurt or liberated depends on our subjective affiliations to colonialism.
- I am also a colored subject, whose embodied "brownness" is a reality, which still is influenced by ideological constructions attached to one's skin color. The effects of my "brownness" are still within and without "whiteness." Denying my "brownness" and the experiences inflicted on this embodied subjectivity hurts me, hurts those who are colored and the "white resistors."
- If I rationalize my interactions with my "colored" vision, I engage with subjects with my "colored" subjectivity. I regard

them as "brown" and "white." This hurts, but at the same time it liberates me and those I engage with. Who gets hurt or liberated depends on our subjective affiliations to our "color."

The key elements of postcolonialism and critical race theory formed the theoretical foundation of my final analysis. And by combining these with poststructural feminist discourse analysis (Weedon, 1987), an analytical tool, I overcame my ambivalence to unpack our subjective discourses. Weedon legitimizes the use of Foucault's form of discourse analysis, as it specifically identifies resistance against dominance at the very individual level, to show where and how alternatives already exist, thus enabling changes to eventuate. Most of all, Foucauldian form of discourse analysis enabled me to work with the ever-pervasive abstract forms of identity constructs that dominate and dictate one's subjective behavior. Hence, I could speak with the slipperiness and the invisibility of "whiteness" that had controlled and still occupies our minds, including mine. Thus, although inquiring Ganga with postcolonial and critical race theories was very personal and emotional, combining discourse analysis to relate to the speakers made it surprisingly less personal.

My Postcolonial Discourse Analysis of Boundary Subjectivities

Any discourse analysis requires the recognition of patterns of statements that are specifically connected to different subjective dispositions of subjects. More specifically, poststructural feminist or Foucauldian form of discourse analysis inquires statements that reflect particular subjective disposition, are mutually bound, strategically formed, and practiced by subjects to realize specific ideals.

Discourses are particular ways of thinking, being, and acting. Although there can be many discourses available, only particular ways of performing specific identities are legitimized by institutions, and therefore, discourses directly relate to power and sanction (Mills 2004; Gee, 2010).

> Discourses are sets of sanctioned statements which have some institutionalised force, which means that they have a profound influence on the way that individuals act and think.
>
> (Mills, 2004 p.5)

Thus, it is this direct and indirect relationship that the institutions have on the performance of one's subjectivity; the subject chooses from the many discourses that are available to perform particular subjective category. To perform one's subjectivity, a subject can be attached to the category to materialize power or sanction, and a subject's discursive practice will hinge upon whether he/she wants to effect power or otherwise. The discourses that are attested by institutions are also powerful, and those that aren't are marginal and therefore can result in sanctions. Although discourses are connected to sociopolitical institutions, the materialization of power or sanction does not require institutional interference, as they can be delivered by subjects who are connected to these institutions in particular ways.

Hence, the categorical identity those subjects speak with, for and about, as "Australian" and "not Australian," becomes their subjectivity. However, the discursive practice of that subjectivity, whether "Australian" or "not Australian" can vary depending on the subjects' attachment to that category, which is also connected to power. Therefore, "Australian" and "not Australian" subjects perform discursively approved practices to retain and maintain power or resist and risk sanctions.

Strategies uphold discourses, as discourses are strategically interdependent, and strategies operate together, change with context and time to maintain particular material effects. Foucault specifically talks about *"tools and methods,"* the strategies, or the constituents that unite to enable certain ideas or *"knowledge."*

> That is to say there may be "knowledge" of the body that is not exactly the science of its functioning.... Of course this technology is diffuse, rarely formulated in continuous, systematic discourse; it is often made up of bits and pieces; it implements a disparate set of tools and methods.... Moreover, it cannot be localized in a particular type of institution or state apparatus.
>
> (Foucault, 1977, p. 16)

As strategies act as a unit to uphold specific identity ideas, the recognition of units of strategies is critical to discussions on how strategies are mutually supportive and morph contextually, especially when dominant discourses are challenged for change. Yet, these strategies are fragmented, scattered, and diffused throughout the social arena of discursive performance. The units of strategies enable specific ideas about what it is to be "Australian" and "not Australian" to be circulated and become more valid than others. And it is these units of strategies that are critical in upholding discourses of "Australian" and "not Australian" to attribute and mobilize particular subjective meanings.

Material effects are the elements that are concretely accessible by the subjects, and therefore these are directly related to discourses and strategies. Strategies work closely with specific discourses to realize specific material effects (Graham, 2005), because they determine the purpose of the statement, their subjective identity, and what material effects are realizable by that discursive practice. As material effects are the final outcomes of our discursive interludes, they are central to all of our subjective performances, and they reveal how we are attached to that subjective category, the subjects, and hence the institutions that guard these categorical behaviors.

In relation to discursive practices of boundary identities of "Australian" and "not Australian," *ideologies* that prescribe these categorical identity behaviors are mobilized by subjects via *discourses*, and are upheld by *strategies* that have the propensity to change contextually in order to realize certain *material effects* by those boundary subjects. Discourse, strategies, and material effects therefore become the key elements of our postcolonial contest of "Australian." The recognition of how discourses of "Australian" and "not Australian" are attached to *power*, and how power is made attainable by specific strategies is necessary to unearth the discursive effects of statements. There is an array of discourses available for both subjects. Subjectively practicing certain discourses result in the realization of more power than others, as these are institutionally attested and therefore dominant and when subjects choose to practice those that are less dominant or marginal, they are sanctioned and brought back to align themselves by dominant subjects (Foucault, 1972). *Power*, which is distinguished by a capital "P" by Foucault (2010) dictates our choice of discourse within any given context. And postcolonial subjects contest the ideological "Australian" via discourses and strategies attached to that "power."

"ØTHERING" SUBJECTIVITIES: POSTCOLONIAL SUBJECTS AND GANGA

I reconciled that there is no escape for me from my postcolonialism and my postcolonial discourse analysis. I now became determined to use *"race talk"* with postcolonial and critical race theories. The current political ideologies did not overtly reinscribe this identity by coloring "whiteness," nor did it ascribe only "whiteness" to this identity. Those who spoke with "whiteness" felt they naturally owned the nation and the national identity, the ideological "Australian" in their real imagi(nation). The "Australian speakers" colonized once by ideology, took control of this identity and in turn colonized the "not Australian speakers." Thus we were all colonized by this ideology "Australian." The conceptions of both "Australian" and "migrant" identities need to be transformed to overcome racism and injustice (Holmes et al., 2007). I set out to transform both, the "Australian" and the "not Australian" identities to steer Ganga toward speaking against racism, to speak with social equity. I transformed "boundary speakers" into postcolonial subjects, "*Other Australian*" (Australian speakers) and "*øthered Australian*" (not Australian speakers). With this naming I acknowledged the extrinsic nature of both identities, as both are structurally constructed by that ideological "Othering." It also represented the overlapping nature of these identities, and discarded the false dichotomy. The "*Other Australians*" are subjects, who "speak" as "Australian," who subscribed to the ideologies of "whiteness" and "Australianness," and "*øthered Australians*" represent those subjects who are differentiated and "øthered" by boundaries of "color" and "culture," ideologically and by "Other Australians."

My inquiry into how cultural identities were contested in Australian early childhood settings took a turn, and I now rebegan to write with and as Ganga. Ganga whispered how Ladson-Billings (2004) amply comments that critical race theory writers use stories to provide the additional voice and power, to enable people of color to speak with their experiential knowledge. She reminded me that many postcolonial authors too agree that working with postcolonialism gives voice to the "other," as the "other" is able to express their worldview (Ashcroft, 2001; Young 2001, 2003; Prasad, 2003; Loomba, 2005; Rush, 2006). The "boundary speaks" clarified that I remained outside what was conceptualized as "Australian," therefore I was an "øthered Australian" subject. In this final process of "speaking" with my Ganga, I did not "speak" about my colonizer, "Other Australian." If I did, as a colonized "self" I would be "othering" like my colonizer, speaking *about* my colonizing "other." Hence, I spoke *as* and *with* "øthered" voices, and how we discursively responded, reacted, and silenced ourselves depending on the discursive practices of "Other Australian." Ganga and I chose just our "øthered Australian" stories to expose the daily material effects realized by us (øthered Australian), as we contested the ideological "Australian" with "Other Australian." As and when we contested the "Australian," Ganga brought to note and reminded us of the discursive elements of "Other Australian" and "øthered Australian" with which our subjective goals were realized.

I split and represented my "voice" with "†," using which † beseeched Ganga, my inner "voice" to make meaning of our exchanges.

Ganga—my inner voice in her absolute postcolonial form—delved deep to surface daily realities that were tossed between postcolonial subjects. Ozkazanc-Pan (2012) recommends postcolonial feminist researchers to not just identify and acknowledge the complexities, but also to engage in this self-reflexive process that exposes the vulnerabilities of "self." Ganga signifies my self-reflexive engagement, as she analyzed our discursive messiness, including mine. The postcolonial estuary of contesting "Australian" surfaced to make visible the messiness of our contest with the ideological "Australian," the idea that ruled our everyday arbitrations. Figure 2.1 represents the complexities submerged in postcolonial Australia, where the discourses of "øthered Australians" converged and diverged with those of "Other Australian."

With Ganga's prompts, ⴕ immersed the "boundary speaks" into my postcolonial discursive analysis to recognize discursive patterns among subjective practices. We now present and explain each discourse and its associated strategies and material effects in our postcolonial discursive contest between "Other Australian" and "øthered Australian" respectively.

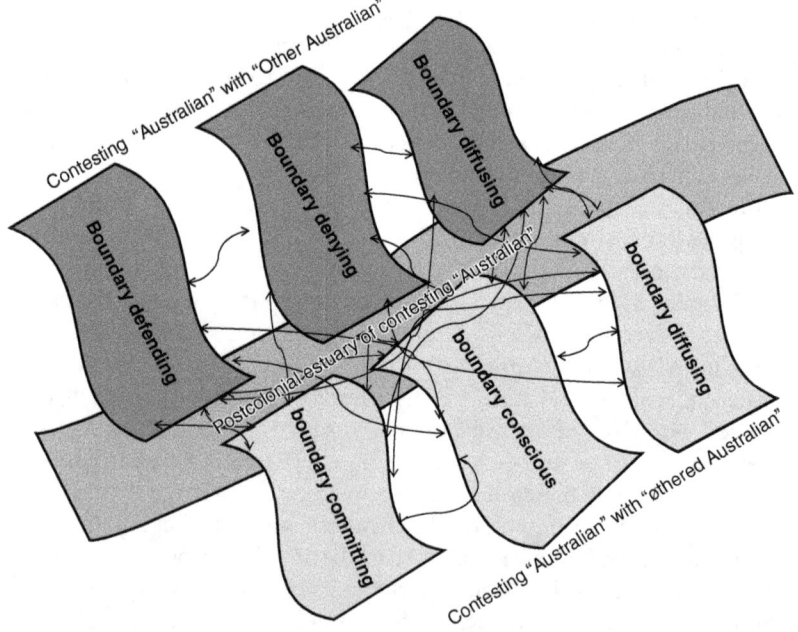

Figure 2.1 Postcolonial estuary of contesting "Australian"

Contesting "Australian": Discourses of "Other Australian"

The major discourses of "Other Australian" are, *Boundary defending, Boundary denying, and Boundary diffusing*. Ganga distinguishes the process of "othering," establishing differences between "self" from "other" by the subjects "Other Australian" as "øthering." The slash represents that the "øthered" have been endured this process twice, once by political ideology and then by "Other Australian." We have used upper case for all the discursive elements attached to "Other Australian" and lower case for those attached to "øthered Australian."

Discourse—Boundary Defending

In this discourse, the subject "Other Australian" speaks as, for, and about the nation and its national identity "Australian," and overtly expresses her/his commitment to maintain this. In openly excluding and maintaining "race" and/or culture–based attributes from what is proposed as "Australian," it resembles "Essentialist racism" (Frankenberg, 1993).

Strategies That Support the Discourse of Boundary Defending

Othering—A strategy used by "Other Australian" to take ownership and control, define the identity of "Australian," what the nation and the national subject stands for. It essentializes "Self" as being superior, and as an attribute that all individuals and groups should aspire to be.

Hierarchical øthering—This strategy supports the one above, and is used to talk about and exclude "øther" (ethnolinguistic, religious groups) from gaining access to what is claimed to be "Australian," by characterizing these groups as dangerous and a threat to national solidarity.

Nationalizing—With the use of this strategy, "Other Australian" is able to position "Self" as the representative of the national subject, which compares and recategorizes individuals and groups to be "as Australian as." The subject is able to dominate by claiming ownership of the nation and its identity unattached to any specific origin and history.

Theorizing—The "Other Australian" uses early childhood theories, media, or personal and public experiences to justify her/his stance. This enables the subject to avert and silence challenges that can initiate change in the current understandings and practices prevalent in that context. This strategy in combination with Western ideologies of individualism and humanism is quite effective especially in early childhood settings. After all, early childhood educators focus on promoting childhood innocence and individual development of children. This strategy also enables the "Other Australian" to discard the impact of colonization, and is able to retain possession and control of the national identity by remaining anonymous, as "Australian."

Sanctioning—The strategy punishes any act or presence of any elements that disrupt the ideologies, attitudes and understandings of nation and the national identity, "Australian." As an ultimate strategy, this is used to silence and overcome alternative practices.

Material Effects Realized by Boundary Defending Discursive Practice

Power—It is a crucial and central material effect, the driving factor of "Other Australian's" statements and strategies. Power is not about strength, but about how closely one's categorical behavior is in accordance with institutionally approved discursive practice. Power enables the "Other Australian" not only to realize the following material effects, but also to feel in control and be satisfied in fulfilling her/his subjective role as "Australian."

Self-Proliferation—The ability to propagate and recruit loyal subjects due to "colonial ambivalence" (Bhabha, 1994), as "Self" engages in training the deficient "øther" to become as close as "Self." Having subjectified the "øthered Australian" as "not as Australian as," this effect is hegemonic, especially through acts of nationalizing and hierarchical øthering, it triggers aspirations in "øthered" to become the national subject.

Ownership—Nationalizing, Theorizing and Othering strategies enable the "Other Australian" to act as an ideological agent, and claim ownership of land and peoples, keeping absolute control of the categorical behavior of all individuals and groups and the nation.

Insulation—This material effect is realized by Theorizing and Sanctioning as the "Other Australian" protects "Self" from being influenced by "øthered Australian" or anything seen as a challenge to the realization of power.

Legitimation—This material effect reifies the control and maintenance of the nation, the national identity, and the privileges this subjective position offers.

Discourse—Boundary Denying

The subject "Other Australian" speaks as and for the nation and national identity "Australian," as in "Boundary defending" discourse. However, in this discursive practice, the subject does not centralize "Self" as superior and anonymously tied to the national identity. The subject "Other Australian" may name the origin of "Self." Yet, through constant comparisons with "øthered Australian," the subject projects "Self" as bland and colorless, but the "øthered" as possessing everything that is lacking in "Self." Therefore, in many ways this discourse is a discourse of covert dominance, as "Self" as the national subject remains undisrupted, with the maintenance of "other."

Strategies That Support the Discourse of Boundary Denying

Othering—This strategy speaks of the attributes of "Australian" as in the previous discourse, but it maintains "Self" with notions of normality and casual presence, and not one of superiority. Therefore, it does not overtly state that being and becoming the same as "Self" is desirable, but positions and maintains groups and individuals as "Australian," and "not Australian" by distinguishing "difference" in color, culture, and celebration and faith.

Øthering—Unlike Hierarchical øthering, the "Other Australian" distinguishes and shows extreme desire for "øthered Australian," yet avoids the influence of "øthered Australian" on daily practices, by keeping this special and distant. The strategies of "øthering" and "Othering," work together usually within a statement to enable the "Other Australian" control the ownership and maintenance of "Australian" identity.

Nationalizing—See Boundary defending.

Theorizing—The "Other Australian" may trace historical and personal events and the evidence of structural understandings in influencing the nation and national identity; however, he does so without unpacking the privileges and discrimination of the past. By drawing upon developmental theories and public and personal experiences, this subject still avoids taking action against prejudice, exclusion, and injustice.

Eluding—The "Other Australian" uses strategies such as structural, spatial, or temporal constraints to divert and avoid taking action that can result in changing current understandings about what and who is privileged to speak as and for "Australian."

Limiting—Used with strategies of eluding and øthering, the "Other Australian" is able to provide special days, space, and specific times to "selectively engage" (Frankenberg, 1993) in celebrating the presence of "øthered Australian." This strategy enables "Other Australian" to show case their commitment to celebrating diversity.

Avoidance—Avoidance affects the subtle exclusion of anyone or any event that critically challenges the relevance of centralizing and neutralizing the national identity, "Australian."

Material Effects Realized by Boundary Denying Discursive Practice

Power—This subjective position of "Other Australian" seems highly generous and accepting due to their repeated naming and negation of "Self," with the acclamation of "øthered Australian." However, "power" is covertly realized by the very same strategies, as they still guarantee the subject invisible control and ownership of national identity and the nation, within the ideological discourse of "democratic multiculturalism" (Vickers, 2002; Leeman and Reid, 2006). The following material effects further guarantee the realization of this "power."

Self-Proliferation—Unlike Boundary defending, this material effect is covertly achieved by Othering and øthering strategies. The "øthered Australian" always feels different and outside what is "Australian," as she/he is positioned as "not Australian." Therefore, to be "Australian," they resort to projecting the same neutrality and normality. Thus, "Other Australian" is able to fortify their dominance, propagate "Self" and maintain control of cultural practices.

Ownership—See Boundary defending.

Insulation—See Boundary defending. Moreover, the realization of Insulation is further guaranteed by Celebration and Avoidance.

Legitimation—See Boundary defending.

Celebration—This effect is realized by strategies of øthering and Limiting. The "Other Australian" feels satisfied in his/her sporadic engagement of celebrating "difference," and continues to maintain the daily practices of "Self."

Discourse—Boundary Diffusing

The Boundary diffusing discourse of "Other Australian" is also about speaking as and for what is "Australian"; however, in this subjective position, the "Other Australian" not only names the national identity, but also critically examines its privileges and its influence on current understandings and practices. The subject opens up conversations with "øthered Australians," within which personal narratives are shared to engage in seeking alternative understandings, to reconceptualize the identity of all individuals and groups. As a collaborative discourse, it is available for "øthered Australian" too.

Strategies That Support the Discourse of Boundary Diffusing

Critical Othering—Unlike "Othering," which speaks as and for the anonymous identity "Australian," this strategy is used by "Other Australian" to name and recognize the "Nationalized" identity "Australian." It critically examines the role of "whiteness" in discriminating "øthered Australian" to redistribute privileges that are unquestioningly linked with "whiteness."

Critical øthering—This strategy, when used with critical Othering, recognizes and names "øthered Australian" to identify inequities, and to speak and act against discrimination. Therefore, although it distinguishes and establishes "difference" between "Self" and "other," unlike the colonial discourse this does not engage in centralization of "Self" and marginalization of "øther" with notions of danger or exoticism.

Risking—This becomes inevitable, as this subjective disposition is outside what is ideologically recommended and supported. Therefore, the subject risks being punished and excluded from institutional power and position by structures and by subjects committed to dominant discourses.

Resisting—The subject uses this strategy along with Critical Othering and Critical øthering to speak and act against dominance, and therefore, collaborates and creates spaces to act with voices of "øthered."

Critical recognizing—This strategy is similar to "Theorizing," which is used by the other two discourses above; however, the "Other Australian" uses personal experiences, historical moments, media, and structures to inform, speak about social issues, and engage in critical action with "øthered Australian." Here, the subject acknowledges the structural power and privileges of her/his subjectivity, and therefore uses this strategically to act for social justice and equity.

Material Effects Realized by Boundary Diffusing Discursive Practice

Diffused Power—The overarching material effect that the subject realizes from this subjective, strategic disposition is the dissipation of power, ownership, and control to reconstitute attitudes and understanding about nation and national identity.

Self-Narration—Affects exchanges of stories and critical historical events to challenge dominance with "øthered Australian."

Critical cognition—Another effect that stems from the above enables rethinking attitudes and understandings with "øthered Australian" to reconceptualize and challenge current understandings about national identity and multicultural practices.

Critical action—This becomes inevitable, as all of the above causes disruption and spaces for collaborative action that reorganizes current identity practices, understandings, and ultimately power.

The following are the elements of the discursive dispositions of us, the "øthered Australian."

Contesting Australian: Discourses of "Øthered Australian"

The three main subjective dispositions that were practiced by us, "øthered Australian" are *boundary committing, boundary conscious,* and *boundary diffusing*. The lower case distinguishes the discursive elements of "øthered Australian" from "Other Australian."

Discourse—boundary committing

We, as "øthered Australian" in this subjective disposition, rather than choosing to retain both identities or subvert both, aspire to be accepted as "Australian" by "Other Australian." Therefore, in many ways this subject is an upholder of the institutional ideology "Australian," and is committed to the national identity unquestioningly.

Strategies That Support the Discourse of Boundary Committing

self-othering—This strategy allows us to alienate "self" from our cultural/ethnolinguistic background, to become assimilated with the national subject. Therefore, in some cases, we discard or talk about "self" and our own group negatively to be accepted as "Other Australian."

self-regulating—The strategy supports self-othering, as we begin to distinguish the "difference" established in "self" by "Other Australian," and erase those by adopting practices regarded as "Australian."

gravitating—The key strategy that finally seals the movement of "øthered" toward the dominant, as we see "self" as "Other," and fail to see otherwise.

Material Effects Realized by Boundary Committing Discursive Practice

subjective power—The key material effect realized by us, "øthered Australian" is "subjective power," as we feel that we have the power of owning and being accepted as a loyal "Australian" subject.

self-alienation—The self-othering and self-regulating strategies contribute toward the realization of being distant from our own collective identity, and gives us a feeling of being "Australian."

submission—We are highly grateful for being accepted as the national subject and become more committed to the nation and national identity by beginning to speak for and as "Australian."

Discourse—boundary conscious

The awareness of being different, in combination with a perception of what is "Australian," causes us, as "øthered Australian," to become acutely conscious of the attributes of "self" in comparison to the nation and the power of ideological "Australian." We either remove "self" from nation and discourses that attribute socio-contextual power as a sign of resistance, or suppress "self" in the company of "Other Australian." Therefore, this discourse does not result in distancing "self" from our collective group, but we as "øthered Australian" are unable to challenge the power of "Other Australian." We choose to publicly display our commitment to the ideology, nation, and national identity, although we believe otherwise among ourselves.

Strategies That Support the Discourse of boundary conscious

self-othering—With this strategy we constantly distinguish the attributes of "self" being different than those of "Other Australian," and unlike the above discourse we speak negatively of "Other Australian," by always positioning "self" outside what is "Australian."

self-regulating—As in boundary committing, we uphold and represent the "Australian" by showing our adjustment and commitment to this nation and national identity outwardly. However, we privatize and reserve the practices of our group and secretly express these practices only within our group.

resisting—With a fear of dilution of our cultural practices, we as "øthered Australian," disengage from sociopolitical and public engagement, and most of all from owning the national identity "Australian."

critical øthering—As noticed in the Boundary diffusing discourse of "Other Australian," we name and recognize the ideological power and origin of the identity, but with no intention of challenging current attitudes and practices in relation to national ideologies. We share this only with another "øthered Australian," ending with reconciliation to change "self" rather than the ideological "Australian."

critical recognizing—As in Boundary diffusing of "Other Australian," we show an awareness of discrepancies in current practices and share historical and personal events. As we are aware of our boundaries, we discuss among ourselves the need to challenge practices.

silencing—This strategy aids the above strategies, and we believe that such silencing is essential so that "self" is not excluded by "Other Australian."

Material Effects Realized by boundary conscious Discursive Practice

subjective power—As defined in Boundary committing, we, as "øthered Australian," realize the power of being accepted by "Other Australian," and this material effect overrides all experiences of suppression and regulated-acceptance.

self-narration—As those realized in Boundary diffusing discourse of "Other Australian." However, here our exchanges are shared only with another "øthered Australian," therefore, critical action does not eventuate.

exclusion—As we become overly conscious of the differences between "self" and those of "Other Australian," we, as "øthered Australian," with resisting strategies, choose to exclude "self" from specific public discourses and negotiations.

regulated-acceptance—Our partial or complete affiliation with our ethnolinguistic and religious origins facilitates our practices to be given permission to be exhibited publically in a sporadic manner by "Other Australian."

suppression—We realize and accept the censorship and marginalization of our attributes by becoming aware of our boundaries as an outsider, being different to what is conceptualized and practiced as "Australian."

Discourse—boundary diffusing

Although this discourse is common to both subjects (Other and øthered Australians), we have differentiated ours with the use of lower case. This is to remind ourselves that our discourses may be similar but our experiences are different due to our subjectivities. We, as "øthered Australian" challenge not just the sociopolitical constructions of the ideological "Australian," but also subjects ("Other Australian" and "øthered Australian") who uphold this ideology. Therefore, this is a marginal discourse, a subjective position that is outside the structurally recommended commitment to the national identity.

Strategies That Support the Discourse of boundary diffusing

risking—We risk being rejected by "Other Australian" and structures that are committed to upholding the ideological "Australian." Yet, we engage in this strategy, and our subjective paradigm to challenge what is "Australian."

resisting—This is similar to the strategy in boundary conscious, but we reinscribe our own identity, without hesitating to speak and practice our difference privately and publicly. *critical øthering*—We name, recognize the origin of the nation and the national identity and the dominant, historical, and political ideologies that maintain its ownership and control, and we share this understanding with "Other" and "øthered Australian" to work toward change. *critical recognizing*—We engage with alternate media information, theories, and literature and we openly confront discourses that essentialize our groups and that of "Australian." We recognize and share our personal and historical events that have influenced our attitudes and understandings about "Other Australian" and we act to change practices and understandings of all subjects in Australia.

Material Effects Realized by Boundary Diffusing Discursive Practice

voice—This is the foremost material effect we realize. We are able to express our experiences and understandings in our own voice and we realize being accepted for what and who we want to be by "Other Australian," with little feelings of compulsion to become committed to national ideologies and national identity. For us, our power is our voice, as we do not yet own that structural power possessed by "Other Australian" to diffuse or share. However, we do become empowered through critical action and change.

self-narration—As a secondary effect, we are able to share the prejudices we had incurred in the past with "Other Australian," who acknowledges and empathizes with "øthered" experiences, by simultaneously recognizing the privileges of "Self."

critical cognition—Through strategies of critical recognizing, we are able to collaboratively acknowledge and identify the realities of "øthered Australian," and with "Other Australian" we plan to reconceptualize the ideological "Australian."

critical action—This is a shared material effect realized with "Other Australian" and "øthered Australian." We collaboratively act upon contextual, current prejudices, hoping to bring about justice and equity for all individuals and groups in Australia.

With Ganga and † clarifying the elements of postcolonial discourse analysis of the "Australian," we move to narrating how each layer of "Australian" and "not Australian" identities were enacted, shaped by "Australian speakers," and finally contested by subjects, "Other Australian" and "øthered Australian."

CHAPTER 3

Complex(ion) Speak: I Am White, I Am Australian. Pookey Is Black, She Is Not Australian

> *But it is difficult to talk about color. If a child comes and asks me, why are you white, I wouldn't know what to say. You say pigments and stuff about your skin when children ask you about color, but what can we say, nothing.*
>
> —Gina, white Anglo-Australian, early childhood educator

Ganga now begins to tell stories of "othering" in early childhood settings, and speaks with the initial strong boundary stream, Complex(ion). Ganga and I begin our "Complex(ion) speaks" with children's "othering" that classified the identities of "Australian / not Australian" using skin color. We then navigate together to trace the ideological origin of such classification and end with identifying the "power" of "whiteness" in the silences and voices of all postcolonial subjects who contested "Australian."

"OTHERING" COMPLEX(ION): ENACTING AUSTRALIAN / NOT AUSTRALIAN

The Complex(ion) speaks did not start with "othering" categories of "Australian / not Australian." It seemed like inquisitive curiosity when Leo (a four-year-old, white Anglo-Australian boy) asked me on the first day he met me at the setting, *"How come you and Pookey are brown and me and Debbie are white?"* Debbie (white Anglo-Australian staff) quickly replied without directly explaining the cause for our skin color differences, "*Don't worry, brown is good, and they don't get sun burnt like you and me,*" as if she was worried that brown skin was being perceived as "bad" by Leo. I explained, "*Actually Leo, it is because we have more pigments in our skin and because my parents and my family also have more pigments in their skin and are shades of brown.*" Leo immediately asked, "*Can you become white, like us?*" I said "no" and moved on to do other things. However, Leo's Complex(ion) curiosities continued and now and again he stopped to ask, "*Your hands are rough, can I touch your cheeks, will they be rough too?*" "*Mmm…'cause you are brown.*" Leo then touched my cheek to reconceptualize, "*No, they are okay, I think you are okay.*" There were other children standing next to us and sometimes they too joined to ask me about the origin of my skin color. Our open conversations on Complex(ion) curiosities continued for a weeks, however amid these was an afternoon during which the curiosities led to Complex(ion) nationalities.

Children who were "white" categorized and named the Complex(ion) of both their personal and collective "self" and "other," and they attached "whiteness" with the national identity of Australia. The divisions were set in bold and clear, and the nationalizing "boundary speaks" divided us into "Australian" and "not Australian" by our outermost layer that we couldn't clad or unclad. It began very casually, "*I am white, so I am Australian. Pookey is black not Australian. Like you she is Indian*" (Feeniyan, a four-year-old, white Anglo-Australian girl). Pookey (a four-year-old, brown Indian Australian girl) insisted, "*No, I don't have brown skin, I don't, I am not Indian. I am white, I am Australian.*" Feeniyan continued, "*No, Australians are white, you are black.*" After all, children's use of language categories to name the collective identities of "self" and "other" is quite noticeable as they develop a sense of who they are (see Kowalski, 2007; Crisp and Turner, 2007; Bennet and Sani, 2008; Epstein, 2009). Therefore, these categorizing remarks can be excused as expressions of children's development of self-identity. Yet, the use of such language categories affected children who were "brown" and it affected me, my "brown self"; and since then for both children and adults, these became their everyday grappling with their "not Australian" realities and "Australian" imaginations.

"OTHERING" REALITIES: "NOT AUSTRALIAN" RESPONDS

Children who were "brown" engaged in "othering," but unlike the children who spoke with "whiteness," it was nothing to do with categorizing their national identities. It was to do with their undeniable "brownness" and their desirable "whiteness." The children who were "brown" categorized "brownness" negatively. The very first day I met and introduced myself to Pookey, she said *"I don't want to play with that brown doll. I don't like brown skin. I am white."* Similar attitudes toward "brownness" were noticeable in others too, *"I like my mum, you have brown skin too. But I don't like my brown skin. I like white skin"* (Seaweed, a three-year-old, brown Indian Australian girl). No amount of coercion could change Seaweed's negative feelings toward her skin color. Moo, one day suddenly burst out to say, *"Prasanna, I don't like you because you have brown skin"* and *"No, I don't have brown skin, I am white"* (Moo, a three-year-old, brown Indian Australian girl). Although Moo's statements were attached to comments made about skin color and food by her peers in the past, she too not only rejected her "brownness," she also desired "whiteness" just like Seaweed and Pookey.

Thus, the children who were "brown" openly admitted their dislike for "brown" skin color. They either admitted that they were "brown" and that they did not like their own "brownness," or they denied the categorization of their "self" as "brown" and named themselves "white." This dislike and denial by children who are "brown" has been identified by many researchers who have conducted studies with young children (see, Tacagni, 1998; MacNaughton, 2001; Targowska, 2001; Skattebol, 2003; Derman-Sparks, Ramsay, and Edwards, 2006; Epstein, 2009). I repeatedly stressed that they were "brown" and not "white"; I continued to insist that there are "white Australians" and "brown Australians" in Australia. The staff in these settings responded with their "whiteness."

"OTHERING" IMAGINATIONS: "AUSTRALIAN" RESPONDS

The white Anglo-Australian staff imagined children's innocence to overlook their "othering," *"But children don't see colors, they are innocent. They may do in some countries where there is a lot of trouble, but Australia being the lucky country such things don't happen"* (Katherine, a white Anglo Australian). In their imagination such "othering" happened in other countries. Yet, the "brown" realities were expressed overtly by children like Pookey, and Katherine clung to her imagination when I took Pookey's voice to her,

> It couldn't have come from here. Her teachers are white. Maybe it is from the family, they probably buy only white dolls for her (Katherine).

Here, the expert educator accused the family of not buying brown dolls for Pookey. Her "whiteness" could not see Pookey, a "brown" child, from a "brown" family with "brown" family and friends expressing her distaste for "brown" skin. All that came to Katherine's mind was that Pookey's family bought only white dolls for her to play with. We, as "white" and "brown," saw the world differently. Katherine was speaking through the "taken for granted" early childhood pedagogical practices. After all, educators are recommended to present early childhood experiences with different skin color dolls to promote acceptance of diversity and eliminate racism. However, responding through the "taken for granted" practices alone without the recognition of "white" power is inadequate, especially to work against "brown" discrimination. I wanted to ask, do "white" families buy "white" dolls for their children to accept their "whiteness"? And would this even be recommended if a "white" child says, "I want to become 'brown.'" I left with these silenced questions, and our "brown" realities that remained submerged within Katherine's "white" imagination. My silencing did not stop children from loudly speaking their Complex(ion) realities and imagination with me, and I labeled the identity of "Australian" with different skin colors with the hope that children would change their conceptions of categorizing "Australian / not Australian" with "whiteness."

It is this naming that shattered their imagi(nation); the "Australian" in them could not remain silent. The "Australian" in Gina and Katherine was awakened,

> "You know, we are both just Australians. Why do you have to call us white? How do you think we would feel when you call us white?" (Gina). "I don't know why you have to tell Pookey is brown, when every other kid in the room is Australian. You tell her she is brown and that she is different" (Katherine). "But the problem is, she is brown and she says she doesn't like brown and that she is white," I added. "Yeah, I understand all that. But telling her she is brown is discrimination. You are making her feel that she is different. You know every other child in the group is white and we are both white teachers, but you make her feel that she doesn't belong (Katherine).

Naming "whiteness" angered the "just Australians," Gina and Katherine. Their national status, "Australian" erased their Complex(ion), and also enabled them to justify their silencing responses. The desire for "whiteness," in Pookey was inferred and accepted as an indicator to belong and become "Australian." Because

I refused to allow Pookey to be consumed by "whiteness," my intentions of contesting our reality, our "brown difference" was imagined as discrimination. These unreal "Australian" imaginations were spoken of as being bigger than "not Australian" realities that despised their own "brownness."

And children continued to see colors and they began to openly compare the Complex(ion) of Gina, Katherine, and me, "*She is black, you are white*"; "*No, hey she is not like you, you are white, Australian,*" and "*She is brown, she is not Australian*" (four-year-old children). These imaginations continued, and "white Anglo-Australian" children commented repeatedly when I read the book, "*The colors of us*" (Katz, 1999),

> "We can't find our color. What about me?" (Feeniyan, See, and Fairy, four-year-old white Anglo-Australian girls). "But you are peachy tan, aren't you?" I asked. "No, see we are white, not peachy tan" (Feeniyan). "It is tricky isn't. There are usually two colors with skin color, like black and white" (Gina whispered).

Children remained subjectified by their "whiteness" and their national identity, "Australian," and never allowed their "whiteness" to be colored as "peachy tan." Yet, in Gina's imagination the dichotomous white/black existed and it was difficult to disrupt this binary vision. I continued to carry children's books on skin color and one day Gina heard Bikky (a four-year-old white, Turkish Australian girl) wanting to know why we had different colored skin. Gina could not escape speaking Complex(ion) and she hastily wondered, "*I wish I had a book*" and I gave the book that I had been carrying in my bag since Leo began to speak Complex(ion) with me. Gina read *All the Colors We Are: The Story of How We Got Our Skin Color* (Kissinger, 1994) with children. As Gina read, she was surprised to find words such as, "melanin, ancestors and pigments" and asked me what they meant, "*mmm...that is surprising, I don't know why they say that in children's book*" (Gina). Gina hastily concluded the book with a moral about sun protection,

> "It depends on how hot it is where you live. The sun can make you go very dark, see you have to protect yourself from the sun, it is very hot in Australia" (Gina).

Lisa, the zebra, (a four-year-old, white European Australian girl) diverted Gina's aspirations to conclude by asking, "*But, how come*

Australians are white, when it is hot here, because sun makes us go brown doesn't it?" Gina hurriedly looked at her watch and dispersed the children for lunch. As I thanked Gina for reading that book with children, Gina took me aside to explain why she ended the book the way she did, *"No worries, can you see children didn't still quite get it. I would have been the same when I was four"* (Gina). However, I thought children got it because Lisa, the zebra, specifically named the color of "Australian." I wanted to speak Australia's "black" Aboriginality and the history of "white" colonization. But, I silently accepted Gina's explanation.

However, Gina's difficulty in speaking Complex(ion) continued and was very evident as children repeatedly compared our skin color and nationalities. Gina privately gave reasons for her discomfort and difficulty in talking about color with children,

> "But it is difficult to talk about color. If a child comes and asks me, why are you white, I wouldn't know what to say. You say pigments and stuff about your skin when children ask you about color, but what can we say, nothing. I remember, last year, you know the hip hop singer, Eminem; he sang this song with the word, Negro in it. That became the buzz word with all the boys in the group. They asked me what does Negro mean. I just said that it is a word used to call people who are dark and didn't make a big issue about it, you know they are just curious. We had a boy who was dark as, and the rest of the boys started calling him Negro. Oh my god, we didn't know what to do, we just were shocked and said don't use that word her" (Gina).

The issue was that Gina, the "Australian" now recognized and accepted her "white" identity, but found it difficult to talk about color, because she had "nothing" in comparison to what I had. We both have the same stuff, pigments; but I have more of that stuff than Gina did. Most of all, Gina and her "whiteness" had the power to call herself "Australian." This "white" reluctance to speak colors with children had resulted in children skillfully using the word "Negro" to engage in racism and prejudice, and yet it was understood as childhood curiosity by "white" imagination. What was conclusively evident was that children used "othering" language of "white" and "black/brown" to categorize and name skin color of both their personal and collective "Australian," "not Australian" identities. It didn't stop there, as children were using racist language to name "brownness."

Gina and Katherine refused to break their silence and children continued to name our skin color and attach "Australian," "not

Australian" tags to "white" and "black" respectively. Katherine became very agitated and explained to us the reasons for her anger,

> "You know, I hate it when people call me white, because I go to great lengths to get a tan. I love tan and I get very angry when people say I am white" (Katherine).

Imaginations of "whiteness" as "nothing" and as something that was less desirable silenced any further discussions about children's "othering." Katherine implied that my concerns about Pookey's dissociation with "brownness" was no different to Katherine's earnest disconnection with her "whiteness." Hence, why talk about that nothing and something that is anyway less desirable. I observed that there was other "brown" staff in the setting who worked with the children and yet, children avoided speaking Complex(ion) with them as they did with me. I clarified this with Gina during our interview, and Gina explained why children spoke color with me and not with any other "brown" staff in the centre,

> Children will never talk about color with Aruna. She wants to be white and she has always said this. When I put my legs out in the sun for a tan, she says, oh you have such beautiful skin and she wishes she was white. She says in front of all the children that she likes only white babies. What luck would one have with her, children will never ask her (Gina).

I realized that it is not that Gina and Katherine have never had Complex(ion) conversations earlier. Aruna (a brown, Sri Lankan Australian staff) had openly expressed her desire for "whiteness" just like Pookey, Seaweed, and Moo and no one contested it. Gina with all her "whiteness" and "Australianness" left this unexplored for children to draw their own imagined conclusions, just like she did when the child used prejudiced language against a very "dark as" peer in the room. Thus staff who were "white" and those who were "brown" did not speak Complex(ion) with children either with their theoretical imaginations, their national imagi(nation), or their "white" desire.

My own experiences and my family's experiences and my theoretical disposition repeatedly intercepted with what was generally perceived about children's understanding of skin color and adults' role in developing such understanding. I became very disturbed when "brown" children overtly expressed their dislike for "brown" skin and believed that they were "white." Most of all, the parents of these "brown" children wanted the educators to speak Complex(ion). Sidya's (a three-year-old, brown, Indian Australian girl) mum angrily said, *"You know what in this country someone has to talk about color"* and Pookey's mum did not know how to make staff speak color, *"Someone here has told Pookey that she is black and yucky, so they won't play with her.... But how do I say this to the staff here. I haven't said anything"* (Pookey's mum). That directly explained Pookey's dislike for her "brownness." Despite being an action researcher, I too did not know how to say this to the staff when I sensed their reluctance to speak Complex(ion). If early childhood is critical for the development of one's self-identity, and if children's identity is constructed by "other" and through "othering," then as an "other" I felt we all had to take responsibility for "brown" children's conceptions of their undesirable "self." Practices that leave "whiteness" unnamed and unexplored, in combination with acting "color-blind" allow discriminatory beliefs about differences to be left unchallenged (Hayes, 2001; de Freitas, McAuley, and Ammon, 2008).

Hence, I couldn't leave it there. It bothered me that they were silencing our "brownness" from being accepted as "Australian," and rather encouraged us to desire "whiteness." It also bothered me that they allowed Australia's colored past and present to remain whitewashed. The process of "othering" that categorizes one's collective identity did not explain what gave the "white Australian" staff permission to accept "white" children's imagi(nation), and "brown" children's eagerness to be "white." I sought that explanation by looking at the past, the ideological conception of that "Australian."

"Othering" Complex(ion): Shaping "Australian Speakers"

The "white Australian" was overthrown with multiculturalism. The national identity of Australia and its subjects should be less attached to "whiteness" with the dethroning of the *White Australia policy* in the 1970s. But the "white Australian" still ruled and this notion was circulated within early childhood settings by children and adults. I now traced the historical moment that dismantled the "white Australian." To establish the presence of ideologies that speak of propagating the "white Australian" is impossible, as these are nonexistent after the demise of the discriminatory policies of the past. However, the "Australian" who then spoke as the owner of this nation and national identity still represented and was represented by "whiteness." And if "whiteness" owned and represented what was "Australian" and recommended the subjects' loyal commitment to this national identity, those who then pledged their loyalty to this ideology would continue to defend to protect not just the "Australian," but also the "white Australian." Afterall, "whiteness" represented this nation's identity when multiculturalism was introduced.

The current sociopolitical statements too do not overtly promote the "white Australian" identity; however, it is also evident that they do not openly disrupt the "white" imagi(nation) of its national subjects. The rewards of subjectification as citizens of Australia are exemplified.

> Australian citizenship is a privilege that offers enormous rewards. By becoming an Australian citizen, you are joining a unique national community. Our country has been built on the combined contributions of our indigenous people and those who came later from all over the world. We celebrate this diversity and at the same time, strive for a unified and harmonious nation.
> (Commonwealth of Australia, 2013, p. 3)

They begin by acknowledging the uniqueness of this nation, its generosity, and the rewards of becoming its national subject. Then this is followed to casually include Aboriginal Australia, along with colonial occupation and later migration as equitable "contributions." This country is indigenous people's land and not a "contribution," as it is referred to, and the loss of indigenous land and cultures can never be measured in terms of "contribution." Moreover, rather than ending with the centralization of multiculturalism, these statements acknowledge and "celebrate" diversity to convey the national subjects' unquestionable commitment to a unified nation. Thus, it leaves it to the subjects to discern, conceptualize and maintain what they visualize as this nation and its identity. As argued by Berman and Paradies (2010) liberal multiculturalism, which is built on the tenants of individual discretion, does not provide a clear tool to effectively identity and combat "racism." Hence, what is needed is critical multiculturalism that actively speaks to work against the residuals of Australia's discriminatory past, which was governed with and by "whiteness."

The absence of speaking against "white" domination in the ideological statements of Australia's sociopolitical institutions can be seen as their discomfort and/or reluctance to engage with uncomfortable, yet undeniable "white" power of the past and present. However, the presence of upholding the identity of Australia and its subjects masks and denies the racism and discrimination that is still in operation within the society. It is this ideological "*Othering*" that epitomizes Australia and "Australian" subjectified, and occupied the minds of Ganga's "boundary speakers," especially those who spoke as "Australian." The ideological "interpellation" that protected and promoted "Australia's Australian" covertly defended "white Australian" imagi(nation), and fuelled and extracted "not Australian" subjection. The ideology subscribers like Feeniyan, Gina, and Katherine, who spoke as "Australian," took control of "*Othering*" "Australian" with their "whiteness" and kept the "white Australian" image alive. Children openly "Othered" and shaped the "white Australian" to maintain the "Australian / not Australian" dichotomy with "whiteness." The adult "Australian speakers" with their discomfort and reluctance to speak against such "Othering" covertly propagated and maintained the "white" power. Disrupting children's conceptions of Complex(ion) meant disrupting the solidarity of the national identity, "Australian." Thus, the "white Australian" desire and denial of "white" power identical to its institutional origin, in combination with their ideological commitment to this identity, influenced both the "Australian" and the "not Australian" subjects to succumb to "whiteness." While the "Australian speakers" exhibited their loyalty by silencing any act that disrupted this identity by naming "whiteness," the "not Australian speakers" exhibited their loyalty to be "Australian" by disregarding and discarding their "brownness." I resolved to shake this ideological submission by "øthering" the Complex(ion) of "Australian." I revoked my postcolonial "self."

"ØTHERING" COMPLEX(ION): CONTESTING "AUSTRALIAN" WITH THEIR IMAGI(NATION) AND OUR REALITIES

The "white Australian" identity was "Othered" not only by political ideologies, but was also mobilized by national subjects, "Australian speakers," the adults and children who "spoke" as and about this identity with "whiteness." Weedon (2004) argues that attaching such stringent attributes to visual clues of one's body is "everyday racism," and Boutte (2008) recommends adults to be honest in embracing children's curiosity with open discussions about such differences. Children scorned and excluded "brownness" as "*yucky*" and positioned "brown" subjects outside the national identity. Yet, there was much silence and silencing that surrounded Ganga's evidence of children's acts of racial discrimination. But, there were "Australian speakers" (Other Australian) who spoke with "not Australian speakers" (øthered Australian) to challenge the nation and national identity being dominated by "whiteness." We, the "øthered Australian" clung to the "white transformers" who aspired for change and we contested the ideological "Australian" not only with our "brownness," but also with our "white transformer." We contested the "Australian" with our postcolonial imagination with and as Ganga and ✝.

Contesting Complex(ion) with Pookey, Thora, Sidya, Their Mums, and Sheri
"You Know What in This Country Someone Has to Talk about Color"

✝ met Sheri (øthered Australian—øA) and Katherine (Other Australian—OA), the two room leaders, and explained my study by saying that ✝ was going to engage with children to gather their attitudes about friendship groups. While Katherine said that it was to do with individual choice, Sheri remarked that Thora and Sidya (øA children) always played together and she encouraged that because they shared the same ethnolinguistic background. ✝ spoke to Sheri later, as ✝ perhaps related to our "øthered" attribute, our "brownness." ✝ shared my concerns about segregating children, especially by color and language.

My first afternoon with Sheri and the children in her room, and Sheri "spoke" Complex(ion).

> It was sleep time and as the children slept "I never thought about this, until you started talking about color. You know I had always dreamt about marrying a white man and I am married to a white man now. Right since I was young, I only wanted to marry a white man. I don't know why I don't like dark skin. May be, it was because I was teased here at school because of my skin color when I was young. But I didn't think that really did affect me, but may be it did" (Sheri). "Sheri, I am very sorry to hear that, because the same thing happened to my children and you are not much older than my son. I am really very sorry to hear that you were teased," I apologized. "No, like I told you it doesn't matter, but you know you can do what you want in the room, change anything, talk about anything with children. I understand, I don't have a problem" (Sheri). "Can I use this as data?" I confirmed. "Yes, because it happened and I didn't think it mattered" (Sheri).

✝ was moved to tears, as we shared our stories and how our color was "spoken" in Australia. ✝ understood why Sheri encouraged Thora and Sidya to play together, as she was deeply affected by what she had experienced when she was young. She spoke of the origin of her current relationship with "whiteness" and "brownness." ✝ decided not to expect Sheri to "speak" colors with children, but ✝ "spoke" Complex(ion) with Sheri's permission.

In Sheri's room, Thora ritualistically picked up books and puzzles to find images of "colored" individuals to talk about "our color" and "our India." Sidya always sat quietly with us. Although ✝ had Sheri's permission to "speak" about skin color with children, ✝ wanted to confirm this with Thora's and Sidya's parents.

> One morning during drop off when I raised Thora's interest skin colors with her mum, she said, "My daughter is like me. She is strong, she talks openly about what is important for her...she speaks what is right and stands up for herself" (Thora's mum).

✝ gathered that Thora's mum had no hesitation in "speaking" colors with children, and believed that this reflected Thora's strong sense of self. ✝ spoke to Sidya's mum.

> Sidya's mum came to pick her up. "Thora has been openly talking about skin color with me and Sidya and many other children around. I don't stop this discussion and I just wanted to know if this is okay with you," I asked her. "You know what in this country someone has to talk about color. I will tell you what happened in my son's school. A few weeks ago, a boy had called my son "blacky" and that he won't play with him. My son was so upset when he came home and he refused to go to school the very next day. I reassured him and I went with him to speak to the teacher. The teacher said that she won't believe my son, as the other boy could not have said something like that. How dare she pass something as serious as being called by names as a lie. It is real for my son and our family, as we go through this every day. I think if you can make Sidya feel that it is okay to stand up for herself and feel it is alright to be who you are that is all I ask of you" (Sidya's mum).

✝ heard another story of discrimination, and the teacher's unwillingness to take action. However, ✝ felt reassured about my Complex(ion) conversations with children and ✝ became even more determined to continue take action.

In the other room, Pookey bluntly said that she did not like brown skin and that she was "white" on the very first day. † was immediately alarmed, and raised this with Katherine, but she felt that she didn't have to address this, as it could have only come from her family. † silenced myself and could not help but speak to Pookey's mum about Pookey.

> It was pick-up time. Pookey's mother and I shared many topics that were common. "Pookey says, she doesn't like brown skin and that she is white," I started hesitantly. "Someone here has told Pookey that she is black and yucky, so they won't play with her. She was so upset when she came home. It took us so long to console her. But how do I say this to the staff here. I haven't said anything" (Pookey's mother).

Pookey had experienced the colored exclusion that many of us had experienced in the past. My postcolonial Ganga lamented that Pookey was gravitating toward "whiteness," and † decided to continue to risk and resist to "speak" colors with children. Therefore, † carried books that reasoned and explained skin colors in my bag daily, and whenever † had conversations of color with children, † purposely involved Pookey as † read with children.

Hearing my free interactions with children about our Complex(ion), Katherine and Gina (OA) arranged for a meeting to question my actions. They accused me of discrimination, because † did not let Pookey believe that she was "white." They defended not just their "whiteness" but also their "Australianness" by nationalizing "Self" as "just Australian." They theorized Pookey's behavior as social development and claimed that my concerns inhibited her sense of belonging. Thus, they took control of my behavior and my interactions with children.

Children continued to "speak" and nationalize colors, as they classified, "Self" as "white" and "Australian," and Pookey and † as "not Australian" because we were "black." Gina and Katherine avoided "speaking colors" with the book, "All the Colors We Are," and theorized that children were too young to understand the concepts. Later, Gina justified her inaction by saying she was "white" and had "nothing" to talk about, and concluded that † could "speak" colors only because † was "brown." Katherine expressed her desire for "tan," and used this to justify her anger about being called "white." Katherine and Gina avoided taking responsibility to contest "whiteness" and "Australian," even as they heard children conceptualizing the "white Australian."

Pookey's contest with "whiteness" and "Australianness" continued.

"No, I am white, I am Australian" (Pookey). "But Pookey, remember what we read in 'Colors of Us', you are like, peanut butter and is it white?" I asked. "Okay, I am Indian like Prasanna and I am from Melbourne. I am both and so I am a bit white" (Pookey).

I was churned, and my postcolonial self wanted to classify and categorize the Complex(ion) discourses of "Other Australians," Gina and Katherine, and question their silence. However, † silenced my postcolonial self to protect my study, my reality. My ripples continued and † wanted to make meaning of these. † beseeched my postcolonial Ganga to break the silence of our Complex(ion) discourses, the discourses of "øthered Australian."

"White" Matters: "Yes, Because It Happened and I Didn't Think It Mattered"

†: Ganga, † was affected when † heard Sheri's story about her past and its current influence on her relationship with "whiteness." Can you explain Sheri's current Complex(ion) discourse?

Ganga: Can't you see that she is discursively committed to the boundaries of "whiteness." Sheri has been teased and she has now submitted to the power of "whiteness." You heard her say that she doesn't like "dark skin" because she was teased, and she had always dreamt of marrying a "white" man. Isn't she "self-othering" and "gravitating" toward "whiteness"?

†: Why didn't she think about this earlier?

Ganga: Can't you see as an "øthered Australian," Sheri has gained "subjective power" by "self-correction" and "submission" to "whiteness" through the discourse of "boundary commitment." She would find it hard to disrupt the power of "whiteness" and she will only contribute to the perpetuation of this "power." That is why she did not challenge Thora's and Sidya's play behavior.

"Brown" Challenges: "but Pookey, You Are Like Peanut Butter and Is It White?"

†: Okay, what about me. My children and † were discriminated. How was † attached to "whiteness" and "Australian" when † decided to practice Complex(ion) with children?

Ganga: You too were discursively responding to "whiteness," but you tried to challenge its "power," by resisting and risking your study and your presence in that centre. That is why you became upset when you heard Pookey say, *"I don't like brown skin, I am not brown, I am white."*

†: But why?

Ganga: This was the subjective disposition that you took because of your postcolonial subjectivity and your role as a participatory action researcher, your "boundary diffusing" discourse acted to disrupt power even though you were "øthered Australian." You did not want Pookey to become boundary committed, as you heard from Pookey's mum that she was teased here at the centre. Remember Sidya's mum's angry outburst, and she wanted someone to talk about color. You know Skattebol (2003) and Atkinson (2009) warn practitioners that children do enact discourses of racism discreetly, when adults fail to acknowledge and address children as sociopolitical enactors. Being a "brown" subject, with your experiences and marginal connections to "whiteness" you decided to "risk" to "resist" the inaction of Gina and Katherine, "Other Australian."

And another couple of ripples churned my postcolonial depths, and † clung to Ganga.

"White" Silences: "Someone Here Has Told Pookey Is Black and Yucky, So They Won't Play with Her"

†: But Katherine and Gina heard children defending the national identity of Australia by "Hierarchically øthering" our skin color, and "Othering" "whiteness." Yet, they maintained children do not see colors in Australia. Ganga, authors caution that the practices that leave "whiteness" unnamed and unexplored, in combination with acting "color-blind" leaves discriminatory beliefs about certain differences to be left unchallenged (Hayes, 2001; de Freitas and McAuley, 2008). What and how did Katherine's and Gina's Complex(ion) practices affect and effect postcolonial subjects?

Ganga: Prasanna, children realized their "power" when they claimed "Ownership" of "Australian" identity, so they maintained their "whiteness" and "Australianness." After all, Gina and Katherine did that too, remember the meeting, "*You know, we are both just Australians. Why do you have to call us white? How do you think we would feel when you call us white?*" (Gina); "*I don't know why you have to tell Pookey is brown, when every other kid in the room is Australian. You tell her she is brown and that she is different*" (Katherine). They were trying to maintain control and "power" by claiming "Self" as "Australian," thus "Nationalizing" and defending their boundary of "white Australian." They were "Theorizing" and "Legitimizing" their inaction to negate your challenge.

†: But after † read the book, "Colors of Us," they heard children's use of dichotomous language, "black/white" and they responded, didn't they!

Ganga: I heard them respond. They just shifted their discourse strategically to retain their "power." With "Boundary denying," they could easily divert children's and particularly your influence from challenging their attitudes and understandings of "whiteness" and "Australianness." I heard Gina say, "*mmm . . that is surprising, I don't know why they say that in children's book.*" When the child asked, "*But, how come Australians are white, when it is hot here, because sun makes us go brown doesn't it,*" Katherine eluded this: "*Hey, I dare you to read those words at the bottom, go on read it.*" Remember how Gina and Katherine gave you a space to put your books and photos of children's hands in a separate corner to be brought out when you were there. Can't you see they were "Limiting" your presence to effect "Insulation" and "Avoidance" for "Self." It is "power."

†: What "power"?

Ganga: The "power" of supporting ideological "Australian," they were being loyal "Australian" subjects. They were reinforcing the structural demands, their commitment toward maintaining the sovereignty of the ideology, "Australian."

"Brown" Submits: "I Am Both and So I Am a Bit White"

†: Is there no way out for "øthered Australian" who resist "whiteness?" Is that why, Pookey and † modified our practices to accommodate "whiteness"?

Ganga: Of course, by now you had both become highly "boundary conscious" of your "øthered Australian" status. With this discourse, Pookey wanted the "subjective power" of owning "Australian," so she chose to have "bits of white." You wanted your study to continue. You realized you will be punished by the "power" of "Other Australian." Both of you, "self-regulated" and effected "self-correction" and "suppression." Move on, get over it.

†: But, Ganga. Listen to Amelia's voice in the following. She is "Other Australian," and she speaks about and with her "whiteness"; but she is different. See how she responded to Seaweed's dislike for our "brownness."

Contesting Complex(ion) with Seaweed and Her Mum, Amelia and Jan

"But I Don't Like My Brown Skin. I Like White Skin"

† met Seaweed's mum for the first time on my very first day at the centre. After † introduced myself, and explained my study and its

theoretical interests, † told her that Seaweed frequently talked about our skin color, and Seaweed's mum responded immediately,

> I know, she goes on about her skin color. The staff here said not to make a big issue about this, as she is doing so for attention seeking. We don't say anything we just ignore (Seaweed's mum).

† believed otherwise, but † kept quiet, as this was my first day at this centre. † had observed Seaweed saying *"I don't like my brown skin,"* and used skin color to categorize people as "Australian" and "Indian." A week later, Seaweed again "spoke" Complex(ion).

> "I don't like brown skin" (Seaweed). "Why, do you say that, I have brown skin just like you and so does your mum, she has brown skin," I said. "I like my mum, you have brown skin too. But I don't like my brown skin. I like white skin," Seaweed replied. "But you can't say that, you should like your own, whatever color. I love my yellow skin, or that is what they say I have and I love it" (Jan, a Chinese Australian staff) hugged Seaweed and looked at me and said "I am shocked to hear this, you should like your skin Seaweed." "Okay, If we draw ourselves what color would you choose?" I asked. "White" said Seaweed and then looked at Jan, "No, purpley white skin color, alright" (Seaweed).

This was not the first time Seaweed commented about her "brown" and "white" skin. † had been concerned, as † observed Seaweed's repeated expressions of dislike for "brown" and a desire for "white." The next time when Amelia (OA), Jan, and † got together, Amelia opened the conversation by "speaking Complex(ion)" with Jan and †.

> "I worry about Plafe and Moo, Prasanna" (Amelia). "Why do you say that," I asked. "I cuddle these children and I protect them. But the outside world is cruel. I know it is different out there. I am from that world Prasanna. I am white, like you say. I grew up in a suburb with many cultures. I used to bring home all sorts of friends from varied backgrounds. My mum and dad were okay with it. But you should have heard my grandpa, grandma and other relatives. They say terrible things against people of color. I just bend my head down and am too scared to say anything. Can't they realize we are all Australians? We first had Sri Lankans and then Indians, they were slowly seen as similar to us and then they were not a problem. Now there are Sudanese and Somalians and that seems to bother everyone, they are right in front of their faces, dark as, and so they don't know how to cope" (Amelia).

"Amelia, Seaweed still says that she doesn't like being brown and that worries me," I said. "I know, I am shocked" (Jan). "We have to do something, I'll have a think" (Amelia).

When † first met Amelia, † could only see Amelia's "whiteness" and categorized her as "Other Australian," and when Amelia said that she worried about Moo and Plafe, † assumed that she was going to point to our "øthered difference," and † was ready to defend our "brownness" and our layered boundaries. But Amelia narrated the "cruel difference" in her "white world" and nothing about us. She reflected on how it affected us in Australia, she spoke with "us," the "øthered." Amelia justified a need for critical action, by drawing upon the attitudes of her extended family toward people of color. She regretfully added that we were all "Australian," despite our colored "differences." † voiced my silenced stories.

> "Amelia, you don't have to share this with me, but you have because you have been there feeling uncomfortable, like me about our silences. This happened years ago. My daughter came home from kinder one day and said that she was called dirty because she was brown, my reaction was anger and to seek justice. But I was silenced when my son who was diligently doing his homework asked her not to worry, because it is not as bad as being called poo for being brown and he was called that at school. Amelia, Seaweed still says that she doesn't like being brown and that worries me," I said. "I know, I am shocked" (Jan). "She sees the reality of colors in her family. This morning I observed children playing with wooden figurines and they made families of the same color and refused to mix up colors, Seaweed just got up and left," I added.
>
> Later, Amelia asked, "Prasanna, can you write up a newsletter for families and we will use EYLF as a reason for making family books, and that way children will see the diversity in families. Because we have it here in our group, we are all different. I will start this by describing my family history, not as just Australians, but as you say, white Anglo-Australians and how we came here many generations ago. Otherwise families will just write about like 'normal' (using her fingers as quotation marks) family" (Amelia). "I want to write it down, white Anglo-Australians. I thought they were just Australians" (Jan).

† shared our stories of discrimination in Australia with her, and Jan joined us, and we decided to engage in "critical action" to challenge "whiteness" and the image of "white Australian." Amelia wanted to break her silence and "speak" for and with us, "øthered Australian" as an "Other Australian," who did not hesitate to name

her "whiteness." With my newly found "voice," ✝ shared critical literature (Derman-Sparks, and Ramsay and Edwards, 2006; Hage, 2000) and websites (Britkids—http://www.britkid.org/index.html; Racism no way—http://www.racismnoway.com.au/; UNICEF—http://www.unicef.org/crc/) with Amelia and Jan, and we planned to circulate newsletters to families on making family books. Amelia decided that to name "Self" as "white Anglo-Australian" would disrupt the "normality" of "whiteness" and its unspoken clench on the identity of "Australian." We contested "whiteness" and "Australianness" together every afternoon for change, and continued to actively make plans and use structures to our advantage. Due to these exchanges, Jan began to name the "just Australian" as "white Anglo-Australian."

✝ reached out to Ganga again, as ✝ heard Amelia's voice tinged with fear.

"White" Fears: "but the Outside World Is Cruel. I Am from That World, Prasanna"

✝: Ganga, Amelia was committed to change, and that wasn't to do with "power." What Complex(ion) discourses enabled Amelia, Jan and ✝ to commit to challenging "whiteness" and "Australianness"?

Ganga: Amelia's affiliation with "whiteness" and "Australianness" was different to Gina's and Katherine's, yet it was related to "power." She discursively practiced to "Diffuse power." Didn't you notice she said, "*I worry about Plafe and Moo... I cuddle these children... But the outside world is cruel. I know it is different out there. I am from that world Prasanna. I am white, like you say.*" Amelia's strategies were "Critical øthering" in combination with "Critical Othering"; she outlined the "difference" in her "white" world and how it affected people of color.

✝: But, she wanted all individuals to be subjectified as "Australian."

Ganga: Remember, you can't avoid this in modern, western societies (Taylor, 2004; Appadurai, 2006), and especially with Australia's political system focused on promoting one national identity to manage diversity (Stokes, 1997; Rizvi, 2005). She did this with "Critical Recognizing"; she didn't automatically claim national ownership of her identity. She planned to name and present the "migrant" origin of her family through family books, just like all "øthered Australian." That is why it was important to name that "Australian" with you and Jan. Didn't Jan reconceptualize how she perceived "Australian"? Didn't this made you speak up and realize your "voice"? You collaboratively shared literature and "critical understanding" to initiate "critical action."

†: Ganga, amongst the same "whiteness," † found my "white transformer" in Amelia, she "Diffused power" with Jan and †, the "øthered Australians." Amelia was ready to engage in a marginal discourse, to reconceptualize "Australian" identity, by challenging the status and "power" of "whiteness."

Ganga: Remember her strategies things will change.

"White Transformer" Laments: "What They Feel and Go through Day after Day Is a Reality"

Yet, things didn't change. Our voices were extinguished later by the "power" of "whiteness," and † remembered Amelia's comments about Katrina (OA). At that time, I did not know that this was going to be my last day at this centre.

> "What does Katrina know? She is white and lives in this white world, but for children like Moo and Seaweed what they feel and go through day after day is a reality" (Amelia).

This is not just Moo's and Seaweed's reality. It is my reality too. † am "brown" and † live in this "white world." Katrina (OA) decided to withdraw the centre from Ganga. She had the power. The "power" of "whiteness" in extinguishing the "voices" that challenged its grasp on "Australian" was repeatedly evident. She discursively defended and denied "white privilege" (McIntosh, 1988), and sanctioned those who tried to recolor the Complex(ion) of "Australian." † left with my Ganga unable to critically share and act to change the Complex(ion) of "Australian." † instead allowed the perpetuation of "white power" through my "silence."

CHAPTER 4

Forbidden Fs Speak: You Know What Australians Think If You Say You Are a Muslim

> *I think of myself as just Australian, so I don't really wonder about that much. But when you ask what it is to be an Australian, like you did once, it is confronting. But what culture do I have to talk about. I am boring, I am nothing. There is no color, celebration or food.*
>
> —Cathy, white Anglo-Australian staff

The "boundary stream" Forbidden Fs—food, faith, and festival, began with the "othering" of "Australian / not Australian" categories. It began in a very abstract manner, and collected strength and form as it united and merged with Complex(ion). Food, Faith, and Festival, the Forbidden Fs, the features central to celebratory discourses of multiculturalism, failed to impress the "Australian." Authoritative and elusive nationalism repeatedly clashed with food and festivals tied to faith. Our emotions and feelings were put under trial and the "Australian" always had reasons and sanctions to exclude the "not Australian" or include at will. Ganga ends this chapter finally to tell her tales of "øthered" silences and whispers.

"OTHERING" FORBIDDEN FS: ENACTING AUSTRALIAN / NOT AUSTRALIAN

Faith was not supposed to intervene with Complex(ion), but it did, very casually. Contradictory to what the staff in this center believed, children's "othering" of "Australian / not Australian" identities using our skin color had become a part of their daily conversation.

It was one such days and Feeniyan casually began "othering" her peers using Complex(ion). Feeniyan looked at Bikky and commented, "*Bikky is Australian. 'cause she is white, Australians are white.*" Bikky immediately stressed, "*No, I am not. I am Turkish. I am white, but I am not Australian, I am only Turkish.*" Feeniyan's repeated attempts to change Bikky's self-categorization from "not Australian" to "Australian" by pointing to her "white" skin color were definitively denied by Bikky. This seemingly "Complex(ion) speak" became intertwined with specific "faith" realities of "not Australian" soon, and silencing "othering" of "faith" and "festivals" began to dominate our conversations.

In another set of "boundary speaks," casual food conversations became superimposed with Complex(ion) as it was narrated. It began as if it had nothing to do with "othering," but it gained momentum, strung with Complex(ion) emotions. I was sitting next to Plafe (a four-year-old, Indian Australian boy) at the lunch table and continued to observe and comment that Plafe always ate very little for lunch. Annie (a white Anglo-Australian staff) directed Plafe as she spoke to me, "*Stop talking and eat. Don't worry about him, he has been doing this since he was 6 months old. He talks too much and he doesn't eat his food.*" As soon as Plafe heard this, he looked at me and said, "*I will if I can have rotis. I love roti.*" At that time it was very difficult for me to conclude whether he commented on *roti* to me because he "othered" and categorized my "boundary identity" with his. Nevertheless, three other Indian Australian children in the room, Tin, Seaweed, and Moo joined Plafe in saying that they would also love to have *roti* for lunch. Jan (Chinese Australian staff) eagerly proposed that we could make *roti* just for Plafe, Seaweed, Tin, and Moo. I immediately suggested that *roti* should be offered to all children for lunch and not just to some children as that would imply that we were segregating and offering "difference" to just some children in the group. Pat (a three-year-old, white Anglo-Australian boy) who was also sitting at the same table said in a strong voice, "*I don't want to have it, I won't like it.*" I insisted that he needed to try before he made decisions about not liking *roti*. Pat exclaimed angrily, "*No, you can't make me. I have bread. Roti is for brown kids. I am not a brown kid. I am white,*" and spat at me. The simple expression of the Plafe's desire for a particular food became central to Pat's "othering" of food with "whiteness." This was a deceptively innocent expression of "othering" food with Complex(ion), and yet the "not Australian" reality and the "Australian" imagi(nation) with which this was responded left a permanent mark on Ganga. Forbidden Fs surged with responses that divided and kept the imaginations of "Australian" from being influenced by the realities of "not Australian."

"OTHERING" REALITIES: "NOT AUSTRALIAN" RESPONDS

Many of us, including me, were directly and indirectly affected by the "othering" of *roti* with "whiteness" and we responded. Moo heard Pat and his peers' repeated ridicule of *roti* after the lunchtime episode. It seemed as if Pat's open outburst gave them all permission to continually mention *roti* as *"yuk"* and *"stinky poo."* After a while, just before pick up time, Moo said, *"I am not having roti tonight Prasanna, I am having rice."* I briefly acknowledged this and left it there as I was too hurt to say anything. The very next morning Moo sat in my lap and said, *"Prasanna, I don't like you because you have brown skin... No, my mum is white and I am white too."* The "othering" of *roti* with "whiteness" not only influenced Moo's food habits, but also her attitude toward our, more specifically my "brownness." Moo became highly emotional when the staff in the room tried to correct her attitude toward her skin color. We all were hurt and shocked, but we responded with silence as we looked at each other.

While Plafe's "boundary speak" was strongly contested with Complex(ion) by Pat and Moo, Feeniyan's "boundary speaks" of Complex(ion) was contested with faith. During pick up time, I informed Bikky's mother about how Bikky contested being categorized as "Australian." Bikky's mother reasoned Bikky's ardent desire for maintaining her "not Australian" status, *"What do you do? But, you know we are Muslims and she knows that."* Once Bikky became aware that I was a Hindu, from the conversation that I had with Pookey, Bikky began to secretly share her faith-based practices with me, *"shhh... I will show you how we pray; my grandpa gave me money after we prayed during Bairam"* (Bikky). Months later, during Christmas celebrations, Bikky again whispered, *"You know we never have a Christmas tree in our house. Because we are Muslims, shhhhh... We only have Bairam, and it is fun."* Thus, Bikky's conscious "othering" of self as "not Australian" became more and more apparent to me as she continually silenced or whispered her "boundary speaks" that spoke of her festival, which was also linked to her faith.

The "othering" by "not Australian" Muslim staff in the setting was similar to that of Bikky's, as they silenced and spoke about the "Australian" by positioning this identity against their faith. It was Ramadan; I knew that Varuna, a Muslim staff, observed Ramadan fast during this period and I suggested that Varuna could share her faith-based experiences with the children. Varuna refused and replied, "*I can't, you know. Yes, that is why some people even hesitate to say they are Muslims. You know what Australians think of Muslims*" (Varuna, Asian Australian staff). Similarly, Selma and Fatima (Muslim, "not Australian" staff) "othered" the identity of "Australian," while categorizing and maintaining their collective Muslim identity "*You know nobody knew that I am a Muslim here, we keep it like that. We all do, Varuna, Fatima all of us*" (Selma, Bosnian Australian staff; Fatima, Iranian Australian staff). The Muslim staff felt this was their "not Australian" reality, as they always "othered" the "Australian" when they spoke of their Muslim identity. This "othering" resulted in the strong masking of their faith, in order to be accepted as "Australian."

Like faith, food too became central to the "not Australian" staff's "othering" of their dual identity status, "*You know we are Sri Lankan, we eat rice and curry. He [her son] has Australian food too and Sri Lankan, so he knows both cultures and adapts to it*" (Sheri, Sri Lankan Australian staff). Such comments were also passed by few more "not Australian" staff, who wanted to showcase their adaptability, "*We go to Bosnian clubs a lot but Aussie restaurants too*" (Selma).

With regard to Muslim faith, embracing this identity meant silencing their faith and hiding it from the "Australian." All Muslim staff and children also regarded themselves as "not Australian" and had mastered the art of masking this layer from the "Australian." However, when it came to food, the "not Australian" eagerly showcased their acceptance of "Australian" and claimed their dualistic status. Being a non-Muslim, I felt I never had the right to speak for or against their realities. However, as an action researcher I wanted to act against this silencing, as I felt troubled about their silences. I took these "not Australian" realities of Forbidden Fs practices, and the "Australian" imagination responded with national fervor.

"OTHERING" IMAGINATIONS: "AUSTRALIAN" RESPONDS

I took these silenced conversations to "Australian" staff whom I perceived as having the power to transform these silences. Whenever I brought up the subject of food, faith, and festival, Gina and Cathy (white Anglo-Australian staff) imagined "Australian" as nothing, and lamented for all its insipidity. They immediately made decisions to fill this identified gap in "Australian" with the celebration of "not

Australian" cultures with children in the setting. Hence, they marked these festivals by their ethnic origin and by making special food, for example: Chinese New Year; Indian *Ganesha* festival; Vietnamese Moon festival). Such "authentic" inclusion and celebration of multiculturalism was responded with explicit anger or implicit silencing by "not Australian" parents, staff, and children, and this shook their imagined nation.

Gina "spoke" as "Australian":

> We used to tell Safeeya's mum that we are coming to her house to have Chinese. She used to tell us that she usually makes lasagna. You can never generalize. You know when you asked us, who is an Australian a week ago, I was totally confronted. I was thrown back. Then I stopped and thought what it is to be an Australian, I couldn't find an answer. It is confronting, because being an Australian is something we take for granted (Gina).

In the imagination of "Australian," Gina very simply could never see Safeeya's (a four-year-old, Chinese Australian girl) mum beyond her Chinese, ethnic box, *"having Chinese."* However, Safeeya's mum reconfigured her identity box deliberately by saying that she cooked *lasagna,* and this disrupted the "Australian" in Gina. Therefore, Gina expressed her difficulties that she faced in unpacking their imagi(nation), the identity of "Australian." This disruption should have resulted in Gina rethinking her categorizing endeavors. During "Multicultural Week," Gina and Katherine celebrated Chinese New Year by inviting a Chinese dancer to the setting. Contrary to their expectations, this practice was responded by Safeeya's mum with much anger and frustration. Gina responded again with her imagi(nation),

> You know it is hard for me. How do I do this, I am only Australian. Like I told you about Safeeya's mum and when I asked her whether she cooks Chinese, she said lasagna. Debbie is an Australian and I am Australian. I know what we eat. It is easy for me to talk about it. I don't know about you and Safeeya's mum. Don't worry, we will find a way (Gina).

Gina knew from her earlier experience that it was wrong to generalize and yet, she was unable to think outside the celebratory discourse of multiculturalism. Such celebratory discourse stereotypes and marginalizes migrant groups and their cultures as being outside the practices of "Australian." The "Australian" found it difficult to think of alternatives, outside practices that stereotyped specific cultures. She went ahead and celebrated Chinese New Year by inviting a Chinese dancer. Again, Gina's imagi(nation) guided Gina to respond as "Australian." The "Australian" ambiguity was evident as it was confronting to explore what was "Australian" and yet, the cultures of "not Australian other" were identified as being definable and knowable. The "Australian" grappled with the unknowable "not Australians." During my interview with her, Gina again imagined the "Australian" as nothing,

> Oh gosh, I wouldn't even know. I think I am an Australian and I don't have anything. Like I am not even a Catholic or anything like that. Just an Australian (Gina).

Cathy's "Australian" imagination was not very different from that of Gina. In Cathy's imagination the "not Australian" possessed all that the "Australian" lacked. Therefore, when I took the "boundary speaks" that spoke of those Muslim silences, Cathy movingly declared how the staff, whom she employed for their color and celebrations, never showcased their backgrounds in the setting.

> I really hire strong women as staff and they are strong, they have been through such difficult experiences and have such wonderful, diverse backgrounds. But they just leave back who they are as soon as they walk into the centre, just out that door (pointing to the entrance). They leave it right there on the foot mat. I keep wondering why can't we celebrate cultures, their colors and festivities (Cathy).

I replied by asking Cathy to name her own background, and the colors and celebrations attached to it. I wanted to disrupt the "Australian" as nothing imagination.

> I think of myself as just Australian, so I don't really wonder about that much. But when you ask what it is to be an Australian, like you did once, it is confronting. But what culture do I have to talk about. I am boring, I am nothing. There is no color, celebration or food. Tell me about it. I am just ordinary. Nothing to talk about. We have nothing. We [Australian] are so blah. Not like you, the food, the celebrations, we are just there (Cathy).

Disrupting the "Australian" was difficult. Although Cathy named her collective "self" as "white middle- class Anglo- Australian," she too believed that she was "just Australian" and felt confronted when asked to unravel its layers. The origin of what was presented and eaten daily in their early childhood settings was left unchallenged. After many such repeated arbitrations, I engaged in purposeful "othering," and as a "not Australian," I overtly named the faith and festival of "Australian." I invited Cathy to name and trace the affiliations of festivals such as Easter and Christmas that are celebrated in a routine manner by all the staff and children in the centre. Cathy maintained its insipidity with its ubiquitous presence. *"But, what is the point, it is not special. There is nothing special about it. It is always there"* (Cathy). I smiled and never again posed this question. Cathy, till the very end, insisted the insipidity of her "white Anglo-Australian" heritage. Bikky, Selma, Fatima, Varuna, and I, as "not Australian," knew what the "Australian" stood for, and we moderated our behavior to be accepted by "Australian." But the "Australian" imagi(nation) continued as nothing, no color, no celebration.

On the other hand, Katrina (white Anglo-Australian staff) was quietly following the change caused by the *roti* incident and my conversations with children since then. One afternoon Plafe and his peers argued about Santa's veracity. Plafe corrected his peers, *"Santa at the shopping centre is not real....A person wears Santa costume and gives you present in the shopping centre. You tell him Prasanna."* I seconded Plafe and told him that Santa at the shopping centers was not real, and it was only someone in a costume. This conversation gave Katrina an opportunity to absolutely defend the Forbidden Fs of "Australian."

> "Did you say Santa was not real? That is so wrong....It is a family value. It is religion and you can't change what 98% of Australians believe to be true...what if I say you can't have *roti*, it is like that....You have to leave things as they are sometimes. Nothing has to change. For some minority Australia does not have to change" (Katrina).

When Katrina equated Santa with *roti*, I realized her "othering" was beyond food, faith, and festival of "Australian / not Australian" dichotomy. The majority had to be safeguarded from the minority. The "Australian" forbade anything or anyone from even slightly disrupting her imagi(nation). My minority status was determined, with my color, my language, my looks, my attire, my faith, or, in totality, my voice. Everything merged and later the "Australian" punished,

> "I am sorry we have to pull out of the project" (Katrina). "I am really sorry. Can I do anything to change? I really only seconded what the child said, as he asked me. I am very sorry," I pleaded. "I know, you spoke the truth and that is very wrong. It is a big mistake...We still like having you here you know. That is not the problem. Saying Santa

is not real is a big problem. That is wrong, I know it is the truth, but it is a mistake to say so." (Katrina).

The problem was not so much speaking the truth; it was about disrupting what was "Australian." The "Australian" had to remain as it had always been. I, the "not Australian," changed, but the "Australian," their Forbidden Fs, and their imagi(nation) thrived.

Thus, questioning "Australian" remained as being confronting for those who regarded themselves as "just Australians," as such questioning would expose the "Australian" myth and shatter their imagined nation. It was interesting to note that those who defended "Australian" spoke with their "whiteness." Critical multiculturalism recommends that educationalists view culture as an abstract phenomenon, beyond symbolic items, such as food, attire, language, religion, and celebrations (see Bennett, 2003; Gilbert, 2004; Derman-Sparks, Ramsay, and Edwards, 2006; Rosaldo, 2006; Grant and Sleeter, 2007; Gorski, 2008). However, when it comes to challenging "whiteness," it recommends that "white" people recognize and name what they celebrate, do, and eat daily as "white culture" (Leonardo, 2004; Rose-Cohen, 2004). I recognized it, but couldn't name it. Many other "boundary speakers" recognized the "Australian" too, but none of us could name it overtly and assertively. Although, I remained silenced, I became determined to find out what fostered this "Australian" imagi(nation) in multicultural Australia.

"Othering" Forbidden Fs: Shaping "Australian Speakers"

The multicultural Australia and "Australian" should encompass and represent varied color, cultural, and religious values. I silently questioned: Australia professes multiculturalism, why then is this "Australian" unable to accept "Chinese" and "Indian" within what is regarded as "Australian"? I began with the dawning of Australia's multiculturalism.

> Something of a conspiracy of silence persists in many quarters about the social impact of other than Anglo-Saxon influences on our national life.... The image we manage to convey of ourselves still seems to range from the bushwhacker to the sportsman to the slick city businessman. Where is the Maltese process worker, the Italian concrete layer, the Yugoslav miner or—dare I say it—the Indian scientist?
>
> (Grassby, 1973, p. 2)

It was during the advent of multiculturalism when the stereotyping or boxing of ethnic attributes in the name of acknowledging cultural diversity began. Grassby, in his eagerness to expose the presence of many cultures, essentialized the groups with stereotypical images and boundary categories. However, Grassby also legitimized representing or "*Othering*" national and boundary categories within particular images, and rather than asking where is the "Australian Anglo-Saxon" process worker, concrete layer, and scientist, he left the national "Anglo-Saxon" and the migrant Maltese, Italian, and Indian in their respective categorical cultural boxes. In fact, Grassby followed this by identifying the "different other," the categorical distinction of the then migrants in the society of Australia,

> They perceive different goals and pursue them in their own traditional ways. In short, they lead a way of life which, while in living touch with its ancient forms and impulses, is imperceptibly coming to terms with—or at least learning to co-exist...in our society.
> (Grassby, 1973, p. 6)

The antiquity and the traditions of the newcomers the "not yet Australians" were thus differentiated, and the then "Australians" were assured that these "not yet Australians" were willing to learn and could be taught to live harmoniously with the perceived owners of the nation. With the statements that followed, encouraging nationalism in the hearts of all subjects for decades to come, the boundary boxes also remained protected, with diversity identified in the outsiders to be taught and subjectified as "Australian" or to be maintained as "not Australian." The set of political ideas that distinguish diversity to recruit and amass committing subjects is still evident.

> Australian multiculturalism recognises, accepts, respects and celebrates cultural diversity...all Australians are expected to have an overriding loyalty to Australia and its people...and...Our commitment to and defence of Australian values of equality, democracy and freedom unite us in our diverse origins, and enhance the ability of us all to participate fully in spheres of Australian society.
> (Commonwealth of Australia, 2003, p. 2)

The political statements that acknowledge, respect, and celebrate diversity in all its forms, including religious diversity, and later recommend that the subjects override these to commit to the nation and national values, still exist. Thus, the politics of Australia since the advent of multiculturalism has struggled with its desire for welcoming diversity and fear of diversifying what is already in Australia. This desire and fear also insulates the "Australian" from learning from the "not Australian" and yet permits the "Australian" to teach the "not yet Australian" to be "Australian." And the insulation and permission royalties protect the "Australian" imagi(nation). This abstract ideological "Australian" now was "*Othered*" by Ganga's "Australian speakers" to defend this from being influenced by "not Australian."

The subjects, "Australian speakers," in Ganga *shaped* the "Australian" by upholding rather than uprooting that "One Australian." While some "spoke" to shape this with definite boundaries, others "spoke" to shape this with indefinable, yet conceivable boundaries. Gina's and Cathy's recognition of "Australian" emptiness and the later celebration of Multicultural Week and employment of vibrant color and cultures in their settings stemmed from the ideological desire to acknowledge and respect diversity. However, their controlled subversion of unraveling the "Australian" also stemmed from the fear of losing the very same ideological "Australian" to the disruptions of "not Australian." Like Grassby, they could not see the celebrations of "Indian" and "Chinese" out of their boundary boxes trickling into those of "Australian." Therefore, both Gina and Cathy as "Australian speakers" continued to shape their "Australianness" as nothing. This label of emptiness enabled them to deny and mask their influence on the cultural arbitrations in Australia, and covertly teach the "not Australian" and overlook the conversion of "not Australian" as loyal subjects. Moreover, the quest to maintain their "Australianness," however insipid and bland it might be, justified this identity remaining uninfluenced by the color and cultures of the "not Australian." After all, protecting this nation and national identity from outsiders was what was recommended by the ideological statements of Australian politics. However, for some subjects of Australia, their "Australianness" was everything that needed to be protected from the outsider, the noncompliant "not Australian," who had come to challenge the integrity of this national identity.

Katrina's unrestrained articulation of faith and festival of "Australian" with Santa originated from the fear of changing "Australia," the nation. Moreover, with "white Complex(ion)" still dictating and dominating the society of Australia, Pat's uncontrolled aversion for *roti* to protect his "whiteness" was overridden by Katrina the "Australian" to protect "Australian values." Katrina surged ahead to teach me, the "not Australian," a lesson to silence my truth. The "Australian speaker" highlighted the religious values of "Australia's

Australian" and reminded me, the "not Australian minority," to leave this alone. She defended and insulated the national identity with notions of majority that gave all "Australians" the right to own and stand up for the nation and national identity as it was and still is. She protected not just the "Australian" but also the ideology of the "white Australian."

Thus, the "Australian speakers" such as Katrina, Pat, Gina, and Cathy who already regarded themselves as "Australian," "*Othered*" this identity by taking control of representing and maintaining "white Australian." The "white Australian" controlled the Forbidden Fs of "not Australian" by maintaining its status outside what was "Australian" with open proclamation or anonymous representation of this identity. Their "Australian boundary speaks" reflected the very same desire and fear while engaging with multicultural "difference," and the reification of the "Australian" imagi(nation) that insulated the "Australian" from learning and permitted the teaching of "not Australian." Thus, the ideology, which is the "Australian" imagi(nation), continued to survive without being tainted by the colors and celebrations of multiculturalism. It overtly and covertly silenced the food, faith, and festival of especially the "not Australian." I wanted to break this ideological myth that enslaved all subjects by "*øthering*" our Forbidden Fs "boundary speaks" with Ganga.

"ØTHERING" FORBIDDEN FS: CONTESTING "AUSTRALIAN" WITH THEIR IMAGI(NATION) AND OUR REALITIES

The dominance of Forbidden Fs "boundary speaks" by "Australianness" that resulted in the restraining and silencing of "not Australian" boundaries was overtly evident. The simultaneous domination of Forbidden Fs boundaries by "whiteness" was more subtle and less discernable. Yet, unidentified, unspoken "whiteness" and "Australianness" still shaped and "Othered" the nation and national identity. The "not Australian" too subscribed and accepted this partial celebration and public silencing of their cultural and religious practices. It seemed like they had willingly accepted their silenced predicament. Leeman and Reid (2006) and Vickers (2002) argue that cultural pluralism that is established around ideologies of liberalism and universalism privileges the unnamed dominant race and covert effects of colonialism, which can be likened to "democratic racism." The postcolonial in me resurged to question the acceptance of "democratic racism" and the exclusion and silencing of some. It is not that all "not Australian" subjects succumbed to being dominated—some did resist. We, the resistors as "øthered Australian," sought the conviction of the "white transformer." And together, we contested "Australian" to rupture the ideological solidarity being controlled by "white" anonymity. Ganga and † "spoke" with "øthered Australian" and the Forbidden Fs of all cultures.

Contesting Forbidden Fs with Plafe, Moo, and Jan

"We Have to Do Something. I Don't Want My Son to Grow Up Thinking Being Chinese Is Bad"

Amelia (OA) greeted me with much enthusiasm as soon as she met me and she introduced me to Jan (øA) in the room. They were both highly interested in the topic and every afternoon we collaborated to share our observations and interpretations of events and they particularly encouraged me to offer my postcolonial interpretations of daily early childhood practices.

My second day at this center, and † observed children playing in the home corner, and they "spoke" Forbidden Fs.

> Sheep and Plafe brought some wooden blocks from the block corner and began to build on top of the fridge. "What are you building?" I asked Plafe and Sheep as they stacked the wooden blocks in the home corner. "I am building a chimney for Santa to come and give me presents," Sheep replied. "Me, too," added Plafe. "Is this for Christmas? But Christmas is at the end of the year, just before you start school and you have many, many days to go," I added. "Yeah, but we are getting ready for Santa," Sheep replied. "Me too," seconded Plafe. "You know I read that you celebrate Diwali too, guess what I do too, Plafe, just like you," I commented. "No, we only celebrate Christmas, don't we Sheep?" replied Plafe.

Amelia (OA) had commented earlier, Plafe was a follower; he copied what Sheep did. † too could sense that he often deliberately avoided speaking to me about his background, and just wanted to be "like Sheep."

> We were seated at the play dough table. "I am making, pronti, pronti." Moo pinched a bit of play dough and kneaded it and rolled out with a rolling pin. "See, Prasanna, have some. This is how my mum and

nannu makes it," offered Moo. "Can I have some, I love *roti*. But I can't have too much, because I get itchy" (Seaweed). Moo said, "It is pronti. I have it all the time. I have it with yoghurt. You tear it like this and dip it and eat." Plafe sits afar with Sheep and watches us talk about *roti*.

This was Moo's favorite activity, she made *roti*, and most children in the room knew this was her favorite dish. Seaweed and Tin (øA) used to join us, to talk about their *roti* preferences, but Plafe never did. His silencing continued. Jan and † were in the yard.

> "Prasanna, this is so wrong. My nephew who goes to school, now does not want to take noodles or rice anymore. He doesn't even talk to my sister-in-law when she goes to school. I feel bad. We have to do something. Everything is food, noodles or bread. He now only takes sandwiches. How bad is that? I am worried. My son might do the same. I don't want my son to grow up thinking being Chinese is bad," Jan said worriedly. "I understand, I used to feel the same too. My son used to bring food home without eating from kinder. During primary school it was hard, he would only take sandwiches but bring the whole thing back, because he didn't like eating them, but would not take anything else. I don't know by the time he got to secondary school he had lots of Indian and Sri Lankan friends, they all used to take rice with vegetables and dhal. He said because there were so many in their group the boys could not tease them about the food. I still felt that is not going to change anything," I said. "I am worried we have to do something. I really am interested in this [my study]. Here in this centre, it is all the same. It is different where I used to work before. They were close to migrant resource centre. They used catering to have different food all the time. So children and staff got used to eating different types of food. Here it is the same, very Aussie" (Jan).

Jan and † shared our "øthered" experiences, and for Jan, rejection of noodles could lead to rejection of one's "Chinese" boundary identity, and she spoke with her experiential knowledge. † told her how my son overcame this by finding safety in peers who ate similar food, those from South East Asian community. Jan challenged current practices at the centre that failed to practice "difference." This was her key concern. † had always questioned just presenting food to include cultures. Jan challenged my understandings; how will children know about practicing "difference" if † don't express and exhibit "difference"? † critically thought about Plafe's behavior and † resolved to engage in discussing my "different" food, faith, and festival practices. Plafe's behavior changed, and he began to engage in conversations that reflected his ethnic origin with confidence. †shared my observation with Jan and Amelia,

> "Plafe has started to speak Hindi, and talk about his background in front of Sheep, and he stands up for himself. He debated with Sheep about Santa the other day, as he continued to argue that Santa at the shopping centre was not real, just a man in a costume. I used to think props are not needed, but if you don't have that food around or someone to talk about different ways of doing things children never seem to then talk about it," I said excitedly.

Amelia too had observed Plafe's recently found confidence. Amelia again suggested using EYLF (Commonwealth of Australia, 2009) to include "øthered" ways of viewing the world, and Amelia, Jan, and † collaboratively worked on strategies to do so. Amelia went on holidays and what followed shattered my confidence in action research, and my own conduct.

> It was lunch time. Plafe was not eating. He continued to laugh, talk and just push the sausages around on his plate. "Plafe, you should start eating. Look most of your friends have finished what was in their plate," I said. "I don't like this, can I leave it?" Plafe asked me. "Plafe eat your food. No, tricks this time, stop talking and eat your food," Annie (OA) spoke to Plafe. "He asked me if he could leave it," I informed Annie. "Stop talking and eat. Don't worry about him, he has been doing this since he was 6 months old. He talks too much and he doesn't eat his food," Annie said. "Did you hear that, Annie says that you have always been not eating your food, come on, what is going to make you eat?" I asked Plafe. "I will if I can have *rotis*. I love *roti*," Plafe replied.

When Plafe turned and said, "*roti*," † wondered whether our shared background and his newly found confidence had made him openly state his desire.

> "What is it, I don't know. I haven't had that before," Jan asked me. "It is just flat bread and it is made fresh and we have it with dhal or vegetables," I explained. "Or even butter," Plafe added. "You can even have it with jam, it is yum" (Tin, øA). "We have to make it then for these children" (Jan). "I don't think we should just make it for Moo, Tin and Plafe, all the children in the group can have it. Then they won't feel different. We have bread and similarly we can have *roti* one day a week in the menu. But it is hard to make Jan, you need practice to roll out the *roti*. It is hard," I said. "No, you can buy it in bulk at the Indian shop. That is what my mum does. She buys lots of it and heats it

up when I go home every day" (Plafe). "My mum does that too" (Tin). "We can do that then, that is not hard" Jan reassured me.

† enacted my role as a participatory action researcher, and † was elated as we planned to make *roti* for all the children regularly. † shook as † heard the voice of "whiteness," Pat (OA), a three-year-old boy, defending the boundaries of "whiteness" and screamingly refusing to have *roti* because he was "white" and *roti* was for "brown kids." † challenged him, "*You should try... I have roti, and bread like you,*" and Pat spat at me. † did not mind being spat at and that he rejected *roti*, but he rejected our "brownness," a fate that we hadn't and can't escape unless "whiteness" gets colored. There was a morbid silence, and the children consoled me. Jan and † quietly waited for Amelia to return.

> The next week when I was in the room, "I am going for my lunch, I am hungry," I said. "What are you having for lunch Prasanna?" asked Kangaroo (øA). "I brought *roti*, remember, the flat bread," I replied. "Oooh, stinky poo, smelly," Pat and Princess (OA) waved their hands in front of their noses and laughed together. I stayed back rather than leave for lunch then. I sat with the children at the lunch table. "I am not having *roti* tonight Prasanna, I am having rice," Moo said.

Pat again ridiculed our "difference." † decided never to speak about *roti* again. Moo too changed her practices, and she said that she was having rice that night.

> The next week, Amelia was back from her holidays. I entered the room and sat down, Moo came and sat in my lap, looked at me and said, "Prasanna, I don't like you because you have brown skin" (Moo). We were shocked, adults and children alike. "You hurt my feelings by saying that. You are sitting in my lap and you also have brown skin," I replied. "No, I am white, not brown" (Moo). "But you are brown, your mum and dad they are also brown," I said. "No, my mum is white and I am white too" (Moo). "No, don't tell my mum. But I am white" (Moo).

† shared the *roti* incident with Amelia, wondering whether Moo's behavior was related to that. After all Moo's favorite food was *roti* (*pronti*, as she calls it). Amelia consoled me and said that we could make *roti* every week with all the children, and she would ask Annie (OA) to get the ingredients. Annie replied that she heard Pat's comments about *roti*, and she believed that it was his personality. Annie asked me to download images of food and laminate this to expose

children to diversity and that making *roti* would destabilize the budget.

The next day, † faced Katrina (OA), and she suddenly questioned the conversation † had with Plafe about Santa. Weeks ago, † agreed with Plafe when he said Santa at the shopping centers was a man in Santa costume. Katrina, the "Other Australian" defended and guarded Australia and the identity of "Australian," by insisting "98% of Australians" are Santa believers. She reiterated, "*Saying Santa is not real is a big problem. That is wrong, I know it is the truth, but it is a mistake to say so,*" and withdrew from the project the next day, and † was devastated.

† still hurt from what happened, and I called Ganga to help me understand.

Forbidden Fs Silenced Voice: *"I Will If I Can Have Rotis. I Love Roti"*

†: Ganga, † am guilty, † could have kept quiet. Should † have left Plafe to emulate Sheep, "Other Australian"? Was my intervention into Pat's food preferences wrong? Why did † say it?

Ganga: When you met Plafe, he was "boundary committed," and he was "self-othering" and "self alienating" you, as you represented his ethnic origin. You saw how he sought the approval of "Other Australian" repeatedly. Taylor (2004) calls this behavior as "existential dizziness" in migrants, which prompts migrants to ignore their own traditions, worldviews and language, and allow to be absorbed by "American whiteness." Plafe wanted to be absorbed by "Australian whiteness." You can't escape your knowledge, experiences and how they contribute to your understandings. You reacted to Jan, your role as an action researcher, and most of all your own boundary experiences of having *samosa, gulab jamun* and singing Hindi songs with Plafe. Jan was there to challenge "whiteness" and "Australianness" with you, and she wanted to "diffuse boundaries" with all the "self narration" and "critical recognizing" you shared. You were both "øthered Australian" but you stood up against dominance, and you wanted your "voice" to be heard. All of these make you who you are, and what you did. Added to this was your postcolonial subjectivity, you saw Pat's "whiteness" as soon as he said *roti* was for brown kids, and that he was white. I can understand your pain and your emotions. Pat, the "white kid" made you, an adult feel like a "brown kid." Such is the "power" of "whiteness" in Australia, you have experienced this before, did you forget?

†: So what did † do wrong?

Ganga: It wasn't wrong, you acted discursively to "resist" and "risk" your presence and your study. You challenged the "power" of "whiteness," and most of all you tried to initiate change in the identity of "whiteness" and "Australianness." Moo, was gravitating to "whiteness" and many do. According to Derman-Sparks, Ramsay, and Edwards (2006), many studies conducted in America have concluded that very frequently, African American children wished or believed that they were "white," while their European American counterparts seldom wanted to be "black." What happened just reflected their studies.

Forbidden Fs Silencing Voice: *"What If I Say, You Can't Have Roti to You? It Is Like That."*

†: But, not everyone reacted to what † said in the same manner. Did Amelia, Annie, and Katrina then subjectively respond to the *roti* incident?

Ganga: Of course they did. Amelia, the "Other Australian" was your "white transformer," who wanted to make hybridity a reality for "white" people too. She embraced what you brought, your "difference," your experiential knowledge, and everything you stood for. Remember, she was ready to challenge "whiteness" and "Australianness" the moment you walked in, and you realized your "voice" with her. Amelia extended her support when she heard Plafe sharing his food and festival practices with you. She collaboratively planned, "*It is the first time I am hearing him talk like this Prasanna. First, let us send a note to parents asking for such material, can you work on that Prasanna.*" Annie was "Boundary denying," so she "Theorized" and "Legitimized" her inaction by justifying what Pat said was his personality. You know how she understood Plafe's reluctance to eat, "*Stop talking and eat. Don't worry about him, he has been doing this since he was 6 months old. He talks too much and he doesn't eat his food*" (Annie). How did she handle Plafe's refusal to eat? She did not acknowledge the culture behind what was being served every day, but blamed Plafe's talkativeness. Therefore, automatically she also suggested that you present food images to reflect cultural inclusion, as if seeing and eating are the same. Katrina took the uppermost control of the nation and national identity, as she was "Boundary defending" fiercely, "*It is religion and you can't change what 98% of Australians believe to be true. Nothing has to change. For some minority Australia does not have to change,*" and she wanted to protect the identity of "Australian," from you, the "minority." You know how Appadurai (2006) talks about minority/majority language and how it creates hierarchical relationship and marginalization. Like Spears (1997) comments, you, Jan, and Amelia were those individuals who could topple the structure, her "power." This "Other Australian," first engaged in "Othering" to outline what was "98% Australian" and she "Hierarchically øthered" you as a threat to children's innocence and "Australian values." Remember, how she connected food, faith, and festival by saying, "*What if I say, you can't have roti to you? How would you feel about it? It is like that.*" She punished you for speaking "Santa difference." She was just being a loyal "Australian" subject, and she retrieved that "power" when she axed you. I still remember her final words, "*We still like having you here you know. That is not the problem. Saying Santa is not real is a big problem. That is wrong, I know it is the truth, but it is a mistake to say so.*" You forgot your color and your origin; after all, you will never be accepted as "Australian," if you practice "difference." Only by pledging your loyalty to this identity, "Australian," you can get closer to being accepted.

†: Ganga, you know how much it affected me. So do you suggest that † behave like the following "øthered Australians"?

CONTESTING FORBIDDEN Fs WITH SHERI, SELMA, FATIMA, VARUNA, ARUNA, SANTA, AND BIKKY

"Otherwise They Will Say, Go Back to Your Country, Go Back to Where You Came from"

This was Sheri's (øA) last day at the centre and she kindly agreed to set aside some time for the interview.

"How does culture affect your daily life?" I asked Sheri. "You know Sri Lankans eat different types of food, you know the food we eat. We eat rice and curry. He (her son) has Australian food too and Sri Lankan, so he knows both cultures and adapts to it and won't be afraid to say he is Sri Lankan (Sheri). "Do you bring your culture outside, to the centre?" I asked. "I don't think I have totally shown my culture. They know I am Sri Lankan and I eat curry, but I haven't brought Sri Lankan food for them to taste" (Sheri).

† was surprised when Sheri classified what she ate as "Sri Lankan," and something else as "Australian." Having distinguished these boundaries, she also ensured that as a family her son was exposed to both cultures through food. Acknowledging her culture with food was about developing a strong sense of identity in her son. † remembered what Selma said in her interview.

"Culture is who you are. Who you are, you want to keep private. When I came to this centre no one asked me whether I am Muslim or this, they just take me. It is because how I present myself. I struggled so hard initially when I came here. But now I have made it here and I want to forget about all that happened before. You know we eat different food and everything being Bosnian, our pans and what we make they are different too. But we have Aussie stuff too, we go to Bosnian clubs a lot but Aussie restaurants too. Like my daily life we do the same things, like everyone, get up and drink coffee and come to work" (Selma). We came to the end of our interview, "Thank you Selma, do you have anything to ask me?" I asked before we brought the interview to a close. "What does cultural identity mean to you, what about you?" (Selma) "For me it is complex. And Selma, I agree with keeping things private. But if we keep things private how will others know about many ways of being in this world and accept many ways of being and thinking. This is where I struggle. Imagine you have a grandchild and you want to send this child to this centre, do you think he or she will be able to grow up knowing who they are, if they come here to this centre?" I asked. "Mmmmmm... I don't know" (Selma).

Ɨ concluded Selma too was strongly conscious of her cultural origin. For Selma, her culture was her religious identity, "Muslim." However, this was something that she privatized, in order to be accepted "like everyone." Sheri and Selma seemed to have reconciled with "hybrid," dual cultural enactments. They had similar perceptions about eating or having "Australian" food, and excluding what was theirs from what was "Australian." Later, Ɨ realized that Ɨ must have slightly disrupted Selma's thoughts with my cultural dilemmas.

> That evening, "You know after the conversation we had, I am seriously thinking about this. But Prasanna, I feel you can't change anything here. You have to change once you are here." Another day, "You know till now, I used to think what is at home is there, leave it when you come out" (Selma). "But you said yesterday (during our interview), culture is who you are and it is everything you do, how can you leave this at home when you come out, because you are you, that culture whether you are in or out isn't it? Otherwise they will say, go back to your country, go back to where you came from. So change is good. We came here with nothing and we have everything now. So we get used to leading two lives. One for home and one for outside. That is how you manage. You have to forget who you are when you come out. But maybe I can change this for my grandchildren. They can then say with pride, I am so and so." (Selma)

Ɨ could sense Selma's silencing, and she feared being rejected by "Other Australian." Selma recognized the "power" of "Other Australian," and Ɨ had kindled her urge to regain her sense of self, yet she felt nothing would change. Ɨ heard fear and helplessness in Selma's voice, and ⸸ decided to work with the most approachable "Other Australian" at that centre.

Cathy, the "Other Australian" named "Self" as "white middle-class Anglo-Australian," and had expressed that she wanted her staff to express their culture, color, and celebration, the attributes she experienced when she participated in their celebrations, in their homes. She believed she had a history that she needed to share with staff to enable equitable practices of all cultures. Yet, Cathy never "spoke" the history of "white Australian" with the staff to explore its influence on current practices. She came back repeatedly and "Othered" her "white middle-class Australian" culture as "nothing" compared to all the color, food, and celebration the "øthered Australian" had. After years of immigration and influences of many cultures, she still believed the identity of "Australian" was still unlike the "øthered." ⸸ silently participated in the "celebration" of multiculturalism, with a "Chinese dancer," Indian festivals, and Vietnamese festivals, with "øthered" color and culture. Cathy's expressions of what was "Australian" echoed in the voice of her staff.

> Aruna walked in to the office from the kindergarten. "Have you returned your questionnaire Aruna" (Cathy). "No, but what do I write, I have no culture. I am just an Australian and those questions are hard and difficult for me to answer" (Aruna). "Really?" I asked. "Yes, I even asked my daughter whether she knew something, but she said the same. We don't have a culture, as we are just Australians" (Aruna). "That is fine, you don't have to do it, if you feel that way," I replied.

Aruna too proclaimed to be "just Australian," "nothing," "no culture." ⸸ wondered why Aruna resorted to imitating the discursive practices of "Other Australian," when many "øthered Australian" spoke how they were influenced by "Australian."

> During my interview with Fatima, "You know this is not my real name. My real name is..." (Fatima). "Really, why?" I asked. "My husband has changed his name too. We gave our children Christian names, because we did not want them to be different from everyone here" (Fatima). "Mmm," I nodded. "You know, my husband says, in this country [Australia] you can't look different or be different. He has changed his name to sound the same" (Fatima). "To sound the same, what do you mean, same as?" I asked. "You know, the same as like the people here [Australians]. We even named our children with Muslim

names and gave them normal, Christian names, so that people do not discriminate them and they don't get hurt" (Fatima).

For Fatima, regulating their Muslim identity was to do with safety. She and her family had to hide their "difference" behind the "normality" of the religious identity of "Australian" and Christian names.

> You know people never knew I was a Muslim here. Even now I don't talk about it. You know how it is if you say you are a Muslim. One day the cook offered me something and I said, it is pork, I won't have it. Then she asked me, why don't you like the taste of pork. That is when I said no, it is because of my religion. I am a Muslim. She was so surprised. One thing is I never bother to tell anyone or show anyone I am one. They [Australians] think if you are a Muslim, you know you have to cover your face, this and that and I am not a Muslim like that. Fatima too and Varuna, we are all Muslims, but we don't fit into that box they expect (Selma).

Selma expressed how she resisted the stereotypical image of her religious identity. ✝ could sense that this was her expression of strength and not her weakness, because she felt that she defied the images constructed by "Other Australian" for Muslims. ✝ definitely couldn't challenge Fatima's and Selma's choice of silencing, as ✝ am not a Muslim and would never know what it is to risk this "difference." I did not want to speak for and about them.

> It was the final week of Ramadan, I mentioned to Varuna about a program on the rehabilitation of terrorists in Indonesia, "That is why some people even hesitate to say they are Muslims. A staff in this centre does not want to be identified as Muslim. You know what Australians think of Muslims. But I tell her, you shouldn't hide who you are." She is worried, she says, "No, Varuna, don't tell anyone, they will think it is not okay" (Varuna)."That is why for me this is complex," I said. "You know you shouldn't talk about religion with others in Australian society" (Varuna whispered).

Varuna too warned me about what "Other Australian" thought of Muslims and silenced any further conversations about religion. Every story of "Muslim" staff approved their silence to be accepted within Australia by "Other Australian." ✝ could not speak about Islam as a non-Muslim, and yet ✝ felt compelled to act with their silences. Id was coming closer and ✝ approached Cathy to celebrate Id at the centre with the staff to transform Islam as "Australian" faith and festival. Cathy diverted my conversation with EYLF (Commonwealth of Australia, 2009), and she again insisted on her blandness in comparison to our, "øthered Australian" color, faith, and celebration. ᵻ explicitly outlined the celebration of "Other Australian," and colored this with green, red, and gold, with carols and bells. Cathy came back to stress on its "everydayness," and eluded by voiding hers. ᵻ smiled and remained silenced.

All the staff including those who were "Muslim" began to prepare the rooms and the children to celebrate Christmas. My postcolonial Ganga surfaced as Cathy and I discussed the relevance of celebrating Christmas at the centre. Cathy promised to challenge the normalized practices of any particular faith in Australia with the staff, but never did. The month of November came and the red, green, and gold in every room spoke of what we celebrated, and whose festival we all took responsibility to celebrate. The "Other Australian," their religious tradition, remained publicized as everyone's religion and tradition.

> Pookey, Bikky, and Santa were waiting for me near the gate and as soon as I entered, Bikky dragged me inside "You know we never have a Christmas tree in our house" (Bikky). "Why?" I asked. "Because we are Muslims, shhhhh…We only have Bairam, and it is fun" (Bikky). "But, why are you whispering?" I asked. "I have to, because everyone has a Christmas tree here" (Bikky). "I don't. Do you Pookey," I turned to Pookey. "No, I don't" (Pookey). "What about Bairam, what do you do?" I asked. "We have lots of sweets. I love this sweet, like it is like Baklava…and I get lots of money" (Bikky). "Hey, I don't have a Christmas tree either. We have Bairam for Christmas. My mum says our Christmas is Bairam. Christmas is Bairam for Australians, my mum says. I have sweets and get lots of money too" (Santa).

ᵻ noticed that Bikky had learnt she had to whisper her food, faith, and festival "difference," baklava, Islam, and *Bairam*. Santa too had learnt from his mum, Christmas was "Australian" and their *Bairam* wasn't "Australian." Their silencing continued, as "øthered Australian" Muslim staff and children self-regulated their identity practices in Australia to mimic what was "Australian." The "Other Australian" food, faith, and festival practices became "everyone's," and therefore represented "Australian." ᵻ could not help but call upon Ganga to solve our Forbidden Fs conundrum.

"Australian" Calls, Cultures Hide: "*Culture Is Who You Are. Who You Are, You Want to Keep Private*"

†: Ganga, Selma and Sheri justified the distinctions of their food and/or faith by centralizing those of "Australian." What affected the discursive practices of Selma and Sheri?

Ganga: They are enacting their "øthered" subjectivities through their "boundary conscious" discursive practices. Remember how Australia's multiculturalism celebrates "migrant cultures" in a similar fashion? It is around an empty space that is regarded as "Australian." It is the most popular public discourse as highlighted by Frankenberg (1993). Therefore, "øthered Australian" who subscribe to this feel that they need to exaggerate their culture and keep this to themselves, as uniquely theirs. But, Selma's discourse was slightly different, as hers was to do with fear of being asked to "go back to where she came from" by "Other Australian." So she worked hard to practice "hybridity" (Bhabha, 1994, 1996) with no power or strength attached to it. Therefore, she not only distinguished hers as "different," but also ensured that this was not exhibited, by an overt expression of her acclimatization to what was "Australian." Every "øthered Australian" above was not exploiting "colonial ambivalence" through "hybridity," as Bhabha (1994) proposes. They effected "suppression" or "submission" through "self-regulation" and "self-correction," they realized the "subjective power" of being accepted as "Australian" without disrupting the dominance of "Other Australian." Thus, ideological dominance remained "Insulated," with added effect of "Self-proliferation."

Cultures Call, "Australian" Hides: "*I Am Just Ordinary. Nothing to Talk about*"

†: Do you mean like Gandhi (1998) claims, postcolonial hybridity is not always empowering? Isn't Australia multicultural, isn't what is Indian, Sri Lankan, and Bosnian a part of what is Australian? How were the cultures of "Other Australian" and "øthered Australian" represented?

Ganga: Yes, hybridity isn't always empowering. Did you see how Cathy (OA) used an empty space to represent what was "Australian," and felt intimidated, "*I think of myself as just Australian, so I don't really wonder about that much. But when you ask what it is to be an Australian, like you did once, it is confronting*." However, she simultaneously branded Selma's and Fatima's "difference," "*It is not that it is not there, when I attend weddings and celebrations of staff like Selma's and Fatima's they are so rich and colorful and vibrant. So different and interesting*" (Cathy). The "Other Australian" was "Nationalizing," "Othering" and "øthering" simultaneously. This is about "Other Australian" maintaining "power" and "Ownership" and, most of all, it affects "Insulation," and they are able to protect "Self" from being influenced by "øthered" boundary practices. I know, you are still puzzled why she came back to say, "*But what culture do I have to talk about. I am boring, I am nothing. There is no color, celebration or food. Tell me about it. I am just ordinary. Nothing to talk about*." Then you mentioned Christmas and she replied, "*But, what is the point, it is not special. There is nothing special about it. It is always there.*" This was to avoid taking responsibility for all her influence in subjectifying individuals as "Australian." You heard Aruna, "øthered Australian," how she discursively committed to the boundary of "Australian," by saying she didn't have a culture, she mimicked the "just Australian." This was to realize that "subjective power" that national identity offers. Again, this is what the structures of Australia recommend, for all individuals to proudly say, "I am Australian." So it is a powerful discourse.

†: But Ganga, the "Other Australian" struggled to reflect their practices of cultural inclusion.

Ganga: I know. I heard Safeeya's mum (øA) confronting Gina (OA) for representing her Chinese culture with a stereotypical dance. Gina was stunned, "*You know it is hard for me. How do I do this, I am only Australian. Like I told you about Safeeya's mum and when I asked her whether she cooks Chinese, she said lasagna. Debbie is an Australian and I am Australian. I know what we eat. It is easy for me to talk about it. I don't know about you and Safeeya's mum. Don't worry, we will find a way.*" What did she do, she "øthered" all the "migrant" groups, by still maintaining what was "Australian" as an empty space, that represented an inert form. She made you celebrate Indian, Vietnamese festivals with "Indian sweet" and "Vietnamese cake." You celebrated all those so called "multicultural" festivals with them, for the same "subjective power." You are guilty too.

†: † agree, but what do † do. † had to protect myself. Ganga, Selma, Fatima, and Varuna too chose to silence their faith practices to protect themselves from "Other Australian." Aren't they "Australian" too, isn't being Muslim another way of being "Australian"? They silenced and excluded themselves by speaking about "Australian." When Muslim staff choose to silence their identity, how do I speak for and about Muslims in Australia?

"Australian" Rules, Muslim Whispers: "You Know What Australians Think of Muslims"

Ganga: I can understand your struggles. Haque (2001), Kunzman (2006), and Martino and Rezai-Rashti (2008) discuss how recent world events have triggered the belief that Islam is a threat to society's solidarity, especially to those in America, Australia, United Kingdom, and Germany. So the "self-regulation" and "suppression" of Muslim staffs and children was no surprise. I also understand that if you speak for and about Muslim staff, it would be like what Spivak (1999) says, usurping the "voice" of "subaltern," as the colonizer and the colonized both speak and decide for "øthered." Alternatively, Kunzman (2006), Hodder (2007), Peterson (2008), and Whittaker, Salend, and Elhoweris (2009) recommend the inclusion of speaking faith "differences" with children as a part of the school curriculum. This, they believe, promotes an understanding of all faiths and of how it influences the daily lives of individuals and groups, and, most of all, opens up discussions to arbitrate internalized prejudices. Why didn't you do that?

ŧ: ŧ tried, you know how Cathy "Theorized" with EYLF (Commonwealth of Australia, 2009), and diverted my conversation and we ended up doing nothing.

Ganga: I told you, Cathy "Other Australian" was covertly avoiding taking responsibility and regulating your influence by "Legitimation" and "Avoidance," and that is to do with "Boundary denying" discourse. She highlighted and guarded "white anonymity."

ŧ: Is "white middle-class Australian" culture really nothing? Should ŧ name the food, faith, and festival of "Australian," if so how ŧ do this? Won't ŧ be engaging in colonial discourse, the practice that ŧ oppose?

Ganga: You know what Leonardo (2004) and Rose-Cohen (2004) comment upon, denying the culture of "whiteness." You are hurting those who have a culture, do you want to become your "white" masters? You observed how every staff, including "Muslims" took responsibility to celebrate the religious tradition of "white culture" in public spaces. Cathy, "Other Australian," eluded when you asked about Christmas celebration, despite all her talk about "fairness" by stroking her cheek. This is what democratic liberalism does to you, it results in "Self-proliferation" of dominant practices. Cathy kept wondering why the staff and families left their cultures at the door. They surely will, if "Other Australian" does not take responsibility to look into their influence on "øthered Australian." Don't you know that cultural pluralism is established with ideologies of liberalism and universalism, and this privileges and propagates the unnamed dominant race (Leeman and Reid, 2006; Vickers, 2002)? Selma, Varuna, and Fatima, they all knew the "power" and religion of "Other Australian" and they feared this "power." Your reluctance to name and speak for the faith of Muslims will only contribute to perpetuating this "power" and privilege of "whiteness."

Ganga Rules, † Whisper: *"What Does Ganga Know"*

† could never break my silence, as I became too conscious of my own identity as a "not Australian." Ganga thinks that she can shift "white Australian" power. But it is not possible with my "øthered Australian" status here. How do † "speak" when † had been slashed by the "power" of "Other Australian"? And † quote Selma (øA),

> But Prasanna, I feel you can't change anything here. You have to change once you are here (Selma).

So † changed. † smiled and silenced my observations of "white" cultural dominance.

Thus, the "Boundary Defending" "Other Australian" maintained the food, faith, and festival of "Australian" with definite ideas about majority and minority. This "Australian" was there to guard and punish anyone who challenged this identity with the realization of ultimate "power." The "Boundary Denying" "Other Australian" on the other hand was soft, and professed the culture of "Other Australian" as invisible and uninteresting, while elating the attributes of "øthered Australian." This maintained the practices of "øthered" as being outside what was "Australian," and swaddled and cocooned the identity of "Australian" with covert "power" of never allowing "øtheredness" to influence the daily practices of "Australian." The "Boundary Diffusing" "Other Australian," worked with "øthered" to change everyday "Australian" practices. But the "power" of "Other Australian" prevailed in punishing all who challenged "white" cultural dominance.

CHAPTER 5

Tongue Ties Speak: I Am Australian, I Speak Australian

I will be the same. If I come to your country and if I am the only one talking in English I won't speak in that language. I am shy. We are both Australians and we will never be able to talk in your language.

—Gina, white Anglo-Australian staff

This chapter discusses how the language of "Australian" silences the tongues of "not Australian." The categorizing "othering" enables children to claim their "Australian" status and effectively assert and maintain speaking "Australian." The "not Australian" children too are aware of how their tongues are "othered" outside what is spoken as "Australian." They struggle to claim this "Australian" status by either self-silencing their tongues to speak only "Australian," or by tightly grouping and restricting their "not Australian" boundaries with fears of becoming "Australian." Speaking "Australian" is also parroted by staffs who educationally care for young children, and being unable to think outside this imagined language of "Australian," they find it difficult to embrace multilingual Australia. The final "øthering" discursive contest with Ganga eventually unties our "not Australian" tongues with much contention. Ganga resists to highlight that this tying imagination is English; the language of Australia's colonizers. But the "Australian" continues to imagine speaking and singing only "Australian."

"OTHERING" TONGUE TIES: ENACTING AUSTRALIAN / NOT AUSTRALIAN

The "othering" spoke with the national language of Australia. The *"othering"* children assertively categorized their national and linguistic identity as "Australian." *"I am Australian, I only speak Australian,"* said Princess (a four-year-old, white Anglo-Australian girl) and *"I am Australian, I speak Australian too,"* said Sheep (a four-year-old, white Anglo-Australian boy). Moreover, when I told the children that I speak more than one language including English, Princess commented, *"It is funny. I am Australian, I speak only Australian,"* and thus continued to make declarations of her "Australian" identity.

The "not Australian" children too engaged in categorizing national identity with linguistic identity, however, the manner in which the categorizing labels were attributed to such identities were different to children's categorization of "Australian." As soon as I introduced myself to Sidya and Thora (three-year-old Indian Australian girls), who spoke fluent Tamil, Sidya said, *"Are you India or Australia. You are India...Because, you speak Tamil, like us."* The staff, Selma and Sheri, who educationally cared for Thora and Sidya, were speakers of English as Additional Language (EAL). They believed that Sidya and Thora had to be grouped together as such grouping supported and maintained children's first language development. While Sidya and Thora played by themselves and me most of the time, Bikky secretly played language games with me whenever I went to her room. Bikky was fascinated when she heard my dog's name for the first time, and I had to repeat *Kizmet,* my dog's name, several times to her. Many weeks later, Bikky asked me, *"That's different, why Kizmet?"* I replied, *"Because it is a Hindi word for destiny. It is a language we speak."* Since then, she continued to find similarities between Turkish and Indian practices by making comparisons of our daily practices such as what we ate, wore, and even how we knelt down.

The "othering" "Australian" children insisted that they spoke "Australian" because they are "Australian," the "othering" "not Australian" children enacted their linguistic identity only with another "not Australian," openly or secretly behind the hearing of "Australian." The "Australian" and "not Australian" responded to these categorizations differently.

"OTHERING" REALITIES: "NOT AUSTRALIAN" RESPONDS

The "not Australian" children responded to the claim and maintained either their "Australian" or "not Australian" status publicly and privately. Amelia (white Anglo-Australian staff) introduced Plafe by saying he spoke Hindi at home. Plafe replied, *"I speak only Australian, like Sheep."* Jan (Chinese Australian staff), a speaker of many languages, was very upset to hear Plafe's expression of speaking "Australian," and his refusal to acknowledge his linguistic background publicly in front of his peers. Jan read a book in Chinese during group time to transform Plafe's conceptions about speaking only "Australian" in Australia. Jan introduced her linguistic background to the children and began to read the book she had brought from home to the children in the room. The children repeatedly interrupted as she read and Jan responded, "*I feel very sad, that you scream when I read a book in Chinese. I am Chinese, that book was in Chinese. You know we all speak different languages in Australia*" (Jan). Jan could never read a book in Chinese without the children's repeated proclamation of being and speaking "Australian." Jan tried to highlight the multilingual reality of Australia, but eventually gave up, as the resisting voice of "Australian" children became louder and louder.

The very first day I met Pookey's mum, she spoke about their family's multilingual background, and that Pookey was fluent in speaking Tamil and Telugu. Yet, when I greeted Pookey in Tamil at the setting, she corrected me, "*No, don't speak to me like that. Tamil only for home and car. Only English here.*" This denial to speak in Tamil in front of her peers continued for weeks at the setting and after many weeks I shared my observations with her family. Her mother commented, "*She doesn't speak to her grandparents anymore because she won't speak Tamil*" and her dad added, "*My in-laws left in March and she came here [the early childhood setting]. Now she doesn't talk in Tamil, even though we insist. She refuses to speak to my parents on the phone, as she has to speak Tamil*" (Pookey's dad). Hence, they both encouraged me to continue to speak Tamil with Pookey at the early childhood setting. Pookey's mum and I spoke only Tamil when we met at the center to show Pookey that it was an accepted practice. Pookey too continued with her silencing, and the probabilities of Pookey's loss of her first language were real, as her family repeatedly lamented about her continued resistance to speak Tamil. Pookey did not avoid me at the centre, and eagerly followed me around when I was there, but her refusal to converse in Tamil at the setting continued, and I persevered.

The responses of "not Australian" Sidya and Thora, who were grouped together based on their linguistic background, was different from Pookey's self-silencing. Sidya and Thora always played together and openly resisted being influenced by English, with fears of becoming "Australian." One day, as Sidya heard me speaking in English, she commented with a worried look on her face, "*Speak more Tamil, otherwise you will become Australia[n]*" (Sidya). When Sidya was absent, Thora always chose to play alone and avoided playing with her English speaking peers, "*I won't play with Puppy, because she doesn't speak Tamil*" (Thora). Although they distinguished the language English from the identity of "Australian," they still strongly related English with being and becoming "Australian," and maintained their "not Australian" status by playing together. Grouping children did enable the continued practice and maintenance of Thora's and Sidya's linguistic backgrounds; however, it also resulted in "othering" peers and adults as "Australian / not Australian." Grouping made them more conscious of their categorical "self" in relation to their "other," and the children thus grouped became highly loyal to their categorical behaviors. They openly resisted moving between language boundaries, and I understood this as one of the realities of ethnolinguistic grouping of "not Australian" children.

Bikky, having learnt that I spoke Hindi, which was similar to the Turkish language she spoke at home, continued to establish similarities between our cultures. To hypothesize the similarities that she had conceptualized, Bikky often whispered in Turkish and asked me to repeat Turkish words and names of her relatives and friends. Bikky inferred, "*You can say it. I thought you can't. I will tell you my real name. My name is not Bikky like they call me. Because my mum calls me...*" (Bikky). As soon as I repeated her "real" name, Bikky softly expressed, "*Because Turkish and Indian are a little bit the same. You can say it, Australians can't.*" Bikky, till the very end, refused to share her "real" name with the staff in the setting, whom she classified as "Australian." The "Australian" staff and children continued to use the anglicized version of her name and Bikky's "not Australian" realities accepted and responded promptly to "Australian" calls.

In the study conducted in Hawaii, Grace (2008) frequently observed young children strongly linking their linguistic identities with their ethnic backgrounds. After all, the two identities are linked and usually termed as one's ethnolinguistic identity. Hence, this form of "othering" one's linguistic identity with her/his nationality can be seen as being common in young children. However, such simplistic categorization influenced the language/s use of "not Australian," as the "not Australian" tied their tongues to speak only "Australian" or excluded themselves from interacting with "Australian." Young children do associate ethnic or national identity with concrete attributes such as food, clothes, and language. But here, our "not Australian tongue ties" became our secret, whispered realities, with the language English dominating the national identity as "speaking Australian." I alerted the staffs about these "not Australian" responses, and this again disrupted the "Australian."

"OTHERING" IMAGINATIONS: "AUSTRALIAN" RESPONDS

By now I had become quite used to the pattern. The "Australian" imagination always responded with nationalism, and by highlighting the attributes of "Australian." At the meeting, I spoke about Pookey's family's concern and how the loss of Tamil in Pookey also meant the loss of intergenerational ties. Gina, Katherine, and Cathy (white Anglo-Australian staff) responded and Cathy believed in "speaking Australian,"

> "Why should Pookey get so attached to you?" Katherine asked. Cathy answered for me, "I went to Singapore, although it is cosmopolitan, and everyone spoke English, I was dying to hear someone who spoke Australian" (Cathy).

The "Australian" reared its head to softly and harshly protect and maintain the language environment of Australia. Cathy implied that "Australian" could be spoken, just like Princess and Sheep. For the "Australian," the language "Australian" existed and they wanted to only hear and speak "Australian." She empathized and equated Pookey's loss of Tamil in Australia with her loss of hearing "Australian" in Singapore. And Gina disbelieved in "speaking not Australian" and spoke for and as "Australian" as she joined the conversation,

> We are both Australians and the rest of the children speak English. We [Gina and Katherine] are both Australians and we will never be able to talk in your language. But, you know when you speak in your language with her mum looking back at Katherine, you can't do that. You are talking about her and isn't that wrong to speak in a language that everyone can't understand. How do you think she would feel? We are both Australians and we treat everyone the same (Gina).

The conversation digressed to vociferously proclaim their "Australian" identity, and the English speaking monolingual environment. Gina spoke emotionally in defense of "Australian" feelings and their identity. Furthermore, Gina justified these nationalistic feelings with "Australian" egalitarian righteousness, "*We are both Australians and we treat everyone the same."* Here, what threatened the "Australian" was the imagined loss of having control over their linguistic environment, and this made them feel insecure. The "Australian" did not want to change their "tongue" and they were quite certain about this as Gina advised me later, *"I think families, work on Pookey's family. They have to support the language and culture, work on them."* The "Australian" ambiguity again was evident. On one hand I was reprimanded for working with the family the way I did and on the other hand I was given permission to work with the family.

This imagi(nation) did not stop here, it continued. During my face-to-face interview with Gina, I spoke about the way Bikky interpreted and whispered the similarities between our ethnolinguistic backgrounds.

> "Yeah, she [Bikky] thinks I say her name right because we are similar, 'Indian and Turkish are a little bit the same,' she says. So she tells me her cat's name and her father's and cousin's names and when Pookey and I pronounce these she is thrilled and believes that her theory is reinforced," I said. "You know why, I think your jaws the way it is shaped that is why you are able to pronounce those names. We [Australians] can't, even if we try, I don't think we can" (Gina).

Gina too reinforced Bikky's theory, by not even trying to pronounce Bikky's name. Gina established physiological "difference" between her collective identity and mine, the shape of my jaw. I wanted to believe in her theory, but I speak English, their language too. The "Australian" imagination was influencing my thoughts, as I was beginning to etch our boundaries more concretely and deeply. I continued to speak Tamil with Pookey and her family, the language that the "Australian" claimed to never speak or understand. Pookey one day replied in Tamil and cast her inhibitions aside, and her family was thrilled.

This was a center with very limited staff who were native English speakers, the "Australian." The bilingual staff at the centre watched Pookey's sudden confidence in publicly speaking Tamil. They too began to freely communicate in the children's first language when they could and noticed remarkable change in these children's self-identity development. The bilingual staff encouraged their colleagues, including those who were "Australian," to learn words and songs in "not Australian" languages. Cathy, the "Australian" immediately grieved,

> "Songs, you know we nowadays don't sing those typical Australian songs in centers anymore. We used to all the time when I was teaching.

Not anymore, it is not fashionable" (Cathy). "Really, Australian, would I know?" I asked. "No, you wouldn't know, 'Road to Gundagai' and many more like that. It is really very Australian. For me I miss that, I wish we would start singing those again, we are losing what is Australian with all this new stuff (Cathy).

Thus the "Australian" imagination continued with proclamations of their national identity repeatedly. Cathy lamented for the loss of what was there by all the newness. The "really Australian" imagi(nation) grew bigger with hearing, speaking, and singing "Australian," and the "not Australian" realities were further silenced. And I could not help but wonder what fuelled this imagi(nation) that spoke and heard "Australian" and not English, and kept the pangs for "really Australian" alive.

"OTHERING" TONGUE TIES: SHAPING "AUSTRALIAN SPEAKERS"

Australia had always been a country of many languages. Multilingualism thrived in precolonial Australia with Aboriginal groups speaking and maintaining many languages of this land. After colonization and especially during the times of the *White Australia policy* (1901), English tests were particularly used to exclude non-Anglo groups from settling in Australia. Since the 1970s, the land that supposedly embraced multicultural diversity, including linguistic diversity, grappled with relinquishing its monolingual English speaking identity. I recall Grassby's famous declaration of multicultural Australia that aspired for all individuals from varied linguistic groups to pledge in a unifying voice, "*I am an Australian,*"

> It is hoped that this [bilingual programs in schools] will reduce family tensions...and evoke a new respect by migrants for their adopted country's proclaimed belief in freedom and equality.
> (Grassby, 1973, p. 9)

Grassby's words even then revealed the desire for the subjectification of national subjects as he stated that bilingual support in schools would kindle this "respect" for Australia's unique value system of "freedom and equality." Supporting children with bilingual programs was more to extract the newer migrants' goodwill toward Australia, and to proclaim its identity. With attitudes that aimed to integrate newer migrants into the nation, most educational institutions aimed to develop English proficiency in all children. Little attention was paid to the loss of the children's first language.

The immigration policies of Australia that followed later overtly "*Othered*" the linguistic identity of multilingual Australia with one national language, English. English was proclaimed as the national language of Australia,

> English is Australia's national language. Because it is a significant unifying influence and the ability to speak English is fundamental to full participation in Australian society.

Recommendations that followed outlined the values of being proficient in Languages Other Than English (LOTE),

> In a multicultural society such as ours, proficiency in a language other than English is more than desirable; it can be a business or social imperative. If we are to engage in global marketplace and derive maximum benefit from it...particularly the major languages of our region and the world.
> (Commonwealth of Australia, 1999, p. 27)

The unifying monolingual proclamation of the national language of Australia was always succeeded by statements that value multilingualism that automatically results from multiculturalism. This recognition and encouragement to become multilingual however is not for the intrinsic values attached to languages; languages are commoditized more as sources of economic gain for all subjects of Australia. Moreover, English tests for aspiring citizens of Australia are currently administered to bind the subjects of Australia, and such imposition is still justified in the name of equal participation for all in the Australian society.

> While we celebrate the diversity of Australia's people, we also aim to build a cohesive and unified nation.
> Australia's national language is English. It is part of our national identity. Everyone in Australia is encouraged to learn and use English to help them participate in Australian society. Communicating in English is also important for making the most of living and working in Australia. Other languages are also valued. In Australia's diverse society, over 200 languages are spoken.
> (Commonwealth of Australia, 2013, p. 9)

Thus, despite acknowledging the presence of multicultural, multilingual Australia, the ideological "interpellation" of Australia (Althusser,

2008) repeatedly bombards the imperativeness of maintaining one language and specifically one identity as a unifying factor for all subjects in Australia. The statements, rather than constructing a multilingual identity for all subjects in Australia, openly declare English as a part of national identity, thus "*Othering*" the categorical linguistic attribute of "Australian" in specific ways. Although the following statement casually recognizes the linguistic diversity in Australia in a tokenistic manner, the monolingual, nationalistic ideological "Othering" automatically ordains superior status and national power to English and native English speakers. And the "Australian speakers," children and adults alike, *shaped* the linguistic identity of "Australian" with this ideological imagi(nation). They imagined themselves as "Australian" and the language English as "Australian." The mobilization of ideological "Othering" precipitated in the everyday voices of the "Australian speakers" for whom hearing many tongues became problematic.

The "Australian speakers," Princess, Sheep, Cathy, Gina, and Katherine heard, spoke, and sang the "Australian" ideology. This idea that maintained English as "Australian," and yet distinguished the same language as identifiably different from English existed for them. Moreover, the national unification with one language to maintain social unity was important for them, and it was a matter of representing "Australian egalitarianism." Hence, rather than focusing on Pookey and her reluctance to speak Tamil at the center, the "Australian speakers" righteously surged to underpin the monolingual identity of "Australian." It was hegemonic and the "Australian speakers" found it difficult to think and behave outside their "Australian" subjectivity, as they repeatedly declared why and what "Australian" speak and don't speak. With such subjective commitment towards unifying all "Australians" with one language being supported by political ideologies of Australia, the committed subjects took control of shaping and defending the linguistic identity of "Australian." My postcolonial voice became stronger and I identified these language acts that dominated our tongues as colonizing. I prepared to contest their now "Othering" imagi(nation), which was so strongly supported with ideological support with our "othered" postcolonial realities.

"ØTHERING" TONGUE TIES: CONTESTING "AUSTRALIAN" WITH THEIR IMAGI(NATION) AND OUR REALITIES

Exploring linguistic diversity in postcolonial societies that remain colonized by English with migrant, multilingual speakers was complex, as we invariably included our "difference," our ethnic background, as "not Australian." The national power that the "Australian" gained as English speakers was always identified by staff who spoke English as an additional language. The ethnolinguistic grouping of children perpetuated dichotomous identity ideas in children, which hypothesized that "Australian" spoke "Australian," and "not Australian" outsiders spoke their respective languages. Those who maintained those restricted friendship groups remained outside what was "Australian," and as this form of segregation kept the friendship groups apart, the power of English remained unchallenged. The children who wanted to be become accepted as "Australian" learnt to silence their first language in public settings. The loss of first language in children is a reality for many children and families living in countries like Canada, Australia, and United States, which are dominated by monolingual practices. Authors caution early childhood practitioners about the loss of generational ties with first language attrition, and, therefore, recommend working closely with families to keep the linguistic ties alive (Siraj-Blatchford and Clarke, 2000; Arthur, 2001; Clarke, 2005).

Moreover, as a speaker of more than two languages who grew up in a multilingual environment in India, I experientially knew that multilingualism was possible and desirable. Beyond my personal experiences, I recognized my own commitment to postcolonial ideas, the lens that I used to deconstruct the colonizing political discourses of Australia that silenced the presence of multilingualism with English in Australia (Srinivasan, 2009). I was seeing the "Australian speakers" in their past, the colonial tradition and its ancient forms of calculated domination, with their "whiteness" and their language. Loomba (2005) too points out that although the "white" settlers try to create an identity separate from their colonizing past, they are still seen as agents of colonialism by the colonized people. Perhaps that was why I saw my colonizer in Gina and Cathy, as they both spoke for the uniqueness of hearing and speaking "Australian," by distancing this from English and from all other languages. With my inner postcolonial ideology becoming louder, I hypothesized the current linguistic domination as being akin to the discriminatory practices that existed in "white Australia." When the *White Australia policy* (Immigration Act, 1901) was in operation, outsiders were excluded not only by their "race," but also by language, as new arrivals were rejected from entering this country with English tests. Discrimination based on "race" and linguistic backgrounds has been guiding the construction of this nation and their subjects for a long time. Authors continue to highlight that Australia had historically been a land of many voices and multiple sounds, and colonization with its emphasis on monolingual discourse usurped this multiplicity through the imposition of one language for all (Nicholls, 2005; Clyne, 2005). My postcolonial will to resist grew stronger and I equated the language ideologies that the "Australian speakers" upheld as acts of discrimination that muted our "tongues." Our voices were silenced by those who spoke only "Australian," and I could not help but chase Ganga to engage in "øthering" that loosened these hegemonic tongue ties. Ganga and † prepared for our postcolonial contest with "*øthered*" voices. We couldn't change the "Australian" imagi(nation), but we changed our realities.

Contesting Tongue Ties with Selma, Pookey, and Pookey's Parents

That Is Why I Tell You Nothing Will Change. They Have the Power

† approached Pookey's mum during pickup and asked her about Pookey's reluctance to speak Tamil at the center with me.

> "Do you know Pookey always says that I should speak in English and not Tamil here? She also says Tamil music for home and car. She doesn't even acknowledge if I speak in Tamil," I commented to Pookey's mum. "Actually, this is something we are noticing too. She always speaks in English to us. It never mattered earlier when my parents were here, as she would speak in Tamil to them and English with us. But now she insists on responding only in English even if we speak in Tamil to her.... She doesn't speak on the phone to my parents, because she has to speak Tamil (Pookey's mum).

My deepest feelings and emotions are linked to Tamil, and † would never be able to share those feelings with my children if they did not speak Tamil. † responded to those feelings of loss in Pookey's mother's voice. † persisted with my Tamil speaking at the centre, and Pookey continued to ignore me. This was brought up during the meeting with Cathy, Gina, and Katherine (OA). Cathy explained her attachment to her linguistic background by saying that she missed hearing "Australian" when she was overseas, and Gina accused me of speaking in a language that everyone couldn't understand, and that † should accept Pookey's reluctance to speak Tamil. † became very conscious of my invested emotions in developing bilingualism in children with EAL, and † wanted to gather the bilingual staff's understandings about the maintenance of children's first language.

> I spoke to Selma, a bilingual staff in another room at the same centre, "Selma (øA), you will tell me if it is not okay to speak in Tamil with families and Thora and Sidya won't you," I requested. "We were told off too, been there Prasanna. That is why I tell you nothing will change. They have the power. Although the Australians are migrants and come from somewhere, they think they own everything. It is to do with power. Otherwise they will say like I told you, 'go back to your land.' Don't get me wrong, I don't want to say I am finding it hard or I have been treated badly, but my experience is just move on. See you need to change" (Selma).

† did not expect this reply from her. Although she did not ask me to stop speaking Tamil, her reply did not permit me to resist "Other Australian" who controlled our linguistic environment. But, she spoke about the power of "Other Australian" that would excommunicate us if we resisted and did not change as expected.

† resisted and continued to speak Tamil with Pookey. After many weeks, she replied to my question in Tamil, without just nodding or shaking her head in front of her peers, and continued to speak Tamil at the center. † shared this with her mum one evening.

> Actually at home too we are noticing that change, she speaks more Tamil. She calls herself Indian Aussie and not just Aussie (Pookey's mum).

This change was acknowledged by many bilingual staff at the centre, and discussions around languages development in children with EAL became central. During the next staff meeting, Bella (Eastern European staff) suggested a change in the early childhood educational practices of all staff. She specifically suggested this to support the cultural identity development of especially bicultural/bilingual children.

> We can sing songs, like I beg of you one thing. Each staff if you could translate one song in the child's language it is so good for the child who is speaking that language. I would like everyone to sing these translated songs (Bella)

Most staff with EAL agreed, but Cathy, the "Other Australian," immediately defended the identity of losing something "really Australian." † had always believed Cathy embraced change and "difference," but this time she was reluctant to invite newness. † felt deeply troubled, and † urged Ganga to respond to my troubled feelings.

Missing "Australian": "Everyone Spoke English, I Was Dying to Hear Someone Who Spoke Australian"

Ϯ: Ganga, all those early childhood theories speak of supporting children's first language, especially to retain generational ties (see, Siraj-Baltchford and Clarke, 2000; Arthur, 2001; Chantler, 2004; Clyne, 2005; Fleer and Raban, 2005). But, Gina and Katherine, "Other Australian" early childhood staff, questioned my attempts to do so. You tell me, should Ϯ have ignored Pookey's first language attrition, and should Ϯ only speak in a language that everyone understood?

Ganga: I don't think you have fully understood the "power" of discursively practicing "Australian." Did you hear Cathy say, "*although…everyone spoke English, I was dying to hear someone who spoke Australian.*" She was "Nationalizing," "Othering" what was "Australian." Then Gina and Katherine followed, and they wanted you to stop talking in Tamil with Pookey's parents and accept Pookey's loss of first language by "Theorizing" to "Legitimize" their inaction and maintain "Insulation" of ideological "Australian." Viruru (2001) questions such attitudes as she equates such restricting attitudes toward languages as dominant acts aiming to colonize the "øthered." However, every "Other Australian" with their "Boundary Defending" discourse took "Ownership" and as I always say, maintained their "power," the power with which they controlled the identity of the nation and their subjects. Gina openly declared by "Othering," "*We are both Australians and we will never be able to talk in your language.*" She "Theorized" with feelings, "*Isn't that wrong to speak in a language that everyone can't understand. How do you think she would feel?*" These tie the "Nationalizing" knot to many tongues in Australia and effect "Ownership," "Insulation," and "power." Even Selma, "øthered Australian," knew that and said, "*That is why I tell you nothing will change. They have the power. Although the Australians are migrants and come from somewhere, they think they own everything. It is to do with power.*" She acknowledged the "power" of "Other Australian," and "critically recognized" their migrant beginnings, to stand powerless, and hence resorted to "silencing." The "Other Australian" wouldn't want to think they are like us, because to be "øthered Australian" is to be secondary citizens, we don't have that ideological support, but they do, as they are protecting what is "Australian," their national language, as law-abiding primary citizens. You know about the citizenship test for migrants (Commonwealth of Australia, 2007, 2013), that tests one's proficiency in English before granting Australian citizenship. Theirs is a powerful discourse. You "risked" and "resisted"; you wouldn't listen; you have to learn to move on, like Selma says. Why do you have to be so tied to your postcolonial ideologies?

IDENTIFYING "AUSTRALIAN": "IT IS TO DO WITH POWER"

†: Ganga, they are not my ideologies, they are real, aren't we in a postcolonial cauldron, isn't Australia a postcolonial nation? Most of all, I don't want to become "boundary committing" or "boundary conscious." Pookey did change and she began to speak in front of her peers in the setting in Tamil with me. Did you hear the elation in Pookey's mother's voice? In fact she felt that this was a sign of Pookey's acceptance of her postcolonial identity, the duality, "*She speaks more Tamil. She calls herself Indian Aussie and not just Aussie.*" † was so happy when the staff in the center began to acknowledge the importance of persevering with the children's first language at the staff meeting. † thought † am going to change this "Australian." But, when † heard Cathy at the staff meeting, † was shocked. You heard what she said, "*Road to Gundagai and many more like that. It is really very Australian. For me I miss that, I wish we would start singing those again, we are losing what is Australian with all this new stuff.*" Isn't this English, sounded very English to me! What was Cathy discursively practicing when she said, "*We are losing what is Australian?*"

Ganga: You stick to your ideologies as "real" and what right do you have to accuse others. Cathy was protecting "Australian," again by "Boundary Defending," as she was overwhelmed with what all the change you brought in with "øthered Australian." As a loyal "Australian" subject she had to maintain the identity of the national subject. Like Loomba (2005) comments, in most settler countries, the group that is politically governing these lands and peoples believes they have an indigenous identity, separate to their colonial beginnings, but the colonized still see them as their colonial masters. Cathy, and many "Other Australian," feel that they have separated from their colonial ties, but you know that their tongues are still tied to our colonial masters, and their "power" is realized as a result of this. The "Other Australian" stopped your "øthered" influence didn't she?

†: Okay, it is all to do with "power." † will tell you how the ideological "Australian" effect and affect the daily "Tongue ties" practices of "Other Australian" and "øthered Australian" subjects in Australia.

The "Other Australians" believe that their national linguistic identity is unique, and this understanding comes from the colonization of Australia's language with English. This political ideology stems from colonial monolingual understandings of nation, national identity, and national language. They defend and guard their national linguistic environment from change. This is how "øthered Australian" succumb and submit to "power," like Pookey, Selma, and Bella and many others. I am still not convinced, change is possible. Jan, "øthered Australian," too resisted monolingual environment, she read and sang in Cantonese at the other centre with all the children. Remember how we decided to add books and magazines in varied languages in the children's library bags to take to their homes. We wanted to rewrite the monolingual ideological image of Australia and "Australian." We were ready to embark on "critical action" together with our "white transformer."

Ganga: I see, you still have your courage and optimism. Selma is much wiser than you are, and I repeat her words, "*That is why I tell you nothing will change. They have the power... It is to do with power.*" It is not so easy when your critical ideas are not backed by political ideologies. You will lose, as the "Other Australian" who proclaims monolingualism for all subjects are supported by political statements.

†know it is still possible to have a multilingual Australia if the structures adequately support and epitomize such understandings. But Australia, this land and its borders "Terra" are strongly and softly protected by those who regard themselves as "Australian." And † reveal soon how † came to that understanding.

CHAPTER 6

Terra Strikes Speak: We Can't Let Everyone in, This Is Our Country, Shouldn't We Have a Choice

> *I really don't think we should let everyone come in to our country. People in boats, can be terrorists. I have a friend from the police force and he says most of these people are terrorists. They come here as asylum seekers in boats, change passports, get comfortable and then turn into terrorists.*
>
> —*Katrina, white Anglo-Australian staff*

Ganga's final boundary stream, Terra strikes trickled and circled the territorial boundaries of Australia by "othering" the precious traits of "Australian" from the ever-threatening infiltration of "not Australian." Narrated only by adults (staff and parents), this boundary stream exposed our innermost desires and fears as we spoke of our categorically defined core values. I find it impossible to suppress my postcolonial thoughts dictating my voice as we exchange our "boundary speaks." Ganga's ultimate episodic contest ends with Terra strikes "øthering" our boundaries to surface our undeniable submission to "whiteness."

"othering" Terra Strikes: Enacting Australian / Not Australian

The physical boundaries of Australia were repeatedly constructed and unified by Ganga's adults, the staff who provided educational care for young children in multicultural Australia. The categorical "othering" by these staff who spoke as "Australian" either expressed fear or desire for the "not Australian" other. The *"othering"* that was attached to fear and desire presented Australia as a land unattached to its colonized histories, and as a generous society that accepted the "otherness" of "not Australian." The "Australian" generosity was expressed through constant comparisons between "self" and that outside "other." The "not Australian" was now either graciously accepted as "Australian" or was maintained as "not Australian" if they tried to disrupt what was "Australian." The acceptance of "not Australian" hinged on how close they were to "self" the "Australian," "*Remi is Indian, she is Sri Lankan and they are as Australian as I am. I think we are all the same*" (Katrina). The "not Australian" difference was momentarily expressed with "othering" and erased with the recognition of sameness. Moreover, the simultaneous reiterations of the "Australian" protected and maintained their collective identity, "*We [Australians] are okay, nothing needs changing. It is in other countries. We are lucky*" (Katrina). Privileging the status of Australia as "lucky country" also followed when establishing the "different not so lucky other," "*They may do in other countries where there is a lot of trouble, but Australia being the lucky country such things don't happen*" (Katherine). The "othering," which also expressed an overwhelming fear of Australia being changed by outsiders, was expressed with a compulsion to convert that change-inducing "not Australian," "*This is what I don't like. When you come to Australia, you have to take on Australian values. You can't try and change us.*" Those who spoke as "Australian" dedicated much of their categorical "othering" to establish "difference" in "not Australian" in comparison to who they were and what Australia was.

The "othering" that was attached to the desire for multiculturalism celebrated and accepted those cultures as "not Australian" against what was "Australian." In this form, the comparison maintained the "Australian / not Australian" dichotomy till the very end. Cathy spoke of her desire for "difference" as objects that her culture lacked, "*I used to walk into their house ['not Australian' neighbor] thinking that my family and I are so different because of all the arts and artifacts they had in their house. I knew I was different the 'other' as I had nothing.*" This categorical "othering" did not exclude or convert the "not Australian" whose practices were different from what was "Australian." The "Australian" rather praised the "not Australian" repeatedly for the colorful differences that they contributed to the otherwise neutral Australia. If one can call the recognized repetitive behaviors in relation to a group's daily practices as culture, culture can never be static or stagnant. These practices are practiced and transmitted by living, breathing individuals, who are influenced by changes around them. Therefore, the repetitive practiced behaviors can only be organic and shifting to accommodate and respond to the changes around. Yet, the "Australian" spoke of groups, "Australian" and "not Australian," as remaining uninfluenced by each other. The individuals remained encapsulated and bound within categories of "Australian" and "not Australian" in multicultural Australia. Interestingly, both forms of "othering" motivated by either fear or desire positioned and accepted the "not Australian" in particular ways, and yet strived to keep the "Australian" intact. And the "not Australian" responded with the realities of such positioning.

"OTHERING" REALITIES: "NOT AUSTRALIAN" RESPONDS

The "not Australian" responses of both staff and parents evidenced "othering" of "not Australian self" in relation to the "Australian other," whom they referred to as "Aussie" or "Western" frequently. Their "othering" too was motivated by emotions and feelings attached to their desires and fears. During an informal conversation, the "not Australian" staff confided, "*Australia advocates multiculturalism, but everything is the same. Because you are so scared to be yourself in fear of rejection, being rejected....I have put it down to just fit in with what is here*" (Filipino Australian staff). The "not Australian" recognized her fear of exclusion in Australia, and its role in extracting the conversion to fit in with whatever that is in Australia. Although one can argue that daily practices of specific groups recognized as culture are always evolving as they are modulated with and by those around, the changes here were driven by fear of rejection. Thus, the reality of "not Australian" was about "othering" what "not Australia self" was in relation to "Australian other" to become what that "Australian other" was by relinquishing the culture of "self."

Sometimes this conscious becoming was also expressed as one's uniqueness, setting the identity of "self" apart from one's collective group of origin. The becoming here was expressed more as a desire to be accepted by the "Australian other." A "not Australian" parent admitted, "*It helps if you are Western, so that you are not excluded and you feel Aussie. I am different from other Chinese here. I am not like them because I am Western. Not so traditional, that way I am not excluded*" (Dora's mum, Chinese Australian parent). Thus, it became apparent that the "not Australian" had to give up their collective boundary identity to be included as "Australian" in multicultural Australia.

Another stronger form of "othering" by "not Australian" adults resulted in favoring the culture of "self" and protecting those attributes from what they had conceived as the culture of "Australian." Such exclusion was attached to fears of cultural dilution by the "Australian" difference established by "othering" the attributes of the two categories. The distinguished "difference" in "Australian" and the fear attached to that "different other" was expressed, "*Aussies don't do that. They are different. Your culture, my culture in all Asian culture, we teach them to respect their parents and grandparents. I am worried Kitten might grow up like them*" (Kitten's mum, Vietnamese Australian parent). And the "othering" by "not Australian" sometimes revealed their rejection of what they had conceptualized as the culture of "Australian," "*I think we prefer our own culture in marriage because of that clash...to get married to another Iranian, because they respect their marriage...but most of Western, when they got a problem with boyfriend or husband, they don't care about what is happening to their children*" (Fatima). Such "othering" repeatedly established "difference" in what was here, "*Look at all this happening. How many percent of marriages break up in this society?*" (Fatima). This comparison and identification of "difference" fuelled a sense of perpetual fear in the "not Australian" about what was "Western" or "Australian" influencing the upbringing of their children and those that they educationally cared for in the setting.

Thus the emotions of fear or desire that stemmed from the process of "othering" by "not Australian" resulted in strongly masking who they were either to be accepted by "Australian," or to exclude "Australian" to protect their "not Australian" culture. It was interesting to note that in this form of "othering," although the "not Australian" maintained their group loyalty by epitomizing their attributes against those of "Australian," they still masked their own attributes outwardly in public spaces to remain included as "Australian." They never felt that the culture they practiced was also another way of representing the culture of "Australian." Therefore, the expressions of varied cultural practices remained suppressed in the daily sphere of multicultural Australia. I took these "othering" realities, including those of mine, to the "just Australian" Cathy, who had expressed much awareness and acceptance of the "not Australian" otherness. This stirred the "Australian" imagination within.

"OTHERING" IMAGINATIONS: "AUSTRALIAN" RESPONDS

I shared the "boundary speaks" that I collected with parents and staff; and particularly those that categorized "Australian" with fears of being influenced by that culture. I imagined as a participatory action researcher that with Cathy's intense desire to embrace diversity, we were going to transform early childhood practices. Cathy always named "self" as "white, Anglo-Australian" right from the start, and she responded as follows,

> "Tell me about it. I was discriminated today at the shops, in my own country. She wouldn't serve me. I felt discriminated. But that is okay" (Cathy). "Why do you say that?" I asked. "This is not the first time I have been to that shop" (Cathy). "Oh, she has, she ignores you always," I asked. "That is life" (Cathy). "I have told you and you say it too, you are a white person. May be she still sees you locked in our histories," I said. "I know all that, but why should I be discriminated, I don't know. She talks to all the Indian customers and doesn't serve me (Cathy).

I had always appreciated Cathy for her readiness to classify herself as "white, middle-class, Anglo-Australian." The non-neutralization of her color, class, and colonial origin represented her willingness to critically make visible the hegemonic power with which the colonizers gained national status. My masked "postcolonial self" could not help but acclaim her voluntary readiness in overturning her assumed neutrality. Yet, Cathy was reluctant to unpack the role of her "whiteness" in her "Indian" experience. She instead proclaimed her ownership of this land and said that she was discriminated in her "own country." With my postcolonial vision, I resorted to highlighting our colonial histories. Cathy quickly discarded my efforts and instead excluded the "exquisite Indian" from her culture, by asserting its insignificance,

> I know looking at the shop I know that I am someone who clearly doesn't belong there. Don't get me wrong. It is a glorious shop, the sequence, and the workmanship was all exquisite. I was relating to my own culture. There is nothing, it is blah like I always say (Cathy).

While Cathy claimed ownership of this nation, she disowned all the glory of the "exquisite Indian" by keeping the "not Australian" outside. These imaginations enabled the "Australian" to exclusively claim cultural ownership of multicultural Australia and thereby evade conversations that recognized and decentralized her culture. Although Cathy named the culture of her "Australian self," the imagination of this "self," as nothing and the "other" as everything, that "self" hasn't stayed with her till the very end. Nonetheless, she guarded this nothing preciously.

The imaginations of Katrina too guarded "self," the "Australian," but she did so with absolute strength and conviction. Unlike Cathy, Katrina spoke as the national "Australian" with her imagined umbrella, "Australia." Katrina's imaginations spoke as follows,

> "When you come to Australia, you have to take on Australian values. You can't try and change us. Like the Muslim girls who want to swim in our community want the swimming pool closed for men on Tuesdays. They can't do that, and that is not fair. Everyone pays their rates, they can't have special permission" (Katrina). "But what are Australian values? Who determines this is what it is to be an Australian," I asked. "I think we are okay. You know Greeks keep to themselves, Italians keep to their own community" (Katrina). "However, in countries like America, Australia, Canada and New Zealand, most number of people are Anglo-white people. Isn't this because this group came in large numbers together and kept together?" I asked. "I know colonization and all that. But we can't go back in history. Like Aborigines they keep to themselves and they don't want to change. I really don't think we should let everyone come in to our country. People in boats, can be terrorists.... They come here as asylum seekers in boats, change passports, get comfortable and then turn into terrorists (Katrina).

Katrina wanted to save Australia and "Australian" from change, and changing Australia meant Australia was not okay. Katrina quickly shut the multicultural gates as soon as any group challenged this space and its ideals. Australia's colonization and colonial occupation, and its discriminatory policies kept this whole land restricted for those from Anglo-Saxon and Anglo-Celtic origin. My postcolonial ideals could not be silenced as they were awakened with Katrina's overt accusations of not just the newer migrants, but also the Aboriginals, the original owners of this land. I challenged the "Australian" and brought up Australia's history of colonization that completely took control of this land and its peoples. My initiatives were immediately dispensed as unworthy of remembering.

Since the founding of National Aborigines Day Observance Committee (NADOC), Australia remembers Aboriginal and Torres Strait Islanders—the people and their heritage—by observing NAIDOC week. Every year in the month of July, the "National Aborigines and Islanders Day Observance Committee" (NAIDOC) celebrates the achievements of Aboriginal and Torres Strait Islanders in Australia. Most educational and sociopolitical institutions participate in activities that are considered as reflecting indigenous culture and heritage. The staff in the room and I made plans to find ways of introducing Aboriginal presence to the children in a manner that acknowledged and respected our recent presence in Aboriginal country. I shared my conversations with Katrina,

> Katrina and I were locking up, "Katrina, Amelia has asked me to find out about the indigenous name of this suburb as we want to start discussing indigenous Australians with children," I started. "It is NAIDOC week soon, but if you are having indigenous flag, we should also have Union Jack displayed" (Katrina). "Okay, I'll see what I can find from the council," I replied.

Katrina was worried that this activity that allocates just one week out of the fifty two weeks in a year to remember the owners of this land might dilute the colonizers' presence. This time she spoke not just to own and protect the nation and the national identity but also to unfurl and hoist the colonial flag. And now she wanted to retain the history and she went "*way back*," something she pledged never to do earlier. Her fear of colonial Australia being eroded by the original owners of this land pushed her to keep the colonial symbol unfurled strongly. The boundaries of Australia were repeatedly constructed and unified by "Australian" as being unattached to its histories, with maintaining one "Australian" as possible and desirable. The "not Australian" realities were further distanced by these "Australian" imaginations.

Both Cathy and Katrina said that they knew about the past colonization, and yet were reluctant to engage with the ruins of colonization. Katrina, like Cathy, not only claimed ownership of this space but she also overtly kept the outsiders who might ever so slightly change this nation and its national identity from its boundaries, "*We can't let everyone in, this is our country, shouldn't we have a choice. Like I told you Australia is an umbrella. We live together as Australians.*" Katrina limited whom the "umbrella" sheltered, only "Australians." As the owner of this land, she had the capacity to limit and warn the "not Australian" strayers within its borders. Thus, Cathy and Katrina protected their imagined "nothing" and "umbrella" with which they represented this nation and its identity.

Every time the "othering" realities disrupted the image of Australia, the "Australian" responded with their "othering" imaginations. In the "Australian" imagination, the nation and the national identity of Australia was represented as something precious and desirable, "lucky" or as "nothing" and yet present in comparison with the "not Australian." The examination of past histories and present realities were quickly silenced with irrevocable control and power on this nation and its identity. Repeatedly, the proclamation of this nation and its identity began and ended with what was now the "Australian" imagi(nation), built on colonization and colonial occupation. Despite the political recognition of multicultural Australia, which opened its doors to varied cultures and colors, the "Australian" asserted and clung to the presence of one nation and national identity and shut its borders to those perceived as threats to national sovereignty. And I set out to seek what fostered this imagi(nation) that allowed such control and maintenance of its physical and identity borders.

"Othering" Terra Strikes: Shaping "Australian Speakers"

I begin with when it all started, when cultural diversity, the outsider, first was allowed to enter Australia.

> The concept I prefer, the "family of nation," is one that ought to convey an immediate and concrete image to all.... The important thing is that all are committed to the good of all.
> (Grassby, 1973, p. 3)

> The flowering of a truly national spirit in Australia is not an optional extra, but a major objective to be sought in the next few decades.
> My personal ambition is that all Australians of all backgrounds will always be proud...to say..."I am an Australian."
> (Grassby, 1973, pp. 8–9)

These were the words with which Grassby declared the *White Australia policy* as a thing of the past and invited multiculturalism by opening Australia's borders to the "non-white other" or the "cultural other." Simultaneously, Grassby spoke as an "Australian" who claimed and maintained the national fervor with unsurpassed passion, and willingly legitimized his desire to convert the "cultural other" as proud national subjects "lucky" to be accepted into this country. This national fervor that embraces cultural diversity and yet demands absolute, subjective loyalty to Australia and "Australian values" through national unification remains in current immigration statements,

> Australian multiculturalism recognises, accepts, respects and celebrates cultural diversity...all Australians are expected to have an overriding loyalty to Australia and its people...Our commitment to and defence of Australian values of equality, democracy and freedom unite us in

our diverse origins, and enhance the ability of us all to participate fully in spheres of Australian society.

(Commonwealth of Australia, 2003, p.2)

The more recent document that specifically encourages Australian citizenship highlights the precious uniqueness of this nation to extract such subjective commitment.

> Australian citizenship is a privilege that offers enormous rewards. By becoming an Australian citizen, you are joining a unique national community.
>
> (Commonwealth of Australia, 2013, p. 2)

> Australian citizenship is an important step in your migration story. Becoming an Australian citizen means that you are making an ongoing commitment to Australia and all that this country stands for. It is also the beginning of your formal membership of the Australian community. It is the step that will enable you to say "I am Australian."
>
> (Commonwealth of Australia, 2013, p. 3)

Thus, the purpose, or what seemed as the purpose of Grassby's speech (1973), and the later multicultural policies (Commonwealth of Australia, 1999, 2003, 2011) was to not just direct all cultural groups in Australia to strive to become "Australians," but also for "all Australians" to become committed to protect this nation and its unique "Australian values." The interpellating ideologies speak of protecting "Australian values" and thereby indicate the presence of conceivable "Australia's Australian," the core characteristics that define the national subject "Australian," and the "lucky" nation Australia. Most of all, by "Othering" the attributes of the nation with unique national "values," the statements continue to justify making such subjective demands of the national subjects. This vigorous aspiration to defend this identity from external influence is more evident in the gradual change in the naming of the government department that is responsible for immigration and multicultural affairs. The Department of Immigration that initially opened the doors of multiculturalism, later changed to the Department of Immigration and Indigenous Affairs, thus signifying the marginalization of not just the migrant groups, but also the Aboriginal groups of Australia. Currently, citizenship and immigration policies are overseen by the Department of Immigration and Border Protection. This gradual change in the naming of the political body reflects the political discourse of fear attached to currently immigrating migrants, the outsiders. According to Burnett (2004), since September 11 the public and political discourse in Australia has reverted to border control policies akin to *White Australia policy* of 1900s, and this has perpetuated feelings of animosity against asylum seekers. Due to the nation's current obsession with protecting its physical borders, this fear of outsiders or "other" predisposes guardianship to the existing citizens of Australia. In fact, this political ideology encourages and shapes the existing citizens to exert vigilance and caution and thereby justifies aggressive elimination of what is perceived as threats to national integrity. Therefore, the process of recategorization, which is promoted by theories of social psychology (Crisp and Turner, 2007) as a strategy to reduce prejudices between diverse cultural groups, had only made the political institutions to become obsessed with creating unified "Australian" subjects.

These national ideas, however compelling they may be, are ideological specificities and hence abstract. Such abstractness allows the interpellated individuals, now the subjects who speak as "Australian," to take control of the configuration and management of this identity and the national borders into their hands. Moreover, the subjects also mobilize this political ideology by committing themselves to fiercely or gently protect "Australian's Australian" from the "not Australian." Hence, those who subscribed to this ideology spoke as "Australian speakers," as they were permitted to decide what could be accepted within its borders. The "Australian speakers" spoke the ideologies and in turn shaped or *"Othered"* the nation and the national subject to keep the "not Australian" in the margins. They espoused similar fear of the "other" by strongly guarding the borders of this nation. They believed that, as owners of this land before the advent of multiculturalism, they had the right to claim ownership of Australia and "Australian." They fervently protected the "white Australian," the colonial image of the past, and went about maintaining the "not Australian other" through constant appraisals against themselves.

In multicultural Australia, a fixed identity for "Australian" must be long gone, as all cultural groups should be influencing each other by exchanging and sharing their cultural attributes. The responses above spoke otherwise, as the "Australian speakers" repeatedly strived to maintain what she had perceived as "Australian." The "white Australian" remained uninfluenced by "difference" despite the declaration of multiculturalism. The desire to maintain Australia, as it was, suppressed the desire to embrace cultural diversity unconditionally.

The centralization of "Australian" identity excluded not just migrants but also Aboriginal Australians, as the "white Australian" hoisted the Union Jack with their fear of Australia being reclaimed by its original owners. The primary shortcoming of Australia's multiculturalism was thus evident, as the Aboriginal Australians and newer migrants were positioned outside the "white Australian," an older migrant who colonized and claimed the political ownership of this nation. The "Australian speakers" refused to let go of their "white Australian" imagi(nation), and continued to *shape* the nation with ideological support.

Katrina respected the cultures of those she regarded as outsiders only if they extended their willingness to be "Australian" without disturbing what was already here. As Grassby (1973) did with the use of "*Family of nation*," she reordered these cultural groups as "Australian," and proceeded to unify and symbolize the nation as "umbrella." As a committed subject, Katrina was enacting the categorical role of "Australian," a subjectivity that she had unquestioningly internalized as "good for all" (Althusser, 2008). And what was already here in Australia was attached to the image of the "white Anglo-Saxon," the colonial roots. She vehemently protected Australia and "Australian" from those whom she believed would change this image. I struggled to remain silent as Katrina, the "Australian speaker" owned this identity, and by speaking as and for "Australian," she shaped it with rigid insularity. I could not hide my loyalty to my postcolonial subjectivity, as she repeatedly justified the ideological "Australian." Burnett (2004) warns that visions of singular "Australian" identity results in seeing "others" as a threat to the current way of life, and Katrina, the "Australian speaker" was doing so. Said (1994) too criticizes encapsulating national identities with culture frameworks. In Australia's case, it was with national values framework. With renewed nationalism her "*Othering*" resulted in repeatedly polarizing what uniquely were "Australian" values. In fact, she wanted to protect the Union Jack from the original owners of this land, the Aboriginal Australians.

Cathy, on the other hand, acknowledged maintained the cultures of new migrants with respect and acceptance just as outlined by the multicultural policies of Australia, albeit outside and "different" from "Australian." Even when she believed that she was subjected to repeated acts of exclusion by the shopkeeper, an "Indian," she glorified the culture of this "not Australian" and nonchalantly accepted and maintained their outsider status. Yet, as an "Australian speaker," Cathy's "*Othering*" shaped her ownership of this nation and its identity fervently and backed this with "white" neutrality. Her "white Australian" neutrality remained unchanged despite the intervention of "not Australian" fineries. Both these "Australian speakers" thus "spoke" only to freeze the image of "white Australian" and thus colonized multiculturalism. Their zealous voices colonized the "not Australian" to portray their adaptability and their utmost commitment to become subjectified as "Australians." This desire to subjectify all individuals in Australia as "Australian" to retain its sovereignty was colonizing and impeding unrestrained practices of multiculturalism, and recent studies conclude that one in ten people in Australia believe diversity is a threat to this nation's integrity (Forrest and Dunn, cited in Berman and Paradies, 2010). My postcolonial "self" could not be contained as it repeatedly contested the incongruous realities of "not Australian" and the imagi(nation) of "Australian." And I equipped myself for our final challenge with "Australian" the colonizing ideology.

"ØTHERING" TERRA STRIKES: CONTESTING "AUSTRALIAN" WITH THEIR IMAGI(NATION) AND OUR REALITIES

The ideologically subjectified voices of the "Australian" controlled this "Terra" its national borders and values to maintain its colonial antiquity by either closing the "not Australian" in exotic boxes or by closing its boundaries to those who disrupted this identity with their "otherness." While the subject "Australian" did not think of "Australianness" without "whiteness," the "not Australian" subjects responded to erase or exclude their colors and cultures—their "otherness"—from "Australianness." Being, becoming, owning, and maintaining Australia and "Australian" was embraced by "Australian" and "not Australian" speakers, and moreover, such commitment was politically expected and supported. Identity discourses that are backed by institutional ideologies also gain power, and thus become dominant (Weedon, 1987; Mills, 2004). Hence, the "Australian speakers" had complete power to oust or softly silence those whom they perceived as a threat to the sovereignty of this nation and its national identity.

The "not Australian" feared the ideologically empowered dominant "Australian" and controlled their identity practices to appease this ideology. If hegemony is a form of dominance that covertly controls subjects by playing on their common sense (Loomba, 2005; Camara, 2008), all our enactments were controlled by the hegemony of "Australian" ideology, and by those who *shaped* this, the

"Australian speakers." Concluding our cultural enactments as hegemonic outcomes does not do any justice to the voices of those who resisted "whiteness" with their "white Australianness," my "white transformers." ✝ did not want to exclude their voices just because they spoke with their "Other Australian" subjectivity. After all these battles, ✝ felt that my "white transformers" were like us, "øthered" due to their resistance by "Other Australians." ✝ had become quite attached to my "white transformers" and we as "*øthered*" contested the "Australian" ideology. ✝ succumbed to exposing all of my subjective layers, and ✝ peeled my mask to reveal my postcolonial subjectivity with all its complexities.

Contesting Terra Strikes with Jan and Amelia

"No One Has Really Attacked Me but I Know Aussies Think I Shouldn't Be Here"

This was my second day with Amelia and Jan. During our lunch break, ✝ shared my concerns with Amelia, especially Seaweed's dislike for her brown skin, and how she spoke of national identities using our skin color.

> "I know we had *White Australia policy* up until the 1970's" (Amelia). Jan joins us as most children are sleeping. "What policy, I don't know" (Jan). "Like people who were not white were not allowed into Australia. People like you [Jan] and Prasanna were kept out of Australia with deliberate policies by the government" (Amelia).

Amelia, "Other Australian," recognized critical historical events that could still attribute "whiteness" with the "power" of owning "Australianness," the national identity, and controlling the national borders. She created an environment of political awareness. ✝ felt extremely comfortable speaking to her and Jan, and at that time, my participatory action research seemed realizable. Our exchange of stories continued, we all found our "voice" as we narrated our "øthered" experiences.

> Oh, I can't believe that really. No wonder, when I walk down the streets or shop, I am always seen as "not normal." No one has really attacked me but I know Aussies think I shouldn't be here. They think Australia is just for them. But we are all here. I work and my son goes to school and we do everything like you but (Jan).

Jan spoke to Amelia as if she was not intimidated or inhibited by Amelia's "whiteness" and "Australianness." As Amelia heard Jan, she empathized and understood how ideologies were circulated by media and traditional practices of multicultural inclusion. ✝ felt and sensed change, a change we could envision, grasp, and enact together.

> See the media doesn't show that. They always say things like "Unaustralian" and that is usually a migrant or an Aborigine. I do talk about cultures and do all that next term but what does that do? We do different countries of the world, but what does that mean? I know these children won't feel so accepted when they go out. But we just do it because it has been done like that always. Let us do Anti-bias curriculum and can you tell me how we can change this. Let us send a newsletter to parents about what we can do next term. We have to start somewhere and I don't want to do what I have always been doing (Amelia).

The "voice" of "øthered" grew louder, as we schemed to change what was perceived and presented as "Australian."

> "I sang in Chinese the other day, you were not here. Some children sang. Princess (OA) asked me, why are we singing this. I told her that this song is Chinese and it is my language. She said immediately, 'oh, Chinese make everything.' I was hurt" (Jan). "What is wrong in saying that?" (Amelia). "No, it is not that. It is what she implied," I corrected. "Yes, that is not what it means, you know how everyone goes on and on about how everything here is made in China and Chinese are taking over, it is that" (Jan). "See, I would have never thought that being what I am" (Amelia).

Jan and ✝ stood together with our "øthered" experiences and understandings, and Amelia stood outside us, and ✝ underlined and named her. Jan and ✝ felt the hurt, inflicted by a young child, with the "whiteness" and "Australianness" she possessed.

> "You are white, how can you like us, your experiences are different," I added. "Yes, I was hurt. I told her, Yes, Chinese make everything because we are clever" (Jan). "I hope it is okay to say you are white Amelia. I don't know otherwise how to say you are different from me, and we are different. I am not the same and I don't want to be accepted only if I am like you. Please let me know if you don't like being addressed like that, we can think of something together," I apologized.

The above stirred my colored visions, and my categorization of individuals. ł called Amelia "white" and later apologized.

> Don't be silly, you are making us think. You will have to tell me, otherwise I just do the same thing done for years and years. If you never have shared this, I would have never thought it is wrong when Princess said, "Chinese make everything" (Amelia).

Amelia willingly entangled herself with our complexities, and she was with "us," the "øthered," and ł excluded her by saying, "*you are white, how can you like us.*" ł recognized my evilness and ł was ashamed of my own practices. ł wanted Ganga to speak about my acts of discrimination,

Sensitive "Øthered": "You Are White, How Can You Like Us, Your Experiences Are Different"

ł: Why did ł call Amelia "white"? Was ł engaging in unwarranted dichotomous understandings of events?

Ganga: Where do I begin, remember the first time you met Katrina, just before this conversation with Amelia, what did she tell you, "*There is nothing wrong with Australia. It is like an umbrella. There, Remi is Indian, she is Sri Lankan and they are as Australian as I am.*" You heard how she defended Australia by symbolizing the nation with an image of shelter and savior, that is "whiteness" and that is colonialism. Katrina, "Other Australian," would only accept those who were loyal to "Australian values." In the name of unification, she wanted to subjectify and dominate all individuals under this "umbrella," the nation and the national identity. The colonial discourse that operates with the establishment of "difference" in the "other" has not died; it has rather morphed to take on a more subtle form to justify the domination of "other" through nationalist discourse. I think you saw that too, and you challenged her vision by asking her to unpack "Australian values." She sensed your postcolonial resistance and she excluded and accused Greeks, Italians and the owners of this land of keeping to their groups, and justified her "Ownership" and "Insulation" of maintaining "whiteness," the "whiteness" that is attached to colonialism, not just the color as "Australian values." You have read Frankenberg (1993), and Katrina practiced that "Essentialist racism"; she definitely believed outsiders as a threat to Australia's solidarity. You heard her when you said that you were going to the council to find out about the name of that land before colonial occupation and what did she say, "*It is NAIDOC week soon, but if you are having indigenous flag, we should also have Union Jack displayed.*" That is "whiteness" and she wouldn't let go of that "power," her control on the color of this nation. The "Other Australian" wanted to retain visions of the "imagined community," the nation that is Australia founded upon "Britishness" and all that was "Anglo-Saxon" (Stratton and Ang, 1998).

ϯ: But Ganga, this country declared that it was multicultural and abolished the *White Australia Policy* (1901), remember the famous speech by Grassby (1973). And ϯ saw and called Amelia "white" that is wrong.

Ganga: Do you remember how Ahmed (2007) and Berman and Paradies (2010) challenge discursive practices that are attached to multiculturalism and diversity. These do nothing to eradicate racism or bring about equity and justice; these are words that superficially reflect the acceptance of "difference." You are nothing more than a colonial clone; you are unable to get past your humanistic "we are all the same" attitude. Allard (2006) calls this a myth, "taken for granted truth," and White (2002) states this understanding stems from western enlightenment discourse of humanism and individualism. You think you are all strong and postcolonial, but you operate within the same discourse and you too are reinforcing the ideological "Australian." Otherwise, why would you have doubts with calling Amelia "white"? Your subjective experiences were different and that did surface from that exchange. The "power" of "whiteness" and "Australianness" possessed by Princess, a four-year-old "Other Australian" could hurt you and Jan, because you didn't and could never own these.

ϯ: But, we had similar visions and hoped for similar changes. She was willing to "Resist" and "Risk" to bring about equity and justice, to empower all individuals and cultural groups as "Australian." Her "Critical othering," in combination with "Critical Recognizing" enabled our "øthered voices" to be heard. She wanted to practice "difference," and for different practices to be acknowledged as "Australian." Wasn't she the "race cognizant" that Frankenberg (1993) talks about?

Ganga: Yes, she was all that, but even she couldn't escape the "power" of "whiteness," and she knew you couldn't as well. Remember Amelia's last words, I still do, "*What does Katrina know about living in this white world? She is white and lives in this white world, but for children like Moo and Seaweed what they feel and go through day after day is a reality. I hope we are able to continue to work on skin colors consistently even after you leave.*"

ϯ: So, "white power" Ganga, is that what influences cultural identities of "Other Australian" and "øthered Australian"?

Ganga: Do you still doubt it. Let me go.

ϯ: One last one.

Contesting "Terra Strikes" with Mary and Cathy

"If We Have Children I Don't Want to Bring Them Up Like Australians"

† heard from many "øthered Australian" staff about the lack of respect, care, and affection as values of, or what "Australian" was. † became more and more concerned, as there seemed to be no end to their dichotomous constructions against, "Australian." † specifically remembered what Mary said when † first met her,

> Because in Australia we are in a bottle. Australia advocates multiculturalism, but everything is the same. Because you are so scared to be yourself in fear of rejection, being rejected. You can't emerge and show who you are. I have a baggage, a baggage I came here with. But I have put it down to just fit in with what is here. To emerge as what is Filipino there is no strength. It will disturb what is already here. I do want to do that but not many people will hold hands with me, if I do that. I am a Filipino and I want to be that. My husband understands me for that and if we have children I don't want to bring them up like Australians. I want them to love and share and show their emotions and feelings (Mary).

† wanted to change this by speaking with Cathy, the "Other Australian." † had become quite attached to Cathy, as we had such lengthy discussions and she repeatedly wondered about cultural participation.

> "You know the funny thing is since you came here I am much more aware of many differences. I am white middle-class Anglo-Australian and I took that for granted. This society fits my values" (Cathy). "You are truly different, when did you become aware of your difference that you are 'other', and began to name yourself as white middle-class Anglo-Australian," I asked. "But, many staff and families don't think about white Anglo culture and values about independence, they think Aussies don't care about their children and it is not that. It is just a different way of caring about children," I said.

Cathy recognized her privileges, and she named her group and how the national culture fits her values. † immediately shared my observations.

> I know but it is childcare, we just have to bring them up like that, that independence is necessary. All theories talk about its importance.

> I was looking out the window this afternoon at the play group with their Chinese mothers. The mothers fed them, wiped their faces. These children will go to school and it is not that they will be failures, because the mothers help them. For some reason here, we think this is not school readiness. But this is Asian culture (Cathy).

Cathy said these were her cultural values and reverted to distinguishing "Asian" culture. For Cathy, the early childhood practices implemented in the setting were tied to theories and had to be followed. These theories, the theorists were unattached to any cultural origin, but those Chinese mothers who wiped the face of their children were.

> Cathy and I met to discuss our focus for my final staff meeting. "Thank you for all your time and understanding. I think sometimes there aren't cultures, because when I speak with you we share similar goals, values, aspirations and expectations. So is culture not there or it doesn't matter," I commented. "No, no, culture is there, we react similarly to an event but we respond differently. Like, you are passionate and fiery and your culture has taught you to respond with so much feeling and emotion, whereas my culture has taught me to be aloof and respond with much more control and diplomacy. I am slow and bland" (Cathy).

Cathy distinguished our cultures, as being not exactly the aspirations and goals that we share, but more to do with how we responded to events. † couldn't see my passion and fieriness, but she could and distinguished this with hers. † felt may be she was stating something that was more obvious to her, because she was seeing my culture as an outsider. † came back to how cultures were segregated by families and staff again.

> "I should write about this conversation, especially because families seem to alienate themselves as if their culture is different to what is Australian. Staff do it too. But we need to show that is not what you want and that you keep wondering why staff do not bring their cultures into their practices," I replied.

Therefore, † underlined perhaps we could enable staff and families to transform what is self-excluded as "not Australian," from being private to public practice. Cathy slipped away by blaming it on the less critical training offered to staff. And † pulled her back.

> "Staff are not trained to think critically, they just do the same thing. You have to do something at uni to train them to think differently"

(Cathy). "Yes, agree it is to do with training, but were you taught differently that you are now thinking differently Cathy? You say white Anglo, middle-class Australian when you talk about yourself" I asked. "Why can't staff see their cultures? Staff do not have the time and are not trained, so they just prod along. Anyway we will make them see cultures" (Cathy).

Again, she said that it was my responsibility and † had to do something different, and this was my last chance and † repeatedly nudged her understandings of her "white culture" and what it stood for in terms of early childhood educational care and cultural inclusion. Cathy agreed to speak with staff, and she spoke and named their daily practices with its cultural roots.

> "I know it is the white Anglo culture to say 'you'll be right mate' to a child who is crying or needs help and it is so white, because we think we all have to." (Cathy). There was silence and restlessness. Cathy stopped and spoke about asthma management.

Cathy risked and named her culture, but she was punished.

> "Do you know, I don't think the staff liked it when I said white-Anglo culture. I know the staff, especially Tina is sensitive. They are Australian and they keep it like that" (Cathy). "I am sorry. I think I started it," I apologized. "No, no. This is what it is. I should not have said it. That took away all the warmth and coziness we had at the start" (Cathy).

She lost their friendliness.

> The next day as Cathy and I were having lunch, "The staff meeting, I didn't feel okay. I should not have said white Anglo, I know it doesn't go very well with staff. I understand what you mean, but the staff here are tired. You have to train them at uni to think critically" (Cathy).

We were back to where we began, and † couldn't understand. † needed Ganga to clarify this.

Sensitive "Other": "They Are Australian and They Keep It Like That"

> †: What happened to Cathy, why did she do this to me? † just wanted her to unpack with staff, the underlying culture of what was practiced in early childhood settings, † didn't ask for much did †?

Ganga: Do you really think that is not asking much. You were asking for a slice of "white Australian power." Didn't you pick up how she eluded and changed her strategies? Go back and refresh your memory with "Boundary denying" discourse. To me she was a perfect example of what Frankenberg (1993) would call discursively practicing "color power evasiveness," akin to colonial discourse. You were blinded by your commitment and your friendship with Cathy. In fact colonialism creates and maintains cultural identities for all who are colonized but the colonizer (Camara, 2008). So Cathy was the masked colonizer, who glorified the cultures of "øthered" and refused to see the layers of "Other."

†: Ganga, you are too severe, remember she began by naming who she was, "white middle-class Anglo-Australian" and she acknowledged her privilege, as a culture that was practiced by the society. She was not evading, this was "Critical Othering" and "Critical Recognizing."

Ganga: But, see then how she named the mother who was feeding her child, as "Asian" culture. Why? For all you know this mother perhaps is a second or third generation Australian. She was practicing "Australian" culture wasn't she, why "Asian"?

†: Yeah, may be. But then why do you say she was practicing colonial discourse? Isn't that just Australian?

Ganga: You are confused indeed. What is nation and nationalism? These are constructs that are propagated to dominate people, by invariably producing the "other" against one central culture (Young, 1995; Ashcroft, Griffiths and Tiffin, 2000; Hage, 2000). Therefore, it is a discourse of dominance. This is about centralizing "Self" through nationhood and national identity and positioning "øther" around the centre. That is what is problematic for many authors as they say it results in racism and hierarchical, comparative relationships (Brooks, 2002; Weedon, 2004; Leeman and Reid, 2006; Connolly, 2008; Merenstein, 2008). Colonialism is a discourse of dominance, and as Loomba (2005) states, one need not necessarily separate the colonizer and the colonized in postcolonial societies, but resisting any form of dominance is resisting colonialism. Therefore, the discourse of dominating groups with narrow constructions of national identity "Australian" is a colonial discourse. Moreover, what about Katrina's "Union Jack" and Cathy's *"Road to Gundagai"* and "really Australian"; aren't these symbols of colonialism? You are contributing to the "power" of "whiteness" and "colonial dominance" with all your confusion.

†: † told you † am confused. But Cathy did it in the end. It is the staff, they were reluctant.

Ganga: You want me to believe this. No, you pushed her and she reluctantly agreed. Remember she started by "Theorizing" with staff training and "Legitimizing" her inaction. She wanted you to act. Remember, rather than acting, she was "Insulating" "Self," and didn't want to lose the "power" of being in the nucleus. She was denying her boundary.

†: Just like Said (1978), you are regarding all acts of "Other Australian" through colonial discourse, and you are working with stringent dichotomies.

Ganga: Okay, so be it. Anyway she was brought back into the system by the staff. They taught her a lesson. Do you think they retracted all the warmth and coziness? No, she lost her "power," the "power" that came from being a loyal "Australian" subject. Hall (2003) specifically underlines how this "power" is directly linked to practicing one's subjectivity, and "power" leaves when the subject fails to practice that subjective behavior. She went on and on about it and came back to "Boundary denying" for that "power." Go on you do it; it is your problem, not hers. She is warm and cozy again with being "just Australian."

†: Tell me, how did the ideological "Australian" effect and affect the daily "Terra strikes" practices of "Other Australian" and "øthered Australian" subjects in Australia?

Ganga: I will say it in one word, "*power*." I quote Foucault below.

> Here the shift did not consist in analyzing power with a capital "P," or even institutions of power, or the general or institutional forms of domination. Rather it meant studying the techniques and procedures by which one sets about conducting the conduct of others.
> (Foucault, 2010, p. 4)

This is the "power" with which the behaviors of "Other Australian" and "øthered Australian" were controlled. Remember Weedon (1987) and Blaise (2005a, 2005b) talk about "power" in poststructural feminism. According to Weedon, power is the vehicle of control or the lack of it in the choice of a discourse by that subject, and subjective identities are made political and central to serve the interest of some groups. Weedon makes identity central, as its performance ascribes that "power" only to specific subjective discursive practices. Therefore, the discourses that maintained the "power" of the nation and national identity effected and affected daily practices of "Other Australian" and "øthered Australian." Not to forget that the national identity of "Australian" is still attached to "whiteness" and colonial symbols of food, faith, and festival, language, cultural, and political dominance. This is what you were contesting as "Other Australian" and "øthered Australian," because for both groups expressing their commitment to the ideology that is "Australian" gave them "power" or "subjective power" respectively. When you Amelia or Jan, resisted and disrupted this, remember, how you were punished, and silenced. Remember what Katrina, "Other Australian," said the day you started, "*We can't let everyone in, this is our country shouldn't we have a choice. Like I told you Australia is an umbrella. We live together as Australians.*" Therefore, at any given time, those who naturally possess the attributes of national subject, are also endowed with "power" (Hage, 2000). The "power" to claim "Ownership," "Self-Proliferate," "Insulate," and "Legitimate" the maintenance of "Australian," the ideological national identity. Now, you think about who had that "power."

> †: I know "white Other Australian." But Amelia challenged the power of "white Australian," she was "white," and possessed all those cultural layers, yet she "Risked" and "Resisted" that "power" of "whiteness."
>
> Ganga: But she collaborated with you and Jan, the "øthered Australian," who "resisted" and were willing to "risk" their "subjective power." Together, you wanted to change current understandings and practices about "Australian" and "whiteness." There are many Katrina, Cathy "white Other Australian," who, with discourses of "Boundary Defending" and "Boundary Denying," control "Australian" and "power," and many Aruna, Selma, and Sheri, "øthered Australian," who, with discourses of "boundary committing" and "boundary conscious," reach out for "subjective power" by becoming and being "Australian." Their discourses are supported by structures, and that is why you couldn't expose or resist colonial dominance. You know what Spears (1997) and Elliott (2010) say, the structures have to support you to resist, or you need large groups of Amelia practicing "Boundary diffusing" discourses with "øthered Australian" like you and Jan.
>
> †: What is all this about then? If all our daily cultural or boundary identities are mere arbitrations of ideological "power," were our efforts to contest ideological "Australian" in "øthered" voices futile? You heard what all those "øthered Australian" parents and staff said. Mary said she would never feel strong practicing her ethnic origin in Australia, and she said Australia's multiculturalism is a fallacy, the "bottle" that is ready to burst. Dora's mum, "øthered Australian" said, "*You know I am not like her, I am Chinese, I am Chinese. I never felt left out in Australia. It helps if you are western, so that you are not excluded and you feel Aussie. I am different from other Chinese here. I am not like them because I am western. Not so traditional, that way I am not excluded.*" Is "power" omnipotent and omnipresent and indestructible?
>
> Ganga: You tell me now, how you see the operation of "power."

†: Ganga, I now acknowledge your revealing power, which is deemed as a myth. If you are a myth, then the abolishment of the *White Australia policy* (1901) too is a myth. You brought to surface our undeniable daily reality, that we were all colonized by the ideological "Australian," who represented, and was represented by the "power" of "whiteness."

My postcolonial Ganga silently surged toward the ocean, and † trundled alone to make meaning of everything that my Ganga was and to speak of that "power." † realized that my journey with Ganga changed my identity permanently and † still remain split as † revisit my identity journeys with Ganga's Australia in what follows.

CHAPTER 7

The "Whiteness Truth": We Have to Do Something

> We do different countries of the world, but what does that mean? I know these children won't feel so accepted when they go out. But we just do it because it has been done like that always. Let us do Anti-bias curriculum and can you tell me how we can change this. Let us send a newsletter to parents about what we can do next term. We have to start somewhere and I don't want to do what I have always been doing. We have to do something.
>
> —*Amelia, white Anglo-Australian staff*

† briefly retrace my voyage with Ganga and all her varied forms, and the cultural identity "truths" (my contextual understandings stemming from that body knowledge) that † encountered with boundary "speakers." † began my voyage in Ganga with hopes of cleansing my sinful postcolonial vision by immersing in her waters. † wanted to wash off my past colonized realities that tainted my vision to seek and maintain the colonizer/colonized, Self/othered dichotomy, my one and only "truth." Yet, my realities remained with me, as my colonizer's imagi(nation) still controlled my tainted vision. However, Ganga was not powerless. As her myths proclaim, my immersion in Ganga transformed my mortal presence and she offered many "truths." And † share my "truths."

The "othered Truth": Our "Australian / Not Australian" Realities

† observed expressions of "othering" in children's (three to five years of age) and early childhood practitioners' or staff's language, and this

form of "othering truth" established "difference," the "Australian / not Australian" reality. This "othered truth" evidenced that we, as "boundary speakers" not only categorized and classified the collective identities of "self" and "other" as "Australian" and "not Australian" (Indian/Chinese/Filipino), we also used "difference" to attribute these identities with layers (boundary streams) that determined which collective identity we could own. Young children classified who was "Australian" and "not Australian" by predominantly using Complex(ion), our skin color. However, staff, especially those who named their collective identity as "Australian," were uncomfortable in speaking Complex(ion) with children, and therefore, "white Australian" attitudes circulated without much discussion and disruption. I sadly gathered that ignoring "whiteness" affected not those who possessed it, but those who didn't, as we were not just excluded as "not Australian," but were shunned with dislike by our own "brown" kind.

Adults, parents, and staff too classified what was "Australian" and "not Australian," and they used concrete attributes such as language, culture, food, faith, and festival, and other abstract values to do so. While some who named their collective identity as "Australian," believed that as "Australian" they possessed specific traits that had to be left undisturbed, there were those who believed that as "Australian" they possessed "nothing" in comparison to "everything" the "not Australian" had. The "not Australian" speakers too conceptualized what was "Australian" and "not Australian" and modified their behavior to express their adoption of what was "Australian." Thus, the desire for nationalizing many ethnic groups to be committed to the collective group "Australian" was evident in the expressions of those who spoke as "Australian" and "not Australian." However, the same desire for nationalizing also resulted in dividing us as "Australian" and "not Australian." Ganga surfaced the most critical "othered truth"; the shaping of that collective group by "Australian speakers" became loud and clear, especially when the identity of "Australian" was disrupted to be reviewed and re-visioned.

The "Othered Truth": Our "Australian / Not Australian" Imagi(nation)

The "Australian" imagi(nation) became central to cultural identity enactments, and having established this "othered truth," † wrestled with the ideological language that was involved in subjectifying all as "Australian." The colonial imagi(nation) Australia, and the colonizing national subject "Australian" was ideologically conceptualized and circulated through the process of "Othering" time and time again. The "Australian speakers" spoke the ideological language, as they shaped, or "Othered" the identity of "Australian" in particular ways. This "Othered truth" showcased the subjective commitment of "Australian speakers" toward this identity "Australian." Such commitment in turn protected and maintained this identity as it was when it was ideologically conceptualized and perpetuated with "whiteness." The fervent desire in "Australian speakers" to protect the "Australian" resulted in this identity being less influenced by "not Australian difference." Therefore, what was established as "not Australian" was "not white / not Australian difference," and these dichotomous understandings were left uninterrupted due to the commitment of "Australian" subjects to the ideology "One Australian."

My postcolonial subjectivity resurfaced with this revelation, and ϯ understood that the identity of "Australian" was "Othered" and shaped by "Australian speakers," both children and staff, with "whiteness" and colonialism, the discourse of dominance. This discourse, or ways of thinking, acting, and being, positioned the "National Self" as superior, with peripheral "outside other," the "migrant," as either dangerous and aversive, or exotic and desirable. These emotions influenced most of our daily cultural practices in hegemonic proportions. This brought me back to the very stance that ϯ tried to cleanse myself of. After all, Ganga's power is an ideology too, perpetuated by her believers, her subjects.

ϯ reconciled with my postcolonial subjectivity that was influenced by my experiences with "whiteness" and colonialism in Australia, and navigated with my Ganga in search of another cultural identity "truth." Ganga and ϯ transformed all boundary speakers into postcolonial subjects, the "Australian speakers" as "Other Australian," and the "not Australian speakers" as "øthered Australian" and resumed our voyage with and as Ganga, my absolute postcolonial inner voice. Ganga ruthlessly analyzed our discursive contest, including those of mine, and she made me feel guilty of my subversions and submissions to "power."

The "Øthered Truth" and Contesting Cultural Identities

ϯ could not convince myself that ideological interpellation of categorical identity was the only destiny for all postcolonial subjects. ϯ re-embraced postcolonialism and not just identified and acknowledged how the ideological "Australian" was discursively reinforced every day, but also recognized and outlined how this was discursively resisted by "white transformer," the "Other Australian" defectors, and "øthered Australian" challengers. My "postcolonial estuary of contesting Australian" imagery kept me afloat in this space that brimmed with our subjective interactions and actions. My Ganga, my postcolonial inner voice enabled me to decipher my ripples, my own trepidations, and made meaning of how we as "Other Australian" and "øthered Australian" reshaped or contested identities discursively.

Ganga surfaced the "øthered truth." Whether we reinforced or resisted, we contested the ideological "Australian" through our silences and voices evident in our daily practices. † came back to where † began, still colonized by "whiteness," as I realized the "power" of "Other Australian" that punished the resisting voices of "Other Australian" and "øthered Australian." † heard my son's voice again tinged with mockery, as my imagination of "white hybridity" remained submerged under the depths of Ganga. With my unrealized imaginations of hybridity as a reality for all individuals and groups, † now contemplated with my "whiteness truth" that my Ganga and I uncovered. The "whiteness truth" governed our early childhood practices with our silences and voices.

† did try to do something by contesting identity constructs such as, "culture," "nation," "ethnicity," and "race" in early childhood settings in Australia. I contested these constructs that have become the central realities of modern nation-states and societies. Yet, my realities remained with me, as my colonizer's imagi(nation) controlled my contesting aspiration. I realized the "power" of "Other Australian," in the name of unity punishing the resisting "øthered" voices that challenged the ideological "Australian." Hence, rather than mutual exchange of cultural understandings blurring and uniting the boundaries of "Australian" and "not Australian," our boundaries were united by this hegemonic ideology still connected to "whiteness." † hear my son's frustrated voice again, as my imagination of "hybridity" for all remains submerged under the depths of Ganga. With my unrealized imaginations of hybridity as a reality for all individuals and groups, † now contemplate with my "whiteness truth" that Ganga made visible.

My Realities: † Can't Question "Whiteness"

Ganga surfaced the bitter "whiteness truth"; as a colored subject I cannot name or challenge "whiteness." It hurts to act collaboratively against the ideological "Australian" as and with "brown" subjects, who have endured discrimination due to their "difference" in terms of skin color, faith and/or language. I also secretly observed the feelings of overwhelming discomfort and uneasiness in "Australian" subjects, when their "Australianness" was disrupted. As "brown" subjects, it is highly improbable to collaboratively challenge the ideological "Australian," as we are not only positioned as "not Australian," but our voices are also discarded and punished with absolute exclusion and we are barred from claiming "Australian" status. Therefore, without claiming the ownership of this identity, "Australian," it is very difficult to challenge it from outside, as the "Australian" fortifies and maintains its insulation. Those who naturally possess "whiteness," the attribute of what is currently conceived as "Australian," also possess the "power" to disrupt this identity and diffuse its "power." Thus, "whiteness" is still invisibly embedded into "Australianness," and this "power" is desirable. This ideology, the "whiteness truth" just like the colonizer, epitomized and juxtaposed nation and national identity, "Australian," against the sporadic celebration of indigenous and migrant identities in the outskirts. It overtly and covertly dominated and subjectified all individuals and groups to practice the abstract "Australian" in a particular manner. We are all affected by "whiteness truth," and the daily early childhood practices of "whiteness truth" affected our silences and voices.

Our Daily Early Childhood Practices Were Silenced by "Whiteness Truth" when,

"*Other Australian*" children overtly claimed the national identity with "whiteness" and excluded "øthered Australian" with "brownness."

- "*øthered Australian*" children denied their "brownness," by developing a dislike for "brownness" and a desire for "whiteness," to show their commitment to "Australianness" and "whiteness."

"*Other Australian*" staff defended "Australian" identity by overtly negating their "whiteness," its presence and its "power," or covertly denying their "whiteness" and its "power" by expressing a desire for "tan."

- "*øthered Australian*" staff and parents, who were discriminated against and whose children were discriminated against due to their "brownness" were silenced because no one would "talk" color in this country.

"*Other Australian*" children defended "whiteness" by coloring food with "white" and "brown," and "Other Australian" staff used this to deny and defend the food, faith, and festival practices of "Australian."

- "*øthered Australian*" children whispered or ignored their food, faith, and festival practices to show their commitment to "Australianness" and "whiteness."

"*Other Australian*" staff repeatedly claimed they have nothing, no color, no culture, no celebration, and nationalized "whiteness" with everyday and everybody's practices, and yet yearned for the color, culture, and celebration of "øthered Australian" as "different" to "Australian."

- "*øthered Australian*" staff and children feared practicing their "different" food, faith, and festival because of their experiential knowledge about the "power" of "Australianness" and "whiteness," and thereby resolved to publicly practicing "Australianness" and "whiteness," to be seen and accepted like "everyone."

"*Other Australian*" children and staff defended "white Anglo-Saxon language" by saying they spoke, heard, and sang "really Australian," when they spoke, heard, and sang in English.

- "*øthered Australian*" children and staff muted their first languages to speak only "Australian."

"*Other Australian*" staff defended and shut the borders of Australia and the identity of "Australian" to all that is outside "whiteness" through "Self" declared "Australianness."

- "*øthered Australian*" staff and parents succumbed to the power of "whiteness" and "Australianness" to be accepted as "Australian."

"*Other Australian*" staff excluded "øthered" cultural practices by naming these outside "Australianness" and simultaneously maintained unnamed practices of "whiteness" as "just Australian."

- "*øthered Australian*" staff, and postcolonial Ganga, walked away with feelings of despair when their "øthered" voices were never accepted as "everyday" "everyone" practices in multicultural Australia, and "whiteness" remained as "just Australian."

Our Daily Early Childhood "Øthered" Practices Were Voiced by "Whiteness Truth" when,

"*Other Australian*" staff named their "white racial identity," and related how "whiteness" had been historically privileged by nationalism, which silenced individuals and groups who did not naturally possess this identity.

- "*øthered Australian*" shared their experiential knowledge with "Other Australian" to work against "white" privilege and racial discrimination that stemmed from nationalizing "whiteness" as "Australianness."

"*Other Australian*" staff observed how "øthered Australian" children were becoming absorbed into "whiteness" and "Australianness," and critically acted with concern and haste to include "øthered" experiences, including food, faith, festival, and languages as "everyday," "everyone" practices.

- "*øthered Australian*" staff communicated their observations and experiences to collaboratively modify their practices and understandings to challenge "whiteness" and "Australianness."

"*Other Australian*" staff showed willingness and eagerness to reconsider and enact changes in current early childhood practices and understandings to reconceptualize the identity of "Australian" with all children and families.

- "*øthered Australian*" staff and postcolonial Ganga felt that their "øthered" voices were valued and heard, to walk away with feelings of pride. Together, they realized their critical multicultural Australia, where "Australianness" and "whiteness" was allowed to be repeatedly questioned to reflect flexibility and multiplicity.

Thus, the "power" of "whiteness" discursively affected and effected our daily early childhood practices to be silenced and voiced. Even young children unleashed the "power" of "whiteness" and expressed this vociferously. And it wasn't just children, as "white" and "brown" adults we too propagated children's attitudes of "whiteness" and

"Australianness." We were less able to respond to children's and adults' divisive expressions, due to being colonized by the ideological "Australian." The adults who spoke with "whiteness" and "brownness" were silenced, or remained silent.

Early childhood is a critical stage for one's identity development in relation to collective identities of "self" and "other" and children are using collective categories attached to "whiteness" to divide individuals and groups into "Australian" and "not Australian." This specifically affects those who are "brown" and are excluded as "not Australian." Therefore, the development of flexible identities, combined with a capacity to challenge narrow constructions of "race," ethnolinguistic, cultural, and national identities in all children is vital for the future of multicultural Australia. However, the development of flexible identities in all children remains a challenge till the very end.

†, as "øthered Australian," could never disrupt the abstract "Australian," and † still re-search my research (re)actions,

- Should † have begun my experience with Ganga from my postcolonial standpoint to deeply analyze the operation of "whiteness"?
- How do † begin to analyze the operation of "whiteness" with "white" researchers when it was still silently embedded in the daily realities of "power" and dominance?
- As a "brown" researcher, with my "brown" realities, experiences, and knowledge, will † ever be able to analyze the operation of "whiteness" and its "power" with "white" researchers?
- If † do, who gets hurt and why, and who gets liberated and why?

Running parallel to these realities of silences and voices are my inspirations. These inspirations compel me to (re)question and (re)imagine contesting identities.

My Inspirations: † Have to Question "Whiteness"

Every time † engage with postcolonial authors and literature, † become emotionally attached to the questions that they pose to challenge "white" domination.

- bell hooks (1998) asks, when will "whiteness" reposition "Self" as "other" to enable the decolonization of "øthered" minds and imagination?

- Gorski (2008) poses, when will "whiteness" turn its attention away from cultural "other" and look inward at "Self" to recognize systems of power and hegemony?
- Arber (1999) proposes, when will "whiteness" and "Australianness" stop being sites that normalize dominance?
- Hayes (2001) pauses, when will "whiteness" just wonder what it means to have "white" racial identity that is seen as secure, safe, normal, casual, and, above all, national?
- Leornado (2004) contests, when will "whiteness" stop dodging scrutiny to acknowledge its multinational dominance?
- Finally, Rivière (2008) prompts, when will internalization of "whiteness" by nonwhites become examined by both "white" and "brown" researchers, to acknowledge our contribution in maintaining the hegemony of "whiteness"?

And, most of all, there are "white transformers," and ✝ internalize these inspirations with their voices. ✝ now imagine practicing with cultures in early childhood settings with my "white transformers."

My Imagination: Without Imagi(nation)

The only way to challenge "whiteness truth" and its imagi(nation) is by holding hands with "white transformers," who work with young children, and want a future with all cultures and colors being equitably practiced in Australia. My "white transformers," as "Other Australians," resist and expose ideological dominance, exploit ideological ambivalence, and look into the influence of ideological "Australian" in the silences and voices of all individuals, and especially in those of "øthered Australian." ✝ imagine that together we ask ourselves the following questions that were suggested by Said (1978),

> How does one represent other cultures?
> What is another culture?
> How do ideas acquire authority, "normality," and even status of "natural" truth?
> (pp. 325–326)

Through this critical inquiry, we clarify our subjective commitment to "whiteness" and "Australianness," and ✝ imagine "white transformers" and ✝ taking early childhood practitioners, "Other/øthered Australian," on a liberating voyage with my Ganga, the data, and my postcolonial "øthered" voice. In this voyage, our commitment to the ideological "Australian" is "different," as we try and reposition "whiteness" as "other" by talking histories of Australia and their relevance in current attitudes and understandings about "Australian." We enable "Other Australian" practitioners to take a look inward, in relation to the daily public early childhood practices (color, food, faith, festival, language, national ownership) and its relationship with "whiteness." Thus, we stop for a moment to imagine what it is to be accepted automatically as "normal Australian," and how this invariably silences "øthered" voices and practices. Thus, as "hybrid Australians," we begin to recognize how we contribute to the propagation of "white dominance," when we ignore how "whiteness" is absorbed and internalized by all individuals in Australia. We unravel how practices of dominance and denial hurt and inhibit the practices that promote multiplicity in the cultural identities of all individuals and groups in Australia.

† imagine, as "hybrid Australians" we take this new knowledge to our settings and we reengage with "whiteness" to challenge its accepted link to "Australianness." We reconsider our daily discursive practices with children, families, and staff in relation to color, food, faith, festival, language, and national ownership in early childhood settings. We reexamine and reconceptualize categorical language used in early childhood guiding documents to reflect our multiplicity as "hybrid Australian." This awareness leads us to constantly question our attitudes and understandings as "hybrid Australian," especially by being vigilant to global movements and contextual events that position particular individuals and groups more prone to exclusion and discrimination in our society. We reteach and relearn our new identity as "hybrid Australian" with children, families, and staff to build a community that embraces many ways of practicing "Australian" publicly. We, as groups of individuals, reclaim the structures to reconceptualize both "Australian" and "migrant" identities, thus keeping the boundaries of "Australian" undulated and stretched to embrace "difference" as they come. My sanctifying dip into my postcolonial Ganga has revealed to me that cleansing my embodied colonialism is impossible, as doing so will also make me oblivious to recognizing its presence, and working against its dominance. Therefore, as long as the "power" of "whiteness" and "Australianness" continues to circulate, so will my Ganga, *"ever changing, ever flowing, ever the same."*

Our Incomplete Inquiry: *Who Are You?*

† know my Ganga and Ganga knows me. We know that in many countries like Australia, New Zealand, Canada, United States, and

the United Kingdom, "whiteness" still has a stronghold in defining their national subjects, the "Other" and the "øthered." Hence, there are "Other" and "øthered" subjects in all these spaces. Now, after your immersion in Ganga, we want to know how you relate to Ganga's subjects.

If You Are an "Other," Do You Know Yourself? How Do You Discursively Practice "Whiteness"?

Do You Engage in Boundary Defending Discourse Like Katrina?

Katrina defined the national subjects with her "whiteness" and was stridently committed to its value system. She fervently engaged in perpetuating this vision by taking ownership of this nation and its identity anonymously with her "white culture." She theorized that colonization was a thing of the past, and she believed that the nation and the national identity had to remain watertight and protected. There was no room for defectors, who were less loyal and committed to this preestablished nation and its identity. She harshly punished anyone who tried to ever so slightly shift this national space. She had the "power," the ultimate "power," which was attached to her "colonial whiteness" and she guarded this "power" as much as she guarded the nation. The early childhood practices had to be left alone, as nothing had to change for the few marginalized. They remained as they are.

Perhaps, You Are More Like Cathy, and You Navigate with Boundary Denying Discourse

Cathy was soft and she loved and celebrated the colors and cultures of the "øthered." She named her "white culture" and its close association with the nation's identity. Cathy's relationship with "whiteness" was ambiguous. She considered it as something that possessed nothing, and it represented nothing for her. She knew the "øthered" were vibrant and possessed everything she lacked. Therefore, now and again Cathy engaged in activities to tease out their colors and make their cultures trickle. Although Cathy knew that her nation was represented through her "whiteness," she was not afraid of the "øthered." Therefore, there was always more room in this nation, but the outsiders always remained as outsiders, with their vibrant passion against her "white" insipidity. Yet, Cathy consciously or unconsciously was also attached to maintaining the purity of "whiteness." Because of her "white ambiguity" and the elusive illusion of her "whiteness," Cathy retained "white power." With that "power," she determined when and how much of the "øthered" could be represented in this nation. Thus, Cathy was able to always guard "white power," its national purity, to remain uncontaminated by colorful cultures. The daily early childhood practices remained unexamined, attached to nothing, and as normal and as usual as they always were.

May Be, You Definitely Think You Are Amelia, the Boundary Diffusing "White Transformer"

Amelia knew the "power" of "whiteness" and its grip on this nation, its identity, and its sociopolitical systems. She named herself and strived with "øthered" to recognize how the anonymous nationality of her "whiteness" discriminated "brownness." In order to reconceptualize the national identity, she wanted to speak with her "whiteness" about and with "brownness." Amelia was there to transform the perpetuation of "white power," and was self-critical. She reexamined everyday happenings and narratives between adults, children, and our interactions with the social media. Her critical consciousness stemmed from examining her personal stories, stories of "white power" and their attachment with covert and overt ideological "power." She stood for change and therefore she was not worried about opening the nation's doors to outsiders. However, she was also conscious of the practicalities of opening the doors to "difference," and was there to critically examine how such "difference" was going to be looked at and overlooked by her "white" world. She risked and resisted with "øthered" to change our daily early childhood practices.

IF YOU ARE AN "ØTHERED," DO YOU KNOW YOURSELF? HOW DO YOU DISCURSIVELY PRACTICE "WHITENESS"?

Can You See a Bit of Sheri in You, as You Practice boundary committing to Fit in?

Sheri had become very conscious of her "øthered" subjectivity, her "brownness" that was scorned and excluded when she was young. She had changed, changed to longingly desire for "whiteness." Having experienced the "power" of "whiteness," she recognized its presence in controlling the nation and national identity. Yet, she never could name it, and consciously or unconsciously overlooked its colonial dominance. However, when her critical consciousness was triggered by an "øthered," she whispered how it had influenced her likes and dislikes forever. It was understandably very difficult for her to think and act beyond her submission and commitment to "whiteness" as she had covertly and overtly experienced "white power." Sheri perpetuated "white power" and nationhood with unquestioning commitment and loyalty, and changed nothing. The dominant early childhood practices prevailed.

May Be, There Is More of Selma Than Sheri in You, as You Are More boundary conscious?

Selma named her culture and all its layers, and its relationship with the nation and the national identity. Being ever-vigilant, Selma carefully conducted her behavior in a manner that she was always accepted by "national power." Outwardly, Selma embraced "whiteness," and yet deep inside she knew who she was and kept her "difference" locked up from public eyes. It is not that she was less critically conscious. She knew very well about the presence of "white power" and how it claimed national status and operated in this society. However, her critical consciousness was also attached to fear; the fear of being rejected by "national power." Although she shared these feelings with an "øthered," she strode elegantly with self-imposed deep silences that hindered her critical consciousness and action. With these silences, Selma perpetuated "white power" and quelled her motivation and desire for change. So nothing changed in the field of early childhood.

Perhaps, You Know That You Definitely Practice boundary diffusing Discourse Like Jan?

Jan was there to challenge "whiteness" and its clutches on nation and national identity. She repeatedly named her "øthered" status and its interactions with national "power." She openly shared personal stories with "Other" and "øthered," with a willingness and motivation to trace their political origin. She was concerned about the future of all cultures and the way in which they were all mitigated by "white power." Jan diligently held the hands of those critical enactors who were motivated to challenge and question "whiteness." Children's expressions of "white power" disturbed her deeply and she immediately acted to change being subjectified by "whiteness." Jan freely exhibited and expressed her "øthered" experiences with children to contest "whiteness" with them. Through critical consciousness, she risked and resisted changing those daily early childhood practices that superficially portrayed cultural tolerance, and was ready to contest "white power" every day in the setting and out in the society. She felt inspired by "white transformers," who were willing to engage in this "Boundary diffusing," contest together.

So, Who Are You? What Is Your Culture? What Is Your Reality? What Is Your Imagination and What Is Your Inspiration?

Ganga's journey ends but continues...

† take snippets of Ganga back to where she was generated. With the voices that re-contested identities, we leave it for you to inquire who has the "power."

Epilogue: But Remember She Is Saying, "I Don't Like Brown Skin, I Am White"

We had very limited time and I took the following three storylines from Complex(ion) speaks to the center where Ganga began. The participants requested me to use their names and not pseudonyms. However, due to my ethical obligation toward maintaining their anonymity, I sincerely apologize to them and use pseudonyms instead. I thank the contribution of all these participants on that evening.

1. *My first day in this room and I found Pookey playing in the home corner. "I don't want to play with that brown doll. I don't like brown skin. I am white" (Pookey). "You are brown, I am brown too" (Cheela, a four-year-old, Latin American Australian). "No, I am white" (Pookey).*
2. *Katherine was cleaning the paint pots and brushes. "Katherine, Pookey says that she won't play with brown doll, because she doesn't like brown skin and says that she is white," I commented. "It couldn't have come from here. Both her kinder teachers are white. Maybe it is from the family, they probably buy only white dolls for her," Katherine replied taking a couple of steps back.*
3. *"Pookey says, she doesn't like brown skin and that she is white," I started hesitantly. "Someone here has told Pookey that she is black and yucky, so they won't play with her. She was so upset when she came home. It took us so long to console her. But how do I say this to the staff here. I haven't said anything" (Pookey's mother). I asked myself, "Do I have the right to disrupt Pookey's mother's silence?"*

Andrea introduced the above narratives to the group and she had circulated a copy of these narratives beforehand.

> Andrea: There are no right or wrong answers, this is just about collecting ideas. So, let us read the narrative and have a think about it for about five minutes.
>
> Prasanna: Thank you for going through these stories with me. As you know I collected these stories or narratives from two centers. Therefore, what we are sharing today could have happened anywhere. I thank you once again for your time.
>
> Andrea: [Reads storyline 1 aloud] I want us to think and say what we would do if this happens in our center, in our rooms.
>
> Viola: I would probably ask her about her family. Like how she sees her family. Like, does she see her family with only brown skin or white? And then may be just go around and sort of point out others. Like, what kind of skin do you think I have, what kind of skin do you think your friends have. Just so that you can understand that there is.
>
> Andrea: So do you actually think that she is not recognizing her skin as brown?
>
> Viola: May be, may be just for herself. She may recognize everyone else's in her family, she may say, my mother, my brother and dad are brown, but I am white. Then it is obvious that she recognizes everyone in the family and not herself.
>
> Nola: But you may see that children who have all white or lighter color in their family may not like that color and vice versa. Therefore, there are all different ranges of color. It is not just black and white. Like when people come from a different background, like from a different country their children might be a different color to their mum and dad are.
>
> Andrea: But remember she is saying, "I don't like brown skin, I am white."
>
> Anne: I find her like a typical child, who can believe what she wants to believe. Like the typical child who might say, I am Cinderella, and I am going to be Cinderella. And you can't tell that child, you can't be Cinderella. So this is how she actually projects herself. I am white.
>
> Elle: I would take it for the group time. That is what I did last year actually, with the children we were just coloring the differences and similarities between all us. Not just the children, but also the educators. Like were actually discussing our skin color, our eyes color and we end up in saying, we are all different. And I have a fantastic book that says okay we are all different, but we are all human beings. So we have the differences but we also have the similarities. And we always try to end up the discussion to say, it is okay. It is

okay to have different color, that is what Australia is all about. That is what is beautiful actually. You can see different people with different skin color, different hair and different eyes color.

Andrea: So you think of perhaps doing a group time, what else could we do?

Nola: If you have got different colored dolls to that doll, like the Asian color and the black color, and a couple of other things, may be have some way of saying look, how beautiful they are, dress them up and say they all look beautiful.

Elle: I would also may be extend it, discuss the families. Looking at our families. Looking at the differences and similarities in our families. And also making sure that all the kinder families are included. So no matter what the structure of the family is, the important thing is that we should accept them.

Andrea: How do you think Cheela felt, when she was observing and saying, I am brown you are brown too. How do you think Pookey would have felt?

Anne, Elle: Confused.

Andrea: So, how do you think as an educator you should help?

Nola: I think sometimes it depends on the child. For a lot of children it just goes over their head and they would often run off and play with something else. Other children you know, they think about things.

Andrea: Cheela was sort of saying, you know she is brown and I am brown too. And so,

Anne: I think I will validate her. Really, you know don't get confused, I will support her.

Nola: You know that little girl can see they are both brown. But the other girl.

Andrea: But as you know it goes on. Katherine, the white Anglo staff member was washing the paint pots and brushes.

(Andrea reads Storyline 2.)

Andrea: Why do you think the person who wrote this narrative was concerned? She was also upset about Katherine's comment.

Viola: I would be upset myself.

Andrea: Why?

Viola: She is just assuming.

Nola: But there is nothing really wrong, if the child walks over and picks a white doll to play. Because that is her choice.

Andrea: Yeah, but.

Nola: She doesn't always have to pick a brown doll because she is brown.

Elle: I do believe as an educator you really shouldn't make such a comment. You have to have a discussion with another educator. I actually as a person coming to Australia from another country would feel actually hurt with such a comment.

Di: But you know, there are parents who say that I don't want my child playing with a brown doll, and what do you say, you know.

Andrea: How did you deal with it?

Di: I don't know, what do you do. It is her request that her child not to play with a brown doll, because it scares her daughter. Her daughter is the same color as the doll and she says that I don't want my child to play with that doll.

Andrea: So what do you suggest Viola and Di might have to do?

Nola: Talk to the family. It is obviously coming from the family.

Sally: It is not fair to put the dolls away as other children will miss out.

Anne: Of course, we need to address if that child has some kind of fear. We cannot just sit back and say it is from the family.

Viola: We have kept the doll out, as other children are playing yeah. And the child has been around it and that has become an issue. Mainly it is coming from the parent.

Sam: So the child is not scared or anything, it is coming from the parent.

Di: We know it is not from the child, because the child can't talk. It is the mother's request.

Anne: So the child plays with the doll, the brown doll.

Viola: She doesn't go out to play with it, she will pick it up or move it.

Di: But when we asked the mum, she just said, oh she is just scared of it and then.

Sam: You know we have it at kinder all the time.

Viola: You know that is what I said, we have it out all the time and it hasn't obviously been an issue.

Sam: So this is obviously coming from the family.

Nola: May be she is an over protective mum and thinks that it will scare her. So, but it doesn't know. She hasn't seen her with the doll.

Di: Now we have got another child, same color. She plays with the doll. Like now we can't have your child have contact with this child, because her mother does not want her to play with that doll. So what do you do, we don't know how she feels.

Andrea: How serious was the mother's comment?

Di: She didn't speak to me actually.

Andrea: So she hasn't actually spoken to you.

Viola: Like we heard when she was talking to another lady. She said like you know, how she looks at it and she cries. Ummm. I said then we have had it out and it hasn't been an issue. She said, well, my child cries every time she sees the doll. But she hasn't really said anything else after that.

Andrea: May be, she is happy after you said that.

Prasanna: So, the family is brown.

Viola: They are Ethiopian.

Andrea: Well getting back to Katherine, so any more comments about what Katherine said. Her teachers are white, maybe it is from the family, they probably buy only white dolls for her.

Ruth: I don't what her kinder teachers being white has to do with her preference to the white doll. Why would Katherine have said, the kinder teachers are white. What consequences, it is their skin color.

Prasanna: For me, it was not just about Pookey saying that she doesn't like brown skin, but she also said that she was white. Because the sentence continues, she is not only saying I don't want to play with that doll, she is saying I don't like brown skin and I am white.

(Silence follows for a minute or two.)

Prasanna: It is not just a matter of doll preference, it is more to do with the skin color.

Nola: The way she is saying she doesn't like brown skin.

Prasanna: Yeah.

(Silence follows for another couple of minutes.)

Viola: It is obvious that Katherine does not want to know much about this. Like that she did not want to have conversations in any form about anything related, because she has just got the assumption now.

Nola: But like Anne said, why can't she pretend that she is white. Children pretend all the time. Like if she doesn't like it now, probably in another couple of weeks, she will change her mind and be something else. You get what I mean, like children want to be dogs and cats and you know they are just children, they change.

Andrea: But, is this an issue in the society that we as educators need to address with the children in our care.

Nola: You probably need to find out why she doesn't like brown skin and ask her and sit down and talk.

Prasanna: Would you think the same, if a white child says I don't like brown skin. Because here the brown child is saying that she doesn't like brown skin and that she is white. Would you think the same if a white child says I don't like brown skin. Would it be the same, because here you are saying it is about pretend play.

Nola: Look, if it was my child, or my grandchild I would tell them off.

Prasanna: No, we are talking about as an educator.

Nola: As an educator, well I can't really comment on what their preference is.

Anne: I am just imagining for example, if a white child says that I don't like brown skin. Personally, I don't like that child's judgment. Mmm, it is definitely not the same.

Prasanna: So, it depends on the speaker, and what gives us the guarantee that a white child is not saying that.

Nola: Well they could.

Prasanna: So what do we as educators might have to do. These are the questions that I had actually. I am very sorry to interrupt, but these questions for me are still unanswered. They came to mind and I thought this is so complex. We can talk about pretend play and all that when the brown child is saying this, but why is she saying that was my question.

Nola: So when she does say that to her mum, then you need to reinforce everything else with it. But for children here to just say it is not a problem.

Anne: You know when I hear that from a white child, I will be judging. I will have an immediate reaction, oh why. I will immediately judge. I will have more reaction on the white child saying I don't like brown. There is something more depth in there than this one.

Nola: All children are going to find, it is not just skin color. Now my daughter has got a scar on her arm. One of my grandsons says it is yucky on you. No, just feel it that is not yucky. My skin will stay like this forever. Then the kids feel it, massage it and they call it the dodgy arm. Well, her parents when that happened, because she didn't say that to the educators, her parents need to reinforce that her skin is not yucky and nobody's skin is yucky.

Andrea: So what as educators should you know?

Nola: But they didn't know.

Andrea: Let us go on to that bit.

(Andrea reads Storyline 3)

The author asks, do I have the right to disrupt Pookey's mother's silence. You are nodding Sally, tell us about it.

Sally: Umm. Well she should. It is her child, but it is also the concern of the educator.

Anne: But if you unearth it, it might unsettle the parents.

Viola: Obviously the mother doesn't feel comfortable talking to the staff. So she can be like the icebreaker. Then the mother might go, I feel a little bit more confident in doing it and it might then bring out more things. If she didn't, the mother does not say anything and no one knows. May be it is alright to break the silence.

Prasanna: For me at that time I asked myself, how we then, as educators, provide spaces for such conversations to happen. Because we may not hear. I am sure Katherine and the staff who were there did not know that this happened. They probably never heard the child actually saying to another child, you are brown you are yucky. When the child goes home and tells the parents, the parents do get upset. And not every parent but most parents would be hesitant to bring this to the staff. Like Anne said, you don't want to upset the balance. Your child is being cared for by the staff. But we all have responsibilities as educators. How do we then bring about spaces?

Ruth: But if you don't know it is happening, how can you do something about it.

Prasanna: I perfectly agree with what you are saying, but if such a thing can happen how do we then enable parents, children and staff to talk about it by giving them a comfortable space. A safe space.

Anne: I will ask them how do they want me to respond. Do they want me to discuss it, do they want me to talk about it.

Andrea: I think what the question is, is it our place as educators, to discuss color with children.

Alisha: Yes, why not.

Andrea: Okay, if it is, how.

Nola: You can only do it if the parent.

Ruth: But children tease about everything, it could be skin color, or a limp or calipers.

Andrea: Let us go beyond, then what about discrimination then. So as educators do we actually talk about discrimination.

Anne, Alisha: Yes.

Andrea: How do we talk about it. What kind of things will we say?

Ruth: I think a lot of it depends on what views are being taught at home. You might have some parents at home who are very set in their ways on who their child should play with what their child should do. I don't want to say anything. But some might be based on skin color. I don't want you playing with that child because she is dark. But I don't want to say it happens in our center, but it is possible.

Nola: We had two parents in kinder. They were both from the same race, but they said I don't want my child playing with her. And that was because of economic reasons. So we can't really change that view because that is what that parent thinks.

Andrea: So what do we do about this.

Nola: I agree with Alisha, we have a discussion about this. What do we have to say? They won't change their mind two seconds flat. I don't know.

Anne: I think we should really address it and so the children know the appropriate reaction. With the parents we cannot educate them. It is the children that we can change.

Nola: We can say what we want, but if the parents tell them at home.

Anne: Because we have the responsibility also, we should really tell them how would you feel.

Nola: But if that child said she was yucky, next week they could be best friends. They are four-year-olds. I am being sensible, I have had three kids and five grandkids, they are four. We expect too much to tell these children. They need to play and have fun. Really and surely. We get too overwrought with what they think and what they should know.

Alisha: Yeah, they do.

Andrea: But wouldn't it be terrible if one of these children came here every day and this was said to the child.

Nola: I am not denying that, but her parents should have discussed it as well with her.

Andrea: But they did. They soldiered and comforted her.

Nola: But as I said, if we haven't been told that. I am sure if I had seen that I will be saying something. But they are four.

Andrea: It goes to show that even a four-year-old can go home and talk about what happens here and be very sad about it. We don't know that, we don't know what is said at home. So do we have an attitude, what we don't know we don't care, or do we think outside the square and think what can possibly be the issues here, within this group of children? And how are we going to address that.

Nola: It is a lot from the family.

Alisha: I think we should also look at separation and things like that. When the child is sitting alone, playing by self because he doesn't want to mix with black skin or brown skin. Then we can think about some activity if we want. Like holding hands, and break that feeling. And little by little talk to the parents and have those conversations with them slowly. And then ask what do you think, just involve the parents. May be they have got something. I can't believe parents in this center are like that. May be there are. We are thinking that it is not going to happen. But as educators we are trying to break off that cycle. Like we can have different animals, different colors. Like black, this is white and we can all be one. It may not happen soon, but little by little they will change. We talk about difference, we can all look different and come from different backgrounds, but we can play together.

Nola: It doesn't have to be skin color. It can even be glasses.

Alisha: In that particular thing we are talking about skin color.

Ruth: But we can start with that and move to glasses. Like I wear glasses because I can't see.

Alisha: Yeah.

Ruth: Like similarities, differences.

Mena: For me each child thinks differently about the skin color. For example for me, one of my children from the group. She asked me, by the end of the year she asked me, Mena why your skin color is dark. She asked me. But I don't know why she didn't realize at the beginning of the year. She asked me nearly end of the year. She said, I think my dad's skin color is the same as yours. I said no. But she said, no Mena it is the same like yours, I think when you are getting

older your skin color goes dark. It was so funny, she said that. That is why each child thinks differently.
(Everyone laughs.)
Nola: But, mind you he might have been out in the sun and got a tan. But she doesn't know.
Mena: She didn't say anything else except this. So, they think differently about skin color. Some children just say it and some children are very quiet. She is the only one who told me and no one else did.
Nola: This was a funny thing that happened. Like this child was outside and people were moving houses. Someone said, gee that is another Yugoslavian, we have a lot of Yugoslavian in Australia. And the child said, maybe we should move then. You are Yugoslavian yourself, her dad said. Then the child said, okay then. See that is how children think. They don't get it.
Andrea: May be they don't, may be they do. I wonder why she said maybe we should move.
(Everyone laughs.)
Nola: But she is four you know. She doesn't know. It is over her head.
Andrea: What she knows is that she needs to go away from Yugoslavians. Well, she made a statement to say, we have to move, there are too many Yugoslavians.
Nola: Yeah but... that is her.
Prasanna: Even when you said that the child had conceptualized that as you grow older you turn brown. I was thinking what is this child going to conclude when she sees a peer who is brown. Is she going to think her four-year-old friend is 40 years old that is why he or she is brown? So, it is much more complex how they have conceptualized and how they have given reasons for why somebody is brown and someone is white. And if they are thinking it is because they are old, how is the child going to treat a peer who is brown?
Andrea: So as educators do we then challenge that?
Mena: But it happens when you get old you turn brown. When I was younger I was a little bit lighter, not little bit, a lot lighter than this color. Now see what has happened. So I am getting darker it is true. Even my husband says that I was so white when we were young, but now look at my color. So he explains like that to my children. Actually it is right.
(Everyone laughs.)
Andrea: It may well be. But would you have taken Stephanie to another child who is brown and said, look Betty has got the same skin color as me, and she is the same age as you. Would anyone say that is a reasonable thing to do?

Ruth: Let me say something here, there is a whole beauty industry on getting darker.
(Everyone continues to laugh.)
Anne: No.
Prasanna: And whiter too. Anne would know.
Caroline: No. It is opposite in Asian societies, you want to get white.
Anne: Really, as a Filipino, I am spending so much till now on whitening lotion and whitening soap. I was always like that I told you.
Ruth: Oh, I wish I had darker skin.
Caroline: I want to say something. In many Asian countries, like North Asian and South Asian countries. I am from Cambodia so I know that in Cambodia all the women we have different sort of like lighter skin and darker skin. So when you see Asian, they are lighter skin, darker skin. But you want more lighter than what you are. So they have these whitening products and so people have different perspectives.
Prasanna: But coming back to the serious side of this, what we know from this is whiteness is desirable.
Ruth: But how can you say that when, in Australia, the whole country is built on going and getting a tan, getting darker.
Andrea: But what Prasanna is saying is through research and study, it is a fact.
Anne: Yes, it is.
Prasanna: For me, I do understand where you are coming from, because that is one thing that media shows and promotes, but the other side of the coin is, Australia was built on *White Australia policy*, desiring whiteness. And that is something we don't want to talk about, because it is history.
Andrea: We have a whole history of our government saying that is what is Australia.
Ruth: I know all that, but that is not how my generation see it. There is also reverse racism.
Prasanna: So there is still friction between groups. I am not here for brown or white. It can be either way, and it is happening around children as young as four and five years old in places such as kindergartens. So as educators what is our responsibility to act against it.
Anne: But Prasanna, are we not allowed to have preference. Like from a young age you like bread.
Andrea: But this is about skin color.
Prasanna: Okay, imagine I am the mother, and I have this family of brown people and my child walks up to me and says, I don't like brown skin, I am white. How would I feel, as a mother? It is beyond liking yellow, green, orange like Alisha said. Race, color has been politically established.

Ruth: I can understand that in India where you have got the hierarchy, where white is considered as better. I can understand for that mother because she is thinking of herself as lesser. But in Australia I don't think we have that hierarchy. You know I don't think any less of anyone else for their skin color, for eye color, hair color. Whether they walk with a limp.

Nola: I think you are expecting a lot from four-year-olds. Yes we can talk about it, but that is a lot to put into four-year-olds. I know that girl would have got on. This was just a little thing and then it all faded away whatever.

Anne: But how do we progress. Because if it is embedded in there, in that child.

Nola: We don't know about this other child who said it or the family, we can't change that family.

Prasanna: This is such a small group and we heard Anne saying whiteness is desirable, Mena saying whiteness is desirable and Caroline saying it is desirable too.

Andrea: When I went to Singapore, a girl in the cosmetic department said, I have got something that will whiten the skin to me.

Nola: It is desirable.

Prasanna: I am from India and the amount of whitening creams and products available is phenomenal. It affects your mind, it is in your head.

Mena: I know, here too.

Andrea: And the question is as educators what do we do? We will wrap it up with that question.

Prasanna: Thank you so much for your time and ideas.

Nina: You know what you say is true. Children know they see differences. Like there is me, Sam and Elle in that room. Children who are brown come to me when they join this kinder, those who are like Asian go to Sam, and those children who are white go to Elle. Even the families, they do it too. They automatically come to those who are similar.

Prasanna: But, what we have here in Pookey is the opposite. She dislikes her own kind.

Nina: But what do you do...

It was time to wrap up and leave. I thanked everyone again, and we left.

I still ask, "*What do we do?*"

Appendix: Ganga's Key "Boundary Speakers"

The following are snippets of background information on the key "boundary speakers" (øthered Australian [øA]; Other Australian [OA]), who encountered and contested identities in early childhood settings with Ganga.

The "Øthered Australian" Speakers

Pookey was a four-year-old Indian Australian girl who mostly played with Cheela, but became very frustrated when Cheela ignored her to play with See and Fairy. Gina (OA) always said that See (OA) and Fairy (OA) were the most powerful girls in the room, and gaining acceptance into their peer group is difficult.

Seaweed (a three-year-old, Indian Australian girl) hugged me as soon as I walked into the room, *"Prasanna you are from India."* Seaweed followed me everywhere, and made artwork and drawings for me to take home. Her favorite sweet was *gulab jamun* and *jalebi,* and we made these at the play dough table.

Bikky (a four-year-old Turkish Australian girl) often would philosophize with me about Allah. She wanted to know whether Allah was real or not, or whether Allah was a boy or a girl. Every time she heard me talk about our Muslim neighbors or I mentioned their names, she became fascinated. She always said, *"Indian and Turkish are a little bit the same,"* and would whisper Muslim names in my ears for me to pronounce. This was her favorite game and we nearly played this every day I was there in her room.

Santa (a four-year-old Lebanese Australian boy), "øthered Australian," had a keen interest in marine biology and botany. We brought our collection of shells, pressed flowers, and leaves to show each other.

Plafe (a four-year-old Indian Australian boy) had been attending this center full-time ever since he was an infant. His best friend was Sheep (a four-year-old Anglo-Australian boy), and he followed and supported Sheep most of the time. Plafe's favorite games were the ones Sheep played and his favorite food was what Sheep ate and so on. They had been together since they were babies.

Moo (a three-year-old Indian Australian girl) was very quiet, a part-timer, and got very attached to me. Moo often played at the play dough table and rolled out play dough *rotis* for us to eat. I commented on Moo's ability to roll perfect *rotis*, and Moo's mother spoke about how much they enjoyed making *roti* together as soon as they got home.

Pookey's mum and † shared not only the same ethnolinguistic background, but also a passion for cooking. We usually talked about our favorite dishes and what we cooked the night before, and we ended up making plans to open a restaurant when I concluded Ganga. Pookey's parents migrated to Australia not very long ago, and they spoke five languages fluently. They said that they wanted Pookey to believe she could be both, Indian and Australian, and it is okay to be both in front of everyone.

Bella (Polish staff) had been most conscious about providing choices for children. She often challenged what this meant, whose choices they were and how these choices were still adult centered. Bella and I had the most intense discussions about poststructural theories, and the practicality of their application.

Thora's (a three-year-old Indian Australian girl) *mum* loved to wear her jewellery, especially her anklets, and Thora did the same too. The staff thought that she was traditional and less modern, but Thora's mum believed that she was very strong and wanted her to be accepted for who she was. She often said that she wanted to raise her daughter to have a strong sense of who she was.

Sidya's (a three-year-old Indian Australian girl) *parents* and I frequently spoke about India's caste system and all the discrimination and injustice that resulted from it. We always wondered whether India would ever be able to come out of this ingrained structural atrocity.

Sheri (Sri Lankan Australian staff) worked with Selma in the room. Her family migrated to Australia when she was very young. Sheri, Selma, and I had the best time when we reorganized the store room. Sheri repeatedly said that she wished she had met me earlier. Selma missed Sheri when she was not around, and often commented that Sheri was more like a daughter to her.

Seaweed's mum spoke to me about Seaweed's dislike for her brown skin color the very first evening I met her. She found my topic fascinating and she wanted to read current understandings and practices about children's identity development.

Fatima (Iranian Australian staff) loved cooking. Being a vegetarian, I seldom ate what was served at the center, and Fatima would bring some of the most delicious vegetarian dishes for me to eat during lunch time. Fatima keenly followed the politics of Iran and we often spoke how the politicians warped common people's minds and will. She believed one day Iran would rise up to overthrow all the corruption and fanaticism associated with their politics to make a fresh start.

Varuna (Indonesian Australian staff) worked part-time, and she loved sweets. Ladoo was her favorite sweet and I always took sweets to share with Varuna. Varuna was very religious and yet made sure that she never expressed her religious identity at the centre. Varuna loved her ideas being challenged and she always warned me about my limits and boundaries within the centre and the society of Australia.

Aruna (Sri Lankan Australian staff) quietly supported Katherine in the room, and seldom spoke to me. When they celebrated multicultural term, she had a small Sri Lankan flag and the national anthem pinned on the notice board in the room. By the end of the year she became more comfortable about my presence and began to share in our fun and laughter.

Jan, "øthered Australian" staff, worked with Amelia closely. As migrants living in Australia, Jan and I shared many conversations that were unique to our experiences in Australia. Jan used to make notes of new ideas and understandings that came from our conversations together.

The "Other Australian" Speakers

Feeniyan was a four-year-old white Anglo-Australian girl. She was one of the girls who held a lot of power in that group and she had been coming to this centre since she was a baby. She usually played with two other girls in the home corner when indoors, or the cubby house when outdoors.

Pat was a three-year-old white Anglo-Australian boy. He was one of the youngest in the group. He was there wherever something interesting happened and immediately became a part of that event. Thus, he usually flitted from table to table and activity to activity. Pat loved singing with me and we sang by taking turns to change rhyming action words.

Cathy welcomed me into her space with much warmth and expectation. She always called me her "exotic other" and I called her my "white Mogul" and laughed about her desire for everything that I was, the color, the food, the celebration, and all my "differences". We had lengthy conversations with each other during which we shared our professional and personal experiences, and I therefore was highly committed to our friendship.

Amelia openly and enthusiastically welcomed my presence. From the very first day, she wanted to know about what I meant by "identity" and we talked about subjectivity, power, and discourse. Every afternoon during her lunch break or sleep time we used to regularly exchange our observations of children and by saying, "*Let us do something to change this,*" Amelia showed her willingness to be challenged and changed.

Gina called herself a peacemaker. She was instrumental in my continued presence in this room, and within a week she acknowledged the complexities, "*You know when you asked us, who is an Australian weeks ago, I was totally confronted. I was thrown back. Then I stopped and thought what it is to be an Australian, I couldn't find an answer. It is confronting, because being an Australian is something we take for granted.*" Although I shared my observations of children with her, we both understood that to trial any action in the room was difficult, and she was always apologetic about this.

Katherine worked in the centre with Gina, Cathy, Varuna, and Sheri. To explain my study, I simply said that I was going to ask why some children play together, and some don't. Katherine replied, "*It is individual choice, they should be able to choose whom they want to be friends with.*" Usually children played, as Katherine supervised them from a distance and would respond to children and staff if approached. Thus, she made it very clear from the start that she would never interfere with children's individual choices and preferences.

Katrina stood up for the upliftment of the marginalized, and she expressed this the very first day I met her, "*You know, this was a staff that no one would employ and I employed her. I am always for change. So, if you think you want to change something you can. But not everything all the time.*" I immediately felt quite comfortable to voice my opinion, as I believed at that time she was open to being challenged.

REFERENCES

Ahmed, S. (2007). "The Language of Diversity." *Ethnic and Racial Studies* 30(2), 235–256.
Alister, A. (1990). *Althusser and Feminism.* London: Pluto Press.
Allard, A. C. (2006). "'A Bit of a Chameleon Act': A Case Study of One Teacher's Understandings of Diversity." *European Journal of Teacher Education* 29(3), 319–340.
Althusser, L. (2008). *On Ideology.* Translated by B. Brewster. New York: Verso.
Appadurai, A. (2006). *Fear of Small Numbers.* London: Duke University Press.
Arber, R. (1999). "Uncovering Lost Dreams: Re-envisioning Multiculturalism through Post-colonial Lenses." *Inclusive Education* 3(4), 309–326.
Arthur, L. (2001). "Diverse Languages and Dialects." In D. E. (ed.), *The Anti-bias Approach in Early Childhood* (pp. 95–113). Sydney: Pearson Education Australia.
Ashcroft, B. (2001). *On Postcolonial Futures: Transformations of Colonial Cultures.* New York: Continuum.
Ashcroft, B., G. Griffiths, and H. Tiffin. (2000). *Post-colonial Studies: The Key Concepts.* London: Routledge.
Atkinson, S. (2009). "Adults Construct the Young Child, 'Race' and 'Racism.'" In G. MacNaughton and K. Davis (eds.), *"Race" and Early Childhood Education: An International Approach to Identity, Politics and Pedagogy* (pp. 139–155). New York: Palgrave Macmillan.
Australian Bureau of Statistics. (2011). "Australia's Population by Country of Birth." From Commonwealth of Australia. Retrieved from http://www.abs.gov.au/ausstats/abs@.nsf/Products/84074889D69E738CCA257A5A00120A69?opendocument.
Australian Curriculum Assessment and Reporting Authority. (2009). *Australian Victorian Essential Learning Standards (AusVELS).* Retrieved from http://vels.vcaa.vic.edu.au/domains/.
Aveling, N. (2002). "Student Teachers' Resistance to Exploring Racism: Reflections on 'Doing' Border Pedagogy." *Asia-Pacific Journal of Teacher Education* 30(2), 119–130.
Bennet, M., and F. Sani. (2008). "Children's Subjective Identification with Social Groups." In S. R. Levy and M. Killen (eds.), *Intergroup Attitudes and Relations in Early Childhood Through Adulthood* (pp. 19–31). Oxford: Oxford University Press.

Bennett, C. I. (2003). *Comprehensive Multicultural Education: Theory & Practice*. Boston: Pearson Education.

Berman, G., and Y. Paradies. (2010). "Racism, Disadvantage and Multiculturalism: Towards Effective Anti-Racist Praxis." *Ethnic and Racial Studies* 33(2), 214–232.

Bhabha, H. K. (1994). *The Location of Culture*. London: Routledge.

Bhabha, H. K. (1996). "Culture's in-between." In H. Stuart and P. Du-Gay (eds.), *Questions of Cultural Identity*. Chicago: Alexander Street Press.

Blaise, M. (2005a). "Performing Feminities through Gender Discourses." In L. Diaz Soto and B. B. Swadner (eds.), *Power and Voice in Research with Children* (pp. 105–116). New York: Peter Lang.

Blaise, M. (2005b). *Playing It Straight: Uncovering Gender Discourses in an Early Childhood Classroom*. New York: Routledge.

Boutte, G. S. (2008). "Beyond the Illusion of Diversity: How Early Childhood Teachers Can Promote Social Justice." *The Social Studies* 99(4), 165–173.

Brooks, S. (2002). *The Challenge of Cultural Pluralism*. London: Praeger.

Burnett, B. (2004). "How Does 'othering' Constitute Cultural Discrimination." In B. Burnett, D. Meadmore, and G. Tait (eds.), *New Questions for Contemporary Teachers: Taking a Socio-Cultural Approach to Education* (pp. 101–112). Frenchs Forest, NSW: Pearson Education Australia.

Camara, B. (2008). *Marxist Theory, Black? African Specificities, and Racism*. New York: Lexington Books.

Chantler, K. (2004). "English and 'Community Languages' in Early Years Establishments." *International Journal of Equity and Innovation in Early Childhood* 2(1), 2–18.

Clarke, P. (2005, June 16–18). *Advocating for Children's Rights: The Challenge for Early Childhood Educators*. Paper presented at the Our Children for the future 4, Adelaide.

Clyne, M. (2005). *Australia's Language Potential*. Sydney: University of NSW Press.

Commonwealth of Australia. (1999). *A New Agenda for Multicultural Australia*. Commonwealth of Australia. Retrieved from http://www.immi.gov.au/media/publications/multicultural/agenda/.

Commonwealth of Australia. (2003). *Multicultural Australia: United in Diversity*. Retrieved from http://www.immi.gov.au/media/publications/settle/_pdf/united_diversity.pdf.

Commonwealth of Australia. (2007). *Citizenship Test*. Retrieved from http://www.citizenship.gov.au/learn/cit_test/.

Commonwealth of Australia. (2009). *Belonging, Being & Becoming: The Early Years Learning Framework for Australia*. Retrieved from http://docs.education.gov.au/system/files/doc/other/belonging_being_and_becoming_the_early_years_learning_framework_for_australia.pdf.

Commonwealth of Australia. (2011). *The People of Australia: Australia's Multicultural Policy*. Retrieved from http://www.immi.gov.au/media/publications/multicultural/pdf_doc/people-of-australia-multicultural-policy-booklet.pdf.

Commonwealth of Australia. (2012). *National Agenda for a Multicultural Australia*. Retrieved from http://www.immi.gov.au/media/publications/multicultural/agenda/agenda89/whatismu.htm#.

Commonwealth of Australia. (2013). *Australian Citizenship: Our Common Bond*. Retrieved from http://www.citizenship.gov.au/learn/cit_test/test_resource/.

Connolly, P. (2008). "Race, Gender and Critical Reflexivity in Research with Young Children." In P. Christensen and A. James (eds.), *Research with Children, Perspectives and Practices* (pp. 173–188). New York: Falmer Press.

Crisp, R. J., and R. N. Turner. (2007). *Essential Social Psychology*. London: Sage.

de Freitas, E., A. McAuley, and R. S. Ammon. (2008). "Teaching for Diversity by Troubling Whiteness: Strategies for Classrooms in Isolated White Communities." *Race Ethnicity and Education* 11(4), 429–442.

Denscombe, M. (2010). *The Good Research Guide*. Berkshire, UK: Open University Press.

Denzin, N.K., and M. D. Giardina. (2007). "Introduction: Ethical Futures in Qualitative Research." In *Ethical Futures in Qualitative Research: Decolonizing the Politics of Knowledge*. Edited by N. K. Denzin and M. D. Giardina. 9–45. Walnut Creek, CA: Left Coast Press.

Derman-Sparks, L., P. G. Ramsey, and J. O. Edwards. (2006). *What If All the Kids Are White? Anti-bias Multicultural Education with Young Children and Families*. New York: Teachers College Press.

Elliott, A. (2007). *Concepts of the Self*. Cambridge: Polity Press.

Elliott, A. (2010). *Concepts of the Self*. Cambridge: Polity Press.

Epstein, A. S. (2009). *Me, You, Us: Social Emotional Learning in Preschool*. Ypsilanti, MI: High Scope Press.

Fairclough, N. (1992). *Discourse and Social Change*. Cambridge: Polity Press.

Fleer, M., and B. Raban. (2005, June 16–18). *"It's the Thought that Counts": A Sociocultural Framework for Supporting Early Literacy and Numeracy*. Paper presented at the Our children the future 4, Adelaide.

Foucault, M. (1972). *The Archaeology of Knowledge*. Translated by A. M. S. Smith. London: Travistock.

Foucault, M. (2010). *The Government of Self and Others*. Translated by G. Burchell. London: Palgrave Macmillan.

Frankenberg, R. (1993). *White Women, Race Matters: The Social Construction of Whiteness*. Minneapolis: University of Minnesota Press.

Freebody, P. (2003). *Qualitative Research in Education: Interaction and Practice*. London: Sage.

Gandhi, L. (1998). *Postcolonial Theory: A Critical Introduction*. New York: Columbia University Press, 1998.

Gee, J. P. (2010). *An Introduction to Discourse Analysis [Electronic Resource] Theory Method*. Hoboken, NJ: Taylor and Francis.

Gilbert, R. (2004). "Studying Culture and Identity." In *Studying Society and Environment: A Guide for Teachers*. Edited by R. Gilbert. Southbank, UK: Social Science Press.

Gorski, P. C. (2008). "Good Intentions Are Not Enough: A Decolonizing Intercultural Education." *Intercultural Education* 19(6), 515–525.

Government of the Commonwealth of Australia. (1901). Immigration Restriction Act. Retrieved from http://www.foundingdocs.gov.au/item.asp?dID=16.

Grace, D. J. (2008). "Interpreting Children's Constructions of Their Ethnicity." *Contemporary Issues in Early Childhood* 9(2), 131–147.

Graham, L. J. (2005, Nov. 27–Dec. 1). *Discourse Analysis and the Critical Use of Foucault*. Paper presented at the Australian Association for Research in Education, Sydney.

Grant, C. A., and V. Agosto. (2006). "What Are We Tripping On? Transgressing the Fault Lines in Research on the Preparation of Multicultural Educators." In *The Sage Handbook of Research in Education: Engaging Ideas and Enriching Inquiry*. Edited by C. F. Conrad and R. C. Serlin (pp. 95–116). London: Sage.

Grant, C. A., and C. E. Sleeter. (2007). *Doing Multicultural Education for Achievement and Equity*. New York: Routledge; Taylor and Francis group.

Grassby, A. J. (1973). *A Multicultural Society for the Future*. Australian Government publishing service. Retrieved from http://www.multiculturalaustralia.edu.au/doc/grassby_1.pdf.

Guajardo, M. A. (2008). "Developing Partnership: The Early Stages of Collaborative Action Research." In S. P. Gordan (ed.), *Collaborative Action Research: Developing Professional Learning Communities*. New York: Teachers College Press.

Gunaratnam, Y. (2003). *Researching "Race" and Ethnicity: Methods, Knowledge and Power*. London: Sage.

Hage, G. (2000). *White Nation: Fantasies of White Supremacy in a Multicultural Society*. New York: Routledge.

Hall, C. (1996). "Histories, Empires and the Post-Colonial Moment.".In *The Post-Colonial Question: Common Skies, Divided Horizons*. Edited by I. Chambers and L. Curti (pp. 65–77). New York: Routledge.

Hall, S. (2003). Foucault: Power, Knowledge and Discourse. In M. Wetherell, S. Taylor, and S. J. Yaes (eds.), *Discourse Theory and Practice: A Reader* (pp. 72–82). London: Sage.

Haque, A. (2001). "Attitudes of High School Students and Teachers towards Muslim and Islam in a Southeastern Australian Community." *Intercultural Education* 12(2), 185–196.

Hayes, M. T. (2001). "A Journey through Dangerous Places: Reflections on a Theory of White Racial Identity as Political Alliance." *Contemporary Issues in Early Childhood* 2(1), 15–29.

Hodder, J. (2007). "Young People and Spirituality: The Need for a Spiritual Foundation for Australian Schooling." *International Journal of Children's Spirituality* 12(2), 179–190.

Hogg, M. A., and D. Abrams. (2007). "Intergroup Behaviour and Social Identity." In M. A. Hogg and J. Cooper (eds.), *The Sage Handbook of Social Psychology: Concise Student Edition* (pp. 335–360). San Diego, CA: Sage.

Holmes, D., K. Hughes, and R. Julian. (2007). *Australian Sociology: A Changing Society*. Frenchs Forest, NSW: Pearson Education Australia.

hooks, b. (1998). "Representations of Whiteness in the Black Imagination." In D. R. Roediger (ed.), *Black on White*. New York: Schocken Books.

Ilaiah, K. (2004). *God as Political Philosopher: Buddha's Challenge to Brahminism*. Kolkata: Samya.

Jupp, J. (1997). "Immigration and National Identity: Multiculturalism." In G. Stokes (ed.), *The Politics of Identity in Australia* (pp. 132–144). Melbourne: Cambridge University Press.

Katz, K. (1999). *The Colours of Us*. New York: Henry Holt.

Keay, J. (2000). *India a History*. London: Harper Collins.

Kissinger, K. (1994). *All the Colors We Are: The Story of How We Got Our Skin Color*. St. Paul, MN: Red Leaf Press.

Kowalski, K. (2007). "The Development of Social Identity and Intergroup Attitudes in Young Children." In O. N. Saracho and B. Spodek (eds.), *Contemporary Perspectives on Social Learning in Early Childhood Education* (pp. 49–82). Charlotte, NC: Information Age.

Kunzman, R. (2006). "Imaginative Engagement with Religious Diversity in Public School Classrooms." *Religious Education* 101(4), 516–531.

Lacan, J. (2002). *The Mirror-Stage as Formative of the I Function as Revealed in Psychoanalytic Experience. Ecrits: A Selection*. Translated by B. Fink, H. Fink, and R. Grigg. New York: W. W. Norton.

Ladson-Billings, G. (2004). "Just What Is Critical Race Theory and What's It Doing in a Nice Field Like Education?" In G. Ladson-Billings and D. Gillborn (eds.), *The RoutledgeFalmer Reader in Multicultural Education*. New York: RoutledgeFalmer.

Leeman, Y., and C. Reid. (2006). "Multi/Intercultural Education in Australia and the Netherlands." *Compare* 36(1), 57–72.

Leonardo, Z. (2004). "The Souls of White Folk: Critical Pedagogy, Whiteness Studies, and Globalisation Discourse." In G. Ladson-Billings and D. Gillborn (eds.), *The RoutledgeFalmer Reader in Multicultural Education*. New York: RoutledgeFalmer.

Liu, Y., and Y. S. M. Owyong. (2011). "Metaphor, Multiplicative Meaning and the Semiotic Construction of Scientific Knowledge." *Language Sciences* 33(5), 822–834.

Loomba, A. (2005). *Colonialism/Postcolonialism.* New York: Routledge.
MacNaughton, G. (2001). "Silences and Subtexts of Immigrant and Non-Immigrant Children." *Childhood Education* 78(1), 30–36.
MacNaughton, G., and K. Davis. (2001). "Beyond 'Othering': Rethinking Approaches to Teaching Young Anglo-Australian Children about Indigenous Australians." *Contemporary Issues in Early Childhood* 2(1), 83–93.
MacNaughton, G., and P. Hughes. (2009). *Doing Action Research in Early Childhood Studies: A Step by Step Guide.* New York: Open University Press.
Makkai, L., and I. McAllister. (1993). "Immigrants in Australian Society: Backgrounds, Attainment and Politics." In *A Sociology of Australian Society.* Edited by J. M. Najman and J. S. Western (pp. 178–212). South Melbourne: Macmillan Education Australia.
Martin, G., lisahunter, and P. McLaren. (2006). "Participatory Activist Research (Teams)/Action Research." In K. Tobin and T. Kincheloe (eds.), *Doing Educational Research: A Handbook* (pp. 157–190). Rotterdam: Sense.
Martino, W., and G. M. Rezai-Rashti. (2008). "The Politics of Veiling, Gender and the Muslim Subject: On the Limits and Possibilities of Anti-racist Education in the Aftermath of September 11." *Discourse: Studies in the Cultural Politics of Education* 29(3), 417–431.
McIntosh, P. (1988). "White Privilege: Unpacking the Invisible Knapsack." Retrieved from http://www.nymbp.org/reference/WhitePrivilege.pdf.
McKinlay, A., and C. McVittie. (2008). *Social Psychology and Discourse.* Chichester, UK: John Wiley & Sons.
Merenstein, B. F. (2008). *Immigrants and Modern Racism: Reproducing Inequality.* London: Lynne Rienner.
Miell, D. (1995). "Developing a Sense of Self." In P. Barnes (ed.), *Personal, Social and Emotional Development of Children* (pp. 187–231.). Oxford: Blackwell.
Mills, S. (2004). *Discourse.* London: Routledge Taylor & Francis Group.
Mills, C., and T. Gale. (2004). "Doing Research with Teachers, Parents and Students: The Ethics and Politics of Collaborative Research." In *Strategic Uncertainties: Ethics, Politics and Risk in Contemporary Educational Research.* Edited by P. Coombes, M. Danaher, and P. A. Danaher (pp. 89–101). Flaxton, Australia: Post Pressed.
Ministerial Council on Education, Employment, Training and Youth Affairs. (2008). *Melbourne Declaration on Educational Goals for Young Australians.* Retrieved from http://www.mceecdya.edu.au/verve/_resources/national_declaration_on_the_educational_goals_for_young_australians.pdf.
Nehru, J. (Unknown), 2013. Retrieved from http://www.webline.co.in/gap_final/ganga_details.php?expID=20.

Nicholls, C. (2005). "Death by a Thousand Cuts: Indigenous Language Bilingual Education Programmes in the Northern Territory of Australia, 1972–1998." *International Journal of Bilingual Education and Bilingualism* 8(2–3), 160–177.

Ozkazanc-Pan, B. (2012). "Postcolonial Feminist Research: Challenges and Complexities." *Equality, Diversity and Inclusion: An International Journal of Behavioral Development* 31(5/6), 573–591.

Pang, V. O. (2001). *Multicultural Education: A Caring-Centred, Reflective Approach*, New York: McGraw-Hill.

Peterson, J. W. (2008). "Teaching World Religion in the Public Schools." *Encounter: Education for Meaning and Social Justice* 21(4), 40–42.

Prasad, A. (2003). "The Gaze of the Other: Postcolonial Theory and Organizational Analysis." In A. Prasad (ed.), *Postcolonial Theory and Organizational Analysis: A Critical Engagement* (pp. 3–46). New York: Palgrave Macmillan.

Reinharz, S. (2011). *Observing the Observer: Understanding Our Selves in the Field*. New York: Oxford University Press.

Reissman, C. K. (2008). *Narrative Methods for the Human Sciences*. London: Sage.

Rivière, D. (2008). "Whiteness in/and Education." *Race Ethnicity and Education* 11(4), 355–368.

Rizvi, F. (2007). "Postcolonialism and Globalisation in Education." *Cultural Studies—Critical Methodologies* 7(3), 256–263.

Rosaldo, R. I. (2006). "Foreword: Defining Culture." In J. R. Baldwin, S. L. Faulkner, M. L. Hecht, and S. L. Lindsley (eds.), *Redefining Culture: Perspectives across Disciplines* (pp. 9–14). Mahwah, NJ: Lawrence Earlbaum Associates.

Rose-Cohen. (2004). "Knowing Ourselves So We May Know Others: Reflections for a White Facilitator of Multicultural Learning." *Adult Learning* 15(1–2), 36–39.

Rush, B. (2006). *Imperialism and Postcolonialism*. London: Pearson Education.

Said, E. W. (1978). *Orientalism*. New York: Vintage Books.

Said, E. W. (1994). *Culture and Imperialism*. New York: Vintage Books.

Schaffer, H. R. (1996). *Social Development*. Oxford: Blackwell.

Sen, A. (2005). *The Argumentative Indian: Writings on Indian Culture, History and Identity*. London: Penguin Books.

Siraj-Blatchford, I., and P. Clarke. (2000). *Supporting Identity, Diversity and Language in Early Years*. Buckingham, UK: Open University Press.

Skattebol, J. (2003). "Dark, Dark and Darker: Negotiations of Identity in an Early Childhood Setting." *Contemporary Issues in Early Childhood* 4(2), 149–166.

Spears, R. (1997). "Introduction." In T. Ibanez and L. Iniguez (eds.), *Critical Social Psychology* (pp. 1–16). London: Sage.

Spivak, G. C. (1999). *A Critique of Postcolonial Reason: Toward a History of the Vanishing Present*. London: Harvard University Press.

Srinivasan, P. (2009). "Languages Matter: My Subjective Postcolonial Struggle." In G. MacNaughton and K. Davis (eds.), *Race and Early Childhood Education: An International Approach to Identity, Politics, and Pedagogy*. New York: Palgrave Macmillan.

Stokes, G. (1997). "Introduction." In G. Stokes (ed.), *The Politics of Identity in Australia* (pp. 1–22). Melbourne: Cambridge University Press.

Stratton, J., and I. Ang. (1998). "Multicultural Imagined Communities: Cultural Difference and National Identity in the USA and Australia." In D. Bennet (ed.), *Multicultural States: Rethinking Difference and Identity* (pp. 135–162). London: Routledge.

Tacagni, A. (1998). "Towards Anti-Racism: Food for Thought." In S. Smidt (ed.), *The Early Years: A Reader* (pp. 52–55). London: Routledge.

Targowska, A. U. (2001). *Exploring Young Children's "Racial" Attitudes in an Australian Context—the Link between Research and Practice*. Paper presented at the Australian Association for Research in Education, Freemantle.

Tavan, G. (2004). "The Dismantling of the White Australia Policy: Elite Conspiracy or Will of the Australian People?" *Australian Journal of Political Science* 39(1), 109–125.

Taylor, P. C. (2004). *Race: A Philosophical Introduction*, Oxford: Blackwell.

Vickers, J. (2002). "No Place for 'Race'? Why Pluralist Theory Fails to Explain the Politics of 'Race' in 'New Societies.'" In S. Brooks (ed.), *The Challenge of Cultural Pluralism*. London: Praeger.

Viruru, R. (2001). "Colonized through Language: The Case of Early Childhood Education." *Contemporary Issues in Early Childhood* 2(1), 31–47.

Viruru, R. (2006). "Postcolonial Technologies of Power: Standardized Testing and Representing Diverse Young Children." *International Journal of Educational Research & Practice: Reconceptualizing Childhood Studies* 7, 49–70.

Weedon, C. (1987). *Feminist Practice and Poststructuralist Theory*. Oxford: Basil Blackwell.

Weedon, C. (2004). *Identity and Culture: Narratives of Difference and Belonging*. Berkshire: Open University Press.

White, C. W. (2002). *Poststructuralism, Feminism and Religion*. New York: Humanity Books.

Whittaker, C. R., S. Salend, and H. Elhoweris. (2009). "Religious Diversity in Schools: Addressing the Issues." *Intervention in School and Clinic* 44(5), 314–319.

Wright, C. S., and D. M. Taylor. (2007). "The Social Psychology of Cultural Diversity: Social Stereotyping, Prejudice and Discrimination." In M. A. Hogg and J. Cooper (eds.), *The Sage Handbook of Social Psychology: Concise Student Edition* (pp. 361–387). Thousand Oaks, CA: Sage limited.

Young, R. C. (1995). *Colonial Desire*. London: Routledge.
Young, R. J. C. (2001). *Postcolonialism: An Historical Introduction*. Oxford: Blackwell.
Young, R. J. C. (2003). *Postcolonialism: A Very Short Introduction*. Oxford: Oxford University Press.

Index

A New Agenda for Multicultural Australia, 31, 172
Althusser, 5–7, 27–30, 34, 108, 127, 171
Australian, 6–12, 26–42. *See also* Australian identity
Aboriginal Australian, 12–13, 127
Australian/not Australian, 6, 23, 27, 39, 55, 58, 75, 81, 101, 104, 117, 141–2
Australian egalitarianism, 109
Australian speaker, 7, 27–43, 54, 62, 64, 82–5, 107–11, 124–9, 142–3
not Australian speaker, 38–43, 64–5, 128–43
Australian speakers, 7, 27–43, 62–5, 82–5, 107–10
Australian values, 15, 31, 83, 118, 122–7, 131
Australianness, 7, 38, 43, 61, 67–73, 84–5, 90–1, 128–32, 145–50
Chinese Australian, 71, 76, 102, 119, 142
Indian Australian, Indian Aussie, 56–62, 102, 112, 114, 142, 168
indigenous Australian, 123, 176
just Australian, 58, 67, 72–5, 80–2, 94, 97–8, 120, 136, 147
migrant Australians, 13
Other Australian, 7, 43–54, 65–72, 90–100, 112–15, 129–38, 143–50, 167–9
øthered Australian, 7, 43–54, 68–74, 86–100, 114–15, 132–49, 167–9
really Australian, 107, 112, 136, 146
speaking Australian, 104, 105
Sri Lankan Australian, 61, 78, 168, 169
white middle-class Anglo-Australian, 80, 121, 133, 136
Australian Citizenship: Our Common Bond, 32, 173

Bairam, Ramadan, 77, 95–6
bilingual, 106–7, 111–12, 17
binary, 23, 39, 59
black, 2, 13, 55, 56, 59–62, 66–9, 91, 155, 162, 172, 175
blackness, 2, 3
boundary committing, 44, 50–2, 114, 138, 152
boundary conscious, 44, 50–3, 70, 97, 114, 138, 153
Boundary defending, 45–8, 91, 100, 114, 138, 151
Boundary denying, 44–8, 70, 91, 99, 100, 136–8, 151
boundary diffusing, 44–5, 50, 53–4, 69, 138, 154
compare Boundary diffusing
Boundary diffusing, 49–50, 100, 152–3
see also Other Australian discourse, øthered Australian discourse
boundary identity, 19, 20, 23, 25, 27, 35, 76, 87, 119
see also cultural, ethnolinguistic, national, "race" identity
boundary speakers, 19–21, 26–7, 43, 64, 82, 142, 143, 167

boundary speaks, 19, 23, 25, 27, 35, 43, 56, 76–7, 80, 85, 117, 120
boundary streams, 19–20, 55, 75, 117, 142
  Complex(ion), Complex(ion) speaks, 20, 26, 55–74, 76, 84, 142, 155 (*see also* skin color, white, black, brown)
  food, faith, festival, 147, 150
  Forbidden Fs, Forbidden Fs speaks, 18, 20, 26, 75, 87–99
  Terra strikes, Terra strikes speaks, 20, 26, 117–39
  Tongue ties, Tongue ties speaks, 20, 26, 101–15
boundary subjects, 42
Brahmin, Brahminic, Brahminism, 1
brown, 38–40, 56–77, 89–90, 144–8, 155–68
brownness, 2, 39, 57, 59, 60, 62, 65, 77, 145, 152

categorical, 30, 34, 41, 46, 83, 104, 109, 117, 118, 127, 143, 150
categories, 5, 15, 24–5, 36, 38, 55, 56, 75, 83, 119, 120, 148
celebration, 31, 47, 75, 77, 82, 84, 85, 94–6, 99, 145, 170
  no celebration, 75, 80, 98, 146
  no color, 75, 80, 81, 98, 146
  nothing, 55, 56, 61, 67, 75, 76–81, 84, 91, 93–4, 97–9, 111–15, 118, 121, 123, 131, 142, 146, 151–3
challenge, challenged, 3, 20, 34, 36–41, 46, 48, 50, 53, 68, 72, 84, 90, 100, 131, 138, 144–50, 153, 172, 177, 178
Chinese, 12, 71, 79–84, 87, 94, 98, 102–3, 130–8
Christmas, 77, 81, 86, 96–9
citizenship, 11–15, 31–3, 63, 125, 173
  citizenship test, 113, 172, 173

colonial, 12, 13, 34, 36–7, 63, 110, 114, 121, 123–8, 137, 152, 179
  colonial ambiguity, 33
  colonial clone, 132
  colonial discourse, 3, 36, 39, 49, 99, 131, 136, 137
  colonial dominance, colonial domination, 17, 23, 39, 136, 138, 153
  colonial resistors, 39
  colonize, colonization, 10, 12, 16, 29, 35–9, 60, 107, 113, 122–4, 151
  colonized, 3, 8–13, 23, 33–9, 42–3, 99, 109, 114, 118, 128, 136, 139, 141, 144, 148, 178
  colonizer, 3, 23, 36–9, 43, 99, 110, 136, 141, 145
  decolonization, 10, 35, 37, 39, 148
  decolonize, 8, 37
colonialism, 1–2, 35–9, 85, 110, 131, 136, 143, 150, 176
  see also postcolonialism
Commonwealth of Australia, 15, 31–3, 63, 83, 88, 96, 99, 108, 113, 125, 171, 172
  See also *A New Agenda for Multicultural Australia*, Australian Citizenship: Our Common Bond, citizenship test, EYLF, Immigration Restriction Act, *Multicultural Australia: United in Diversity*, *National Agenda for a Multicultural Australia*, *The People of Australia: Australia's Multicultural Policy*
Critical Discourse Analysis, CDA, 7, 34
critical race theory, 2, 7, 38–43, 175
  see also Frankenberg

INDEX

culture, 1–5, 11, 14, 28, 45, 47, 80, 92, 94, 118, 120, 122, 127, 133–6, 146, 151–3
 cultural diversity, 13, 29, 31, 83, 124, 126, 178
 cultural identity, 1, 5–11, 15–19, 37, 93, 141–3 *(see also* ethnolinguistic identity, linguistic identity, migrant identity, multicultural identity)
 cultural identity development, 14, 17, 112
 cultural pluralism, 85, 99, 172, 178
 culture narrators, 1

desire, desire for, desire to, 20, 32, 33, 47, 57, 58, 61, 64, 67, 71, 84, 107, 117–21, 124, 126, 142–5
difference, 19, 26, 30–8, 45–53, 62, 72, 87, 92–9, 118–20, 131–3, 153, 156, 162, 170, 178
different, 3, 5, 12, 24, 37, 58, 94, 98, 102, 103, 109, 118, 130–2, 146, 156–7, 162–4
discourse, discourses, 1, 11, 13, 36, 40–3, 45–54, 68–73, 79, 97, 114, 128, 136–8, 151–3, 172–6
 dominant discourse, 41, 49
 marginal discourse, 53, 74
discrimination, 47, 49, 58, 63–4, 145–7, 161, 168, 172, 178
dominance, 23, 36, 39–40, 47–9, 85, 90, 137, 149–53
 colonial dominance, 23, 136, 138, 153
 cultural dominance, 100
 ideological dominance, 37, 97, 149
 "white" dominance, 38, 150
dominant, 12, 38–42, 49–54, 85, 99, 113, 128, 153

dominant race, 85, 100
dominant "Self," dominating "other," 36

early childhood practices, 17, 86, 121, 134, 144–54
early childhood setting, 1–11, 15–18, 43, 46, 81, 103, 135, 144, 149–50, 167, 177
early childhood staff, 113. *See also* Chinese Australian, Muslim, Sri Lankan Australian
 white Anglo-Australian staff, 55, 57, 75–8, 81, 101, 105, 117, 141
English as Additional Language, 102
ethnic, ethnicity, ethnolinguistic, 10–19, 24, 28, 79, 83, 104, 110, 138, 142, 144, 171, 172, 174, 177
EYLF, 15, 72, 88, 96, 99

Fairclough, 5, 7, 34, 173
 see also Critical Discourse Analysis, CDA
families, 9, 15–21, 35, 58, 72–3, 99, 106, 110–12, 133, 147–50, 157, 165, 173
fear, fears, fear of, 1, 20, 32, 52, 73, 84–5, 93, 100, 101, 103, 117–23, 126–8, 146, 153, 158, 171
focus children, 18–21
Foucault, 5, 40–2, 137, 173–4
 see also power
Frankenberg, 5, 38, 45–8, 97, 131–6, 173
 see also critical race theory

Ganga, 1, 4–8, 29, 37–43, 44–5, 54–5, 64–73, 84–100, 111–17, 131–44, 150–5, 167, 176
Grassby, 9, 29–35, 82–4, 107, 124–7, 132, 174

INDEX

Hall, 5, 10, 26–7, 174
hegemony, 23, 28, 34–5, 128, 149
Hindi, 18, 88, 90, 102, 104
hybridity, 3, 8, 37, 91, 97, 144
   see also white hybridity

I, 7, 43–74, 86–100, 111–15,
   129–39, 141–54, 168
identity, 6–7
   Aboriginal identity, 14 (see also
     indigenous identity)
   Australian identity, 13–15,
     26–32, 47, 63–9, 74, 102,
     127, 145
   collective identity, 10, 23, 34, 51,
     62, 106, 118, 142
   English, English speaking
     identity, 13, 29–33, 101–15,
     146, 172 (see also national
     language)
   ethnolinguistic identity, 23, 25,
     45, 51, 104, 106, 110, 148,
     168 (see also ethnic, ethnicity,
     ethnolinguistic)
   indigenous identity, 114
   linguistic identity, ethnolinguistic
     identity, 33, 102–15
   migrant identity, 13
   multicultural identity, 33
   national identity, 9, 10, 14, 20,
     23, 26–49, 54–73, 85, 102,
     115, 123–4, 145, 151–3
ideology, 3, 27–39, 45, 50–3,
   63, 109–15, 126–9, 137,
   143–5, 171
imagination, imaginations, 2–6,
   9–12, 16, 57–61, 65, 77–80,
   101, 105–7, 120–3, 144, 148,
   154, 175
   imagi(nation), 6, 12–21, 27–33,
     58, 61–4, 80–5, 106–11,
     127–8, 141–4, 149
   othering imaginations, 57, 78,
     105, 120, 123
Immigration Restriction Act, 29, 174

Indian, 2, 10, 56–71, 76, 79,
   82–8, 98–106, 121–7,
   167, 177
inspiration, 148, 149, 154
interpellated, interpellation, 28–34,
   64, 108, 126, 143

Lacan, 5, 24, 175
Languages Other Than
   English, 108
liberalism, 85, 99

majority, 81, 85, 100
marginal, marginalization,
   marginalized, 41–2, 49, 53, 69,
   74, 79, 125, 151, 170
material effects, 7, 41–54
   critical cognition, 50, 54
   critical consciousness, 152–4 (see
     also power: power, sanction)
   Insulation, 46, 48, 70, 84, 98,
     113, 131, 145
   Ownership, 46, 48, 69, 98, 113,
     131, 138
   regulated acceptance, 97, 99
   Self-proliferation, 46, 48, 97, 99
   self-regulation, 97, 99
   submission, 51, 64, 68, 97, 117,
     143, 153
   suppression, 52, 70, 97, 99
metaphor, 4–5, 175
   see also Ganga
minority, 81, 85, 91, 100
multicultural Australia, 16, 27, 82,
   117–26, 147–8
*Multicultural Australia: United in
   Diversity*, 31, 172
multiculturalism, 7, 10–15, 25–7,
   48, 62–3, 82–5, 94, 119,
   124–8, 132–3, 138, 171,
   172, 175
multilingual, multilingualism, 3,
   33, 101, 107–10, 115
Muslim, 75–80, 92–100, 122, 167,
   174, 176

INDEX • 185

NAIDOC, 122–3, 131
narrative inquiry, 16, 17, 19
narratives, 6, 7, 10, 16, 18–21
National Agenda for a Multicultural Australia, 173
national language, 31, 33, 101, 108, 113–15
nationalizing, 45–7, 56, 67–9, 98, 113, 142, 147
nation-state, 10–11, 14, 29, 33, 144
see also national identity
normal, normality, normalization, normalizing, 3, 6, 36, 38, 47–8, 72–3, 95–6, 149–52
not normal, 129

Other, Othered, Othering, 7, 27, 31, 33, 43–54, 62–72, 82–100, 107–9, 112–15, 124–37, 142–53, 173, 176, 177
other, othered, othering, 1–6, 11–23, 24–7, 35–9, 55–66, 75–84, 90–8, 101–5, 117–26, 132, 142, 172
øther, øthered, øthering, 7, 23–4, 45–8, 64–9, 85, 98–101, 109–11, 117, 124–8, 143, 176
different other, 30, 37, 83, 120
self-othering, 51–2, 68, 90
(*compare* Othering, øthering, critical Othering, critical øthering, self-othering)
See also Other Australian, øthered Australian

participatory action research, 16–19, 69, 89, 129, 143, 150, 171, 174, 177–8
political, socio-political, 6, 7, 11–16, 25–37, 41–5, 52, 83, 109–15, 122–9, 137, 152, 175, 178
politics, 13, 36, 83, 169, 171, 173, 175, 176, 178
postcolonial, 1–18, 24, 30, 36, 44, 65, 124, 143

postcolonial discourse analysis, 40, 42, 54
postcolonial estuary of contesting "Australian," 6–7, 44, 144
postcolonialism, 35–43, 143, 176, 177–9
compare colonial, colonialism
postcolonial vision, 3, 39, 121, 141
postsructural feminist, 5, 7, 40
power, 7, 12, 27, 28–35, 39, 48–54, 58, 68–74, 91, 98, 100, 109, 112, 121, 132–41, 143–54, 169–70
Diffused power, 50, 74
national power, 109–10, 153
power, 42, 46–8, 111, 114, 174
subjective power, 51–2, 68, 70, 97–8, 137–8
white power, 38–9, 58, 63–4, 74, 132, 152–4
privilege, 7, 32, 47–50, 74, 85, 100, 147, 176

"race," 11, 14–16, 28, 38, 42, 45, 110, 132, 144, 148, 164, 171, 173, 174, 175, 177, 178
racism, 7, 15, 38, 43, 58, 63–4, 69, 73, 132, 136, 164, 171
democratic racism, 85, 86
essentialist racism, 45, 131
realities, 2, 4, 6, 9, 11, 19, 36, 44, 54–9, 64, 76–8, 85, 102, 104, 107, 109–11, 119–23, 128, 141, 144, 148
othering realities, 56, 77, 102, 119, 120, 123
resistance, 35–40, 51, 103, 129–31, 171
colonial resistors, white resistors, 35, 38–9, 86
resist, resisting, resisted, 5–6, 34–6, 41–53, 67–70, 90–5, 101–4, 111–15, 136–8, 144–54
roti, 76–7, 81, 84, 87–92, 168

sanction, 40–2, 74–5
 see also Sanctioning
Santa, 18, 81, 84–92, 96, 167
Self, 23, 24, 36, 45–50, 67, 69, 73, 94, 99, 136, 143, 146–9, 173, 176
self, 1, 3, 6, 9, 26–35, 43–5, 51–6, 62–90, 96–106, 112, 121
 Australian self, 39, 46, 51, 52, 119, 121
 migrant self, 13
 national self, 13, 143
shaped, 13, 54, 64, 84, 85, 106, 126–8, 143–4
shaping, 5, 7, 33, 62, 82, 107, 109, 124, 142
skin color, 2–6, 20, 39, 55–77, 129, 142–5, 156–68, 175
social psychology, 5–6, 16, 23–8, 126, 173–8
stereotypes, stereotyping, 25, 83, 79, 178
strategies, 7, 17, 25, 38, 41–54, 73, 74, 88, 136, 173
 critical Othering, critical othering, critical øthering, 49–53, 73, 132–6 (*see also* nationalizing)
 Hierarchical øthering, 46, 47
 Legitimizing, 69, 136
 Limiting, 48, 70
 Privileging, 118
 Risking, risking, 49, 53, 68
 Sanctioning, 46
 silencing, 27, 52, 58, 62, 76, 78, 79, 85–7, 91, 95–6, 101, 103, 113
 Theorizing, 46, 47, 49, 69, 113, 136
subjects, 1, 4–7, 28–30, 33, 40–9, 63–4, 83–6, 107–15, 144, 151

 Australian subjects, 30–1, 33, 128, 137, 148, 145
 national subjects, 10–4, 27, 33, 35, 37, 124–7, 151
 postcolonial subjectivity, 7, 21, 35, 39, 69, 90, 127, 129, 143
 postcolonial subjects, 5–7, 42–4, 55, 69, 143
 subjectified, 2, 27, 32–5, 46, 59, 64, 73, 83, 128, 142, 153
 subjectivity, 39–41, 50, 90, 109, 129, 137, 152, 170

Tamil, 18, 102–6, 111–14
The People of Australia: Australia's Multicultural Policy, 31, 173
truths, 4, 5, 7, 18, 141

universalism, 85, 99

Weedon, 5, 40, 64, 128, 136–7, 178
 see also poststructural feminist
white, 3, 12–16, 29, 38, 57, 58–68, 69, 72–6, 85–9, 91–100, 127, 135, 143, 148–53
 white anonymity, 86, 99
 white culture, 38, 82, 99, 135, 151
 white hybridity, 144
 white resistors, 39
 white transformer, 35, 38, 65, 74, 86, 91, 129, 144, 149, 152–4
 white truth, whiteness truth, 5, 141, 143–53
 whiteness, 3, 11, 29, 38–43, 55, 64–77, 82, 89–99, 130–9, 143–53
White Australia policy, 13, 29, 62, 107, 110, 124, 129, 132, 139, 164, 178

GPSR Compliance

The European Union's (EU) General Product Safety Regulation (GPSR) is a set of rules that requires consumer products to be safe and our obligations to ensure this.

If you have any concerns about our products, you can contact us on

ProductSafety@springernature.com

In case Publisher is established outside the EU, the EU authorized representative is:

Springer Nature Customer Service Center GmbH
Europaplatz 3
69115 Heidelberg, Germany

www.ingramcontent.com/pod-product-compliance
Lightning Source LLC
LaVergne TN
LVHW051912060526
838200LV00004B/97